M. J. Davy.

from

P. M. L. for Feb 19th 1951.

JAN VAN EYCK

BY LUDWIG BALDASS

PHAIDON

DETAIL FROM PLATE 116

JAN VAN EYCK

BY

LUDWIG BALDASS

PHAIDON PRESS

MADE IN GREAT BRITAIN
TEXT PRINTED BY GEO. GIBBONS LTD · LEICESTER
PLATES PRINTED BY HENRY STONE & SON LTD · BANBURY

CONTENTS

FOREWORD

WHEN we consider the work of Jan van Eyck within the framework of Netherlandish art, we notice at once that the artist, while the greatest of his century, fits into the development of Flemish painting. But taking European art as a coherent whole—and such it is—we can have no doubt that he opens a new chapter in the history of occidental painting. Jan van Eyck's work was a decisive turning point in the long and not always straight line of development that starts with Giotto and ends with the great Impressionist painters of the late nineteenth century.

A kindly destiny has preserved for us a very considerable number of paintings executed by Jan van Eyck during the last fifteen years of his career. Thanks to his exceptionally thorough technique most of these have come down to us in a good state of preservation. It is true that their full charm can be appreciated only by a close examination of the originals, but good reproductions, wherever possible in the size of the originals, enable us to obtain an idea of the wealth and beauty of the individual pictures, and consequently of the scope and significance of the whole œuvre. In the plates of this book, both coloured and monochrome, the Phaidon Press have taken pains to achieve such a result as far as was possible.

The foundations of our knowledge of Jan van Eyck's art were laid by the art historians of the nineteenth century. Since that time only a few works have come to light. The literature on the subject, however, has continued to grow, to such an extent that it is now difficult to make a comprehensive survey of it. Distinguished scholars have contributed much to the clarification of sundry points, especially as regards the inner significance of certain pictures. On the other hand, the formulation and acceptance of purely subjective opinions, sometimes having scant foundation, have sometimes tended to obscure the issue, so that opinions concerning the limits of the artist's personality and the course of his development often differ widely. Following Max Dvořák's example, I have here made another attempt to give a concise solution of the controversial points. The arrangement of the text which follows upon this intention is clearly displayed in the table of contents. In the catalogue portion of the book I have separated the few faithful copies of lost pictures and drawings from the works which I consider authentic, but in the text itself and in the plates I have inserted them so far as possible in the place where the lost original would belong. At the end of the plates I have placed reproductions of those works which, judging by their design and execution, I cannot recognize as works of Jan van Eyck or of his brother Hubert, but which competent scholars have claimed as works of one of these two painters. Since in the notes, and more especially in the catalogue, the opinions of experts as to attribution and dating have been extensively quoted, the book will also be of use to those who are of a different opinion of the genesis and scope of this art and wish to retain it.

The publishers have arranged for the translation of my original German manuscript. I have endeavoured to check the English text with regard to factual accuracy, and I have to thank Dr. Bruno Fürst, Oxford, for looking over the proofs and for making a number of suggestions to improve the clarity and precision of the translation. Moreover, Mr. Paul Oppé had the great kindness to read the whole translation and to suggest further alterations, which have been very gratefully accepted. In spite of the valuable assistance I have thus enjoyed, I refer the reader, in all cases where scientific accuracy is concerned, to the forthcoming German edition of this book.

* * *

It is incumbent on me to express my heartfelt thanks also to all those who have given me their kind assistance in other ways. In particular, I would thank the Phaidon Press, whose generous director, Dr. B. Horovitz, has invariably shown understanding and readiness to help. I have also to thank all those who have made it possible for me to study the originals with the aid of the scientific means available. In this respect I owe a special gratitude to the former Austrian Minister in Brussels,

FOREWORD

Baron Wimmer, to the director-general of the Cinquantenaire in 1948, and in particular to my good friend, Baron Joseph von der Elst. To Messrs. P. Coremans and A. Janssens de Bisthoven I am indebted for enabling me to study the two hundred and sixty X-ray photographs made at the Archives Centrales Iconographiques d'Art National of the whole of the two parts of the Ghent altar-piece. I also thank Messrs. P. Coremans and A. Philippot for allowing me, in May 1951, to examine from close at hand all the panels of the Ghent altar-piece, which were brought to the Cinquantenaire (even the four panels of the centre portion during their careful restoration by M. Philippot). I have thus been able to include certain results of this examination in the text and, more especially, in the catalogue. The interesting report by P. Coremans, A. Philippot and R. Sneyers (*L'Adoration de l'Agneau, elements nouveaux interessant l'histoire d'art*, Brussels, 1951) and the essay by Cesare Brandi (*Il restauro dell' 'Adoration de l'Agneau Mystique' di Van Eyck*, in *Bolletino dell' Istituto Centrale del Restauro*, Rome, 1951) appeared unfortunately too late to be taken into account by me.

In all questions relating to painting technique I have benefited from the advice of that outstanding connoisseur of old painting techniques, Professor Josef Hajsinek, of Vienna.

I would also thank the staffs of all the museums and libraries I have had occasion to use, especially Messrs. Eberhardt Hanfstaengl and Peter Halm (both of Munich), M. Vanderquenne (Versailles), Miss Esther Preiswerk (Basle), Miss Margaretta Salinger (New York), the director of the Institute of French Culture in Vienna, M. Eugen Susini, and Messrs. Ludwig Münz, Ortwin Gamber and Eckhard Knab (all of Vienna).

Peter Baldass has rendered me valuable assistance in the formulation of the text and the catalogue.

* * *

On behalf of the publishers, I also express my thanks to Canon van der Gheyn in Ghent, who gave us special permission to make colour plates, and to the directors of the National Galleries in London and in Washington for similar permissions. The National Gallery in Washington also placed at our disposal colour negatives of a detail from the *Annunciation*. The authorities of the Metropolitan Museum in New York and of the Wadsworth Atheneum, Hartford, Conn., Mr. and Mrs. S. van Berg of New York, and Messrs. Duveen have likewise helped the publishers by word and deed. For the excellent detail photographs of the Ghent altar-piece we are greatly obliged to A.C.L., Brussels, and to M. Bijtebier, Brussels. Other photographs have been provided by E. Irving Blomstrann, New Britain, Conn. (*Figs.* 79-80), by Messrs. Bruckmann, Munich, and by the authorities of the National Gallery, London, the British Museum, London, the Metropolitan Museum of Art, New York, the John G. Johnson Art Collection, Philadelphia, the Detroit Institute of Arts, the Robert Lehman Collection, New York, the Kunsthistorische Museum, Vienna, the Rijksmuseum, Amsterdam, the Museums of Antwerp, Brunswick and Turin, and others, to all of whom we express our gratitude.

Vienna, October 1951   LUDWIG BALDASS

CHAPTER I: THE PRECURSORS

1. *Melchior Broederlam and Franco-Flemish Art about* 1400

IN 1604 Carel van Mander began his ' Lives of the Netherlandish Painters ' with those of the brothers van Eyck. Obviously they were the oldest artists whose memory at that time was still alive. But even down to our own times almost every history of Old Netherlandish painting, has begun with the art of these two personages, despite the fact that more than forty-five years ago Max Dvořák[1] demonstrated convincingly how deeply their work is rooted in Franco-Flemish art as practised between 1390 and 1425.[2]

In Flemish painting the first tangible personality for us today is Melchior Broederlam, who lived in Ypres. The only work of his that has come down to us is also the first important panel-painting produced in Flanders or France, for in 1392 he was commissioned to paint at Ypres the reverses of the wings of a carved altar-piece, destined for the Chartreuse de Champmol in Burgundy, which he delivered in 1399. It is quite possible that the architectural and figure carvings were executed in Dijon and fixed to the wings after their arrival in that city.

There have been preserved in Italy from the twelfth century, and in Germany from the thirteenth, numerous painted triumphal crosses and reliquary shrines, pictures of the Virgin and composite retables, but we possess only a few isolated fourteenth-century panel-paintings from the western sphere of culture and among these there are no works of outstanding artistic merit.

From the emergence of Gothic art until the beginning of the fifteenth century, sculpture occupied the leading place among the pictorial arts. During Broederlam's lifetime the greatest individual artist was a sculptor—Claus Sluter, who worked in Dijon. In his chief work, the fountain of Moses for the Chartreuse de Champmol, he achieved, fifteen years before Donatello, a free and full development of plastic form. The artistic conception of his last work, the tomb of Philip the Bold, Duke of Burgundy, which was completed after his death by a pupil, Claes de Werve, is of almost equal grandeur. To surround the sarcophagus with figures of mourners, known as ' pleureurs', was an old tradition, but there is something completely new in the way in which Sluter brings out in forty figures, though giving all of them identical costumes, individual variations in the manner of experiencing and bearing grief for the same person (*Fig. 41*). Mighty draperies sheathe their bodies and sometimes almost completely conceal them. The figures are placed in pairs in deep niches, the shadows of which provide a dark foil to the bright gleam of the white stone out of which the figures are hewn. To Sluter we also owe the most animated and grandiose figures of donors produced by late mediaeval art (*Fig. 39*). He carved them for the jambs of the portal of the church of the Chartreuse de Champmol, the burial place of the first dukes of Burgundy. They show psychological profundity in the rendering of the features.

In the fourteenth century French painting took the second place, coming after sculpture. In all its branches and in every kind of technique the same conception prevailed, the development of which can best be followed in the many miniatures, that is to say in works of a more private appeal. The predominance of line is preserved almost until the end of the century. The figures are developed in the flat and set against neutral backgrounds, in most cases patterned like a wall-paper. The contrast to contemporary Italian painting,[3] as regards the representation of space, could not, therefore, be greater.

At the beginning of the fourteenth century the Florentine artist Giotto created a spatial scene in which fully moulded figures combine to form carefully balanced compositions. In his frescoes in the Arena chapel at Padua he sometimes even equips an interior with contemporary furniture and

---

[1]*Cf. Das Rätsel der Brüder van Eyck*, in *Jahrbuch der kunsth. Sammlungen*, XXIV, Vienna 1904; in book form, Munich 1925.

[2]An exception is Sir Martin Conway's book: *The van Eycks and their Followers*, London 1921.

[3]Note, for example, how Jean Pucelle on occasion—*e.g.* in the Bréviaire de Belleville, executed before 1343 (Paris, B.N., Lat. 10484)—gives absolutely flat reproductions of Trecento architectural motives. In the Bible de Jean de Sy (Paris, B.N., MS. Franç. 15397), which was begun by order of King Jean (†1354), the roof of a house is on the same level as the heads of the figures in the same plane and a door from which a figure has just emerged is lower than the figure's shoulder.

embellishes it with objects suggestive of still-life painting, or gives plastic volume to window-recesses. We realize that he is anticipating something that did not achieve permanent significance in painting until the days of Robert Campin and Jan van Eyck.

It is noteworthy that for almost a century French painters appear to have been influenced hardly at all by this artistic development. It is only just before the end of the century, with the emergence of the so-called 'weiche Stil' or 'international' style, which spread throughout the whole Occident, that we find in French painting increasing evidence of the influence of Italian Trecento ideas of spatial construction. It was not Giotto's creation of a spatial image, but the transformatian of it by Sienese, and later by Northern Italian painters, that exercised this influence. More attention was now being paid to panel-painting and, moreover, the topographical centre of artistic production had shifted. The leading artists were no longer French, but Flemish. Between 1390 and 1420 most of the artists, whether sculptors or painters, working for the two most important art patrons in France— the Duke of Burgundy and the Duke of Berry—came from the Low Countries. Since, however, they were active mainly in France and since they carried on French tradition along the old lines, we may now speak of a Franco-Flemish art. It was not until about 1420, at the height of the disruption caused in France by the war and at a time when the political and cultural power of the Duchy of Burgundy, whose young ruler had just removed the seat of his government to Flanders, was at its zenith, that there occurred a clear and definite separation between the Flemish and the French practice of art.

Melchior Broederlam's wing-panels in the museum at Dijon (*Figs. 1, 2*) which we have already mentioned, were the first important product of the new style. When the wings are opened, we find inside a work of wood-carving by Jacques de Baerze, a richly decorative ensemble of architectural elements adorned with little statuettes and enclosing representations carved in the manner of reliefs. Everything glitters with gold. The representations reveal in their composition a well-balanced linear style, such as is found in the ' Parement de Narbonne ' now in the Louvre. In these figures there is no trace of Claus Sluter's monumental grandeur. Broederlam's paintings are more advanced than the carvings.

1. Melchior Broederlam: *The Annunciation and the Visitation.* Dijon, Musée

2. Melchior Broederlam: *The Presentation in the Temple and the Flight into Egypt.* Dijon, Musée

3. Ambrogio Lorenzetti: *The Presentation in the Temple.*
1342. Florence, Uffizi

4. Altichieri and Avanzo: *St. George slaying the Dragon.*
Padua, Oratorio di San Giorgio

The profusion of detail displayed in this work has much of the intimacy of fourteenth-century French miniature-painting, but in place of the flat Gothic style we find a complete spatial image. Each of these two wings (*Figs.* 1, 2), separated by the borders of the frames, consists of two scenes, of which the left-hand one in each case takes place in an interior, while the right-hand one is set in a landscape. In accordance with Trecento usage, both the exterior and the interior of the building are shown at the same time, this being done by omitting the front, and sometimes one or two of the side walls. The forerunners of these bright, pink and white buildings, with their gay roofs, their multi-coloured gold-ribbed vaultings, their slender little columns with richly decorated bases and capitals, sometimes bearing little figures, are to be found in Sienese painting of the middle of the fourteenth century, especially in the works of the brothers Lorenzetti—cf., for example, Ambrogio's Presentation in the Temple, painted in 1342, now in the Uffizi (*Fig.* 3). The courtyard in which Broederlam's Angel kneels is in the foreground on a plane parallel with the surface of the picture, whereas the diagonally placed chamber of the Virgin recedes into the background. Thus by the very disposition of the buildings the representation achieves its spatial effect. The landscape consists of a rising terrain painted in warm brown tones, with vivid green plants and tiny trees, beyond which are whitish rocks. The vegetation is shown only in an abbreviated form. The leaflike serrations of the terrain and other details of the landscape can be traced back ultimately to Byzantine art. Its construction, however, is closely akin to that of the landscape of the frescoes in the Oratorio di San Giorgio at Padua, founded in 1377, which were executed by the Veronese artist Altichiero Altichieri in collaboration with the painter Avanzo. In these frescoes, too, we find a steeply rising rocky terrain, enlivened with little plants, stretching upwards from the foreground and, in the fresco of St. George slaying the Dragon (*Fig.* 4), reaching nearly to the top of the picture.

Broederlam inserts his figures in the buildings and landscapes. With their gentle and expressive movements, which have lost all trace of Sienese austerity, and with the gay and vivid colouring of their draperies, which flow around them (in accordance with the 'international' style), they dominate the scene despite their relatively small dimensions. The gold in the haloes, in the wings of the Archangel Gabriel, in certain details of the draperies and buildings and in the narrow strip

5. Franco-Flemish Painter, about 1395: *The Resurrection.*
Antwerp, Musée, Mayer van den Bergh

6. Franco-Flemish Painter, about 1395: *St. Christopher.*
Antwerp, Musée Mayer van den Bergh

of background, heightens the festive effect of the whole. In the manner in which the lily, the donkey, certain utensils and the details of Joseph's costume are depicted, we see the beginnings of 'naturalism', a novelty for Burgundy and Flanders. The genre-like elements of Joseph's figure go back to Italian Trecento painting, for example, to the cook in Giotto's fresco of the Marriage at Cana in the Arena Chapel and even more to the dishwashers by the fireside in Pietro Lorenzetti's fresco of the Last Supper, in Assisi (*Fig.* 20). They are, however, only a secondary motive. The idealistic character of the conception is in the main preserved.

'Idealistic' and 'naturalistic' elements of style are thus fused in Broederlam's work. The independent existence side by side of these two artistic conceptions can be detected in a second creation of the new art of panel-painting executed at about the same time.

Four scenes from the Life of the Saviour with stippled gold grounds have been preserved from the front of a small altar-piece.[1] These paintings (*Fig.* 5), some of which may reveal indirect Italian influence, show us the first stage of the 'international' style in its clearest form. The wellnigh incorporeal figures have been almost completely idealized by the artist, who reduces the setting to the minimum necessary for its comprehension, *e.g.* in the Resurrection by showing only the sarcophagus with its cover lying at an angle.

In the two pictures from the outside of this little altar-piece, however, though they were painted by the same hand, there are 'naturalistic' elements. Let us glance at the St. Christopher (*Fig.*6). Here the scene is set against a coloured background and extends to the top edge of the picture, which the trees rising on the horizon actually touch, but it is not conceived, as it is in the works of Altichiero and Broederlam, as a rocky landscape, but merely as an inclined plane, and there are thus no undulations

[1]The Annunciation and the Crucifixion are now in the Walters Art Gallery, Baltimore; the Nativity and the Resurrection in the Mayer van den Bergh Museum, Antwerp. On the back of the Resurrection is a painting of St. Christopher. The counterpart to the St. Christopher, a Baptism of Christ in a similar landscape setting, is likewise in Baltimore. According to the catologue of the 1930 exhibition in Antwerp, the Antwerp picture came from the Chartreuse de Champmol near Dijon. The six panels of this little altar-piece (Grete Ring, *A Century of French Painting*, London 1949, Nos. 19, 20, claims that they are of Flemish origin) constitute a perfect stylistic parallel to the pictures of the Passion, now in Prague, executed before 1395 by the Bohemian Master of Wittingau.

in the terrain. Little houses, trees and plants, looking as if they had been taken out of a child's box of toys, stand on the bank of the river, in the waters of which numerous fish can be seen. A bush twines its branches round the wickerwork walls of the thatched hut. It is quite clear that the painter, apparently without knowledge of late Trecento painting in Northern Italy, where we find for the first time a natural rendering of plants and animals, or of the secular frescoes in Avignon, has endeavoured to create a real landscape out of an assemblage of details.

The construction thus belongs to an earlier stage of stylistic development than Broederlam's. The painter of this little picture of St. Christopher is here following an old French tradition. In the works of illuminators during the third quarter of the fourteenth century we occasionally find behind the figures disposed in the pictorial plane a similar landscape, compounded of separate details, which unrolls itself like a carpet until it almost reaches the top of the picture.[1]

Many of the landscape details in the picture of St. Christopher are stereotyped artistic forms and remind us of stenographic symbols, but others, such as the terraced steps which the Child Jesus is descending or the blossoms of the foliage, reveal a certain observation of nature. The very animated figures are set in the middle of this landscape. The idyllic character of the whole is also revealed by the moment which the artist has chosen to represent. He shows us, not the giant Christopher carrying the Child, but the scene immediately preceding this, when the little Jesus standing on the bank appeals to St. Christopher to carry out his duties as ferryman. Everywhere in this picture we perceive that intimate trait characteristic of French book-illumination during the fourteenth century.

The most famous miniature-painter about 1400 was Jacquemart de Hesdin (or Houdin), who from 1384 on was frequently employed by Duc Jean de Berry. The inventory made in 1401–2 of the 'livres et joyaux' belonging to the Duke mentions the miniatures in the 'Très belles heures', now in the Bibliothèque Royale at Brussels (MS. 11060–61), as being by Jacquemart's hand.[2] They form a stylistic parallel to the art of Broederlam. By the time he created his most mature works Jacquemart had doubtless, like Broederlam, seen examples of Italian art, but he transforms the little Trecento houses into Gothic forms. Owing to the fact that he took for his models the works of various artists, his method of composition is not very homogeneous. Often we find slender and elegant figures together with others of shorter stature on the same page (*Fig.* 7). The stumpiness of the latter is probably to be construed as an attempt to be 'naturalistic'. Apart from this peculiarity, the stylistic relationship to Broederlam's wing-panels in Dijon (*Fig.* 1), is particularly close in the miniature of the Visitation. The existence of a common model seems probable. Jacquemart de Hesdin strives to attain a more logical representation of space by putting overlapping rocky coulisses on either side of the foreground. A dovetailing of separate motives is noticeable, but the numerous landscape motives with which the

7. Jacquemart de Hesdin: *The Visitation.*
Brussels, Bibliothèque Royale

[1] *Cf.* the miniatures in the 'Poésies de Guillaume de Machaut' (Paris, B.N., Cod. Fr. 1984). On account of the trees, grouped together in clusters to form tiny coppices, H. Martin (*La Miniature Française*, Paris and Brussels 1923) calls the painter of these miniatures the 'Maître aux boqueteaux'.

[2] As is well known, two miniature-painters from different schools collaborated in the illumination of the Brussels book of hours. Experts do not agree as to which of the two is the 'Jacquemart de Odin' mentioned in the inventory. Although no exact critical study of the style has been made (bibliography in Ring, *op. cit.*, No. 46), I follow the opinion of Tolnay and Panofsky, who obviously think it easy to establish a link between these scenes from the Life of the Virgin and the miniatures in the 'Grandes Heures du Duc de Berry' (Paris, B.N., Lat. 919), which according to the inventory are by Jacquemart de Hesdin, unless we accept Hulin de Loo's theory (*Académie Royale de Belgique, Bulletin de la Classe des Beaux-Arts*, Bruxelles, 1925, p. 125) that the entry in the inventory refers to full-page miniatures only, which he assumes have since disappeared from the volume. It is, however, difficult to find such a link between the two frontispiece miniatures in Brussels, showing the kneeling Prince and his patron saints before the enthroned Madonna, and the existing miniatures of the 'Grandes Heures'. According to Panofsky, these frontispieces were sewn in afterwards.

The miniatures of the 'Grandes Heures', which, according to a statement by the ducal secretary (*cf.* Ring, No. 43), were not completed until after 1409, show the same types, movement and gestures and the same concise, vivid narration as the pictures in the Brussels manuscript, but—possibly on account of the smaller format of the Paris miniatures—an even greater reduction of the landscape, which often gives no more than an idea of the scene of the episode. On the other hand, we find in the 'Grandes Heures' one of the earliest examples in Franco-Flemish art of the 'box-like' room and the beginnings of an arrangement of inanimate objects in the manner of still-life painting. I cannot, therefore, agree with A. Boeckler (*Handbuch der Bibliothekswissenschaft*, ed. Milkau, Leipzig 1931, p. 210), who finds the style of the 'Brussels Hours' much more advanced.

miniaturist embellishes the scene reveal no signs of having been observed direct from nature. In the modelling of details miniature-painting does not yet reveal that craftsmanship which we already find in panel-paintings of the same period, but confines itself to achieving an illustrative effect, merely indicating the object.

On the other hand we notice attempts to observe nature in the work of another painter, who executed the miniatures of a manuscript now in the Bibliothèque Nationale, Paris (MS. franç. 619), the 'Livre de la chasse'.[1] To a considerable extent this painter is still bound by fourteenth-century tradition, as is shown by the fact that only a few of his miniatures have 'natural' blue skies, the remainder having merely that patterned ground which is a relic of the usage of thirteenth-century Gothic. Nevertheless, these miniatures cannot have been painted before the first decade of the fifteenth century. The seemingly improvised manner of representation seeks to establish contact with the spectator. This desire for directness is undoubtedly derived from the 'drolleries' which often adorn the borders of fourteenth-century miniatures. It was doubtless a great achievement to remove these naturalistic details from their isolation (in the borders), to introduce them into the composition and, in the more advanced miniatures (*Fig.* 8), to combine them to form a genre picture.[2] The landscape is composed partly of conventional Italian Trecento set-pieces and partly of details drawn from nature. This observation of nature is revealed in the way in which vegetation is reproduced and to an even greater degree in the representation of animals.[3] The settings in which the animals and human beings move are often terminated by a wall of vegetation running parallel to the pictorial plane. This method of terminating the setting comes from Italy and can be already found in the late Trecento, *e.g.*, in a Lombard miniature showing the grain harvest.[4]

The panel-paintings and miniatures we have discussed belong to the first phase of that idealistic period, distinguished alike by its charm and by its power of expression, which we call the 'international style. To it even an outstanding personality like Claus Sluter paid homage in parts of his works such as his figures of angels for the Fountain of Moses. Throughout Western Europe its current was fed in the main by two sources: fourteenth-century French Gothic and Sienese Trecento painting. In Franco-Flemish art the effort to achieve animation is characteristic, deliberate stylization of the figures being found more rarely than in Germany or Italy. The relationship between the figures and their surroundings is not reduced to a rigid scheme, as it is in Italian Trecento painting, but becomes the chief problem of the pictorial construction, in the development and the embellishment of which the artists were indefatigable.

Cy deuise comment on doit aler en queste entre les champs et la forest.

8. French School, early 15th century: *Miniature from the Livre de la Chasse*. Paris, Bibliothèque Nationale

[1]To judge by the number of extant copies, this book must have been a literary success in its own time. It was written by Gaston Phébus, Comte de Foix (1331–1391), whose court at Orthez offered hospitality to, among others, the famous chronicler Froissart. The manuscript mentioned here must have been executed after the death of the author. Unfortunately we do not know who commissioned the book (MS. fr. 616) or who made the illustrations.

[2]There is a parallel to this genre-like manner of representation in the scenes depicted in the miniatures of a manuscript of Boccaccio's 'Livre des femmes nobles et renommées' (Paris, B.N., Fr. 12420), executed between 1401 and 1403. Here we see against a neutral patterned ground veritable incunabula of genre-painting, concisely executed and also attractive on account of the similarity to still-life paintings (reproduced in Martin, *op. cit.*, Pl. 86). O. Pächt (*Journal of the Warburg and Courtauld Institute*, Vol. IV, p. 88, note 1) holds the miniatures to be early works of the 'Bedford Master'. Closely akin are the illustrations of a Terence manuscript in the Bibliothèque de l'Arsenal in Paris. B. Kurth (l.c.) noted affinities to Northern Italian works of the late Trecento, *e.g.* the miniatures in the 'Tacuinum sanitatis' of the Veronese family Cerrutti, now in Vienna (publ. by J. Schlosser, *Jahrbuch d. kunsth. Sammlungen* XVI, *Vienna*).

[3]The book can be divided into two parts, of which the first deals with game animals and sporting dogs and the second with hunting itself. In the first part each miniature is devoted to one animal and aims at showing 'toute sa nature'. The painter endeavours to do this by giving five or six views of the same animal in different attitudes. It is not until the second part that human figures are included in the miniatures.

[4]Published by O. Pächt, *Journal of the Warburg and Courtauld Institute*, XIII, 1950, Pl. 12c, Paris, Bibl. Nat., nouv. Acqu. Lat. 1673.

2. *The Limbourg Brothers and the Style of the Second Decade*

THE efforts made about the year 1400 by Franco-Flemish artists to arrive, with or without borrowings from Italian models, at a new method of representing the spatial setting and at the same time a more accurate reproduction of nature, were continued on a broader basis during the second decade of the fifteenth century by younger artists, with ever-increasing success. Miniature-painting is the chief branch of art in which we can study this phase of development today and for the last time in the long history of mediaeval art it occupies the foremost place.

Closely related to the style of about 1400 are the miniatures of the 'Heures du Maréchal de Boucicaut', now in the Musée Jacquemart-André, Paris. This book of hours, containing many full-page illustrations, can be dated, from the coats of arms, between 1390 and 1416. As the painter has progressed far beyond the stage of development reached by Broederlam and Jacquemart de Hesdin, we may conclude that the illumination of this manuscript can hardly have been executed before 1410.[1]

In the miniature of the Visitation (*Fig.* 9) the artist follows Broederlam's construction of this group, while modifying it slightly. In Broederlam's version (*Fig.* 1) the combination of two scenes in one picture explains the fact that the action does not take place on the threshold of Elisabeth's house, but in a wild and rocky landscape. Here (*Fig.* 9) the lack of architecture becomes comprehensible only if we are aquainted with the model. The lines of the rocky coulisses are brought into relationship with the group of figures, which they enframe—a motive that goes back to Jacquemart de Hesdin (*Fig.* 7) —thus making it the focal point of the composition. This emphasis is necessary, for the landscape has become much richer in motives. The rising slope of the terrain is bordered by the waters of a lake. The shore on the far side of the lake is no longer conceived as an ideal landscape. Familiar Flemish motives, such as a windmill—imitations of nature, though still abbreviated to such an extent that they look like toys—are enlivened by the addition of human figures rendered in a bucolic, not to say genre-like manner.

Very similar landscapes are reproduced on other pages of this book of hours. In one case, where the subject (God the Father appearing to King David; *Fig.* 10) involves the representation of a divine apparition occupying the whole of the top half of the page, the artist even eliminates the inclined plane and achieves, with the sole aid of overlapping rocky coulisses, an almost natural effect of spatial depth, the modernity of which, however, must not be unduly stressed. From this we perceive that in the other miniatures, too, the artist is not primarily concerned with the spatial effect, but rather with the insertion of many varied motives, in other words that this setting is not first of all an imitation of the inclined planes found in the works of Altichiero (*Fig.* 4) and Broederlam (*Figs.* 1, 2), but an echo of the 'carpet-like' landscapes of the indigenous French tendency (*Fig.* 6) at the end of the fourteenth century. That this is really the case is proved by the narrow strip of ground in the extreme foreground (*Fig.* 9), which occupies the whole width of the picture. This is the only part of the whole landscape given in normal perspective. With the plane in which the figures stand the unrolling of the 'carpet-like' landscape begins. Like the illuminator of the 'Livre de la chasse' the painter sometimes combines a conventionally composed foreground with a decorative background consisting mainly of coats of arms, into which in one case (*Fig.* 29) a 'gloria' with a spatially foreshortened crucifix is inserted.

In the rendering of interiors, too, we find, side by side with incorrectly foreshortened buildings of which both the interior and the exterior architecture is shown, modern spatial constructions almost giving the impression of being representations of reality, in which the figures are quite correctly proportioned to the size of the buildings (*Fig.* 14). To these we shall return later.

There is one other respect in which the illuminator of this book of hours, who has a marked preference for central compositions (*Figs.* 9, 10), surpasses his precursors. He combines his figures with the landscape or with the interior to form a whole, so that the effect is no longer that of an illustration, as it is in Jacquemart's miniatures, but of a picture.

The artist seems to have had only second-hand knowledge of Italian art. As an example of the distance between him and his first Italian model, let us consider his St. Francis receiving the Stigmata

---

[1]Grete Ring (*op. cit.*, No. 36) believes that the miniatures were probably painted after 1409. This book of hours must have been commissioned before the Battle of Agincourt (1415), where the Marshal was captured by the English. He died in England in 1421. Panofsky (*Art Bulletin*, XVII, 1935, note 80) explains the mature style of the Boucicaut master, as displayed in this book of hours, by assuming an assimilation to the art of Jacquemart de Hesdin, who, in his turn, approached his Italian models 'à travers le tempérament d'un peintre monumental'.

9. Miniature from the Book of Hours of the Maréchal de
Boucicaut: *The Visitation*. Paris, Musée Jacquemart-André

10. Miniature from the Book of Hours of the Maréchal de
Boucicaut:*King David*. Paris, Musée Jacquemart-André

(*Fig.* 29), which could never have been painted without Giotto's version of the theme. The pose of
the Saint's head and the movement of his arms, however, have a sentimental note which is alien to
Giotto, but very characteristic of the 'international' style. In the architecture, too, French Gothic
forms are far more prevalent than those of the Trecento. And lastly, the style of the figures is derived
entirely from Franco-Flemish tradition. This suppression of Italian elements[1] constitutes the main
difference between the paintings in the 'Heures du Maréchal de Boucicaut' and the miniatures of the
Limbourg brothers, whose workshop at this time rose to a leading position.

The Limbourg brothers created their masterpiece with the miniatures in the 'Très riches Heures
du Duc de Berry', now in the Musée Condé at Chantilly.

Paul de Limbourg and his brothers Hennequin and Hermant are known to have been in the Duke's
service at least from 1411 on. About this time they began the elaborate illumination of this magnificent
book of hours, which for us is the greatest achievement of Franco-Flemish art during the second
decade of the fifteenth century. When the Duke died on 15th June 1416, the work had not been
completed. From the fact that several miniatures begun by the brothers were not completed until 1485
and that new ones were then added, we may assume that the death of the Duke also signified the end
of the brothers' participation in this work.

The manuscript consists of two parts—the calendar[2], with pictures of the twelve months, of which
ten were executed by the brothers and an eleventh was at least designed by them, and the book of

[1]This circumstance would seem to disprove the identification of the miniaturist as Jacques Coëne, who was summoned to Milan in 1399 and
is known to have been working in France again in 1404. Moreover, the numerous buildings in the book of hours do not look as if they were
designed by an architect who even collaborated in the plans for Milan Cathedral. In them we find neither a coherent sense of form nor a
real absorption in architectural problems (*cf.* also B. Kurth, *Kunstgeschichtliche Anzeigen*, 1910, p. 103 ff.).
[2]B. Kurth (*Kunstgesch. Jahrbuch der Zentralkommission*, Vienna 1911, Fig. 57) and, still more emphatically, O. Pächt (*Journal of the Warburg
and Courtauld Institute* XIII, 1950) draw attention to a Franco-Flemish prayer-book in an English private collection, the calendar miniatures
of which—the theme appears still earlier in Northern Italy—show a less advanced style than Paul de Limbourg's.

hours proper, embellished with numerous illustrations from Genesis, the Psalms, the Gospels etc. In each of these two parts the work of several hands is clearly discernible, but most of the miniatures, and the most beautiful among them, were the work of the chief master, who in all probability can be identified as that Paul de Limbourg who is given the place of honour in the inventories. His two brothers were very close to him in style.

The art of the Limbourg brothers does not reveal the influence of the work of Broederlam and Jacquemart de Hesdin to the same exclusive degree as the book of hours in the Musée Jacquemart-André. Another factor makes itself very strongly felt, namely a renewed interest in Italian Trecento painting. With Paul de Limbourg, who probably visited Italy[1], it is not so much the art of Altichiero, but rather that of the great Sienese painters, the brothers Lorenzetti and Simone Martini, and sometimes also that of Giotto's Florentine followers, that leaves clear traces.

The pictures of the months are, with one exception, set in the open air. To a much greater degree than in the works of Broederlam and his followers we see here a product of courtly art. The progress of the year is depicted in its relationship to the pastimes of the ladies and gentlemen of the ducal court and to the work, as dictated by the seasons, of the peasants who are their thralls. Thus a new genre element makes its appearance, not just indicated or relegated to a modest position in the background, but fully displayed.

Nine of the miniatures painted by the Limbourg brothers in the calendar portion have as background a castle or a town belonging to the royal family or to the Duke's own domains. As some of these buildings can still be identifed today, it seems reasonable to assume the existence of instructions that the castles should be represented in a clearly recognizable way.

In some of the miniatures, e.g. the boar–hunt (December) and the Cavalcade (May), we find in the landscapes reminiscences of a style earlier than that of the miniatures in the 'Heures du Maréchal de Boucicaut'. This is all the more surprising since it is precisely in the Cavalcade (*Fig.* 36) that the free and natural disposition of the figures seems already to anticipate the art of Jan van Eyck. The treatment of space, however, is still approximately the same as in the more advanced miniatures of the 'Livre de la chasse' (*Fig.* 8). In both cases a wall of vegetation running parallel to the pictorial plane shuts off the area in which the figures move. In the picture for the month of May there are, in addition, towers and roofs visible behind the conventional wall of trees and through a narrow gap in this wall we catch a glimpse of the bright yellow field lying behind the little copse. Paul de Limbourg thus fashions a link between the foreground and the complex of buildings in the background.[2]

Some of the other calendar miniatures (February, July, August) are on the same stylistic level, as regards landscape design, as those in the book of hours at the Musée Jacquemart–André (*Fig.* 9). Here, too, we see a steep inclined plane, lateral coulisses and motives from the artist's own country.

The greatest advance in the representation of space is found, however, in those pictures of months (June, October) in which the setting does not follow any of the already existing types. In these the artist aims at representing a 'naturalistic' landscape, to a much greater degree than in the miniature for May (*Fig.* 36). He is obviously carrying to a logical conclusion his above–mentioned corrections to the settings of an earlier style; he omits the line of trees between the foreground and the castle (October; *Fig.* 11) and replaces it by a spacious field, the Seine and the Quai du Louvre. The landscape almost produces the effect of being foreshortened from a given viewpoint. The master even attempts to characterize the material quality of the ploughed field, the river, the stone wall etc. This he does, in accordance with the technique of illumination, using his hair-brush like a draughtsman.

We realize the importance of Paul de Limbourg's spatial images, if we compare his solutions with the landscapes of the frescoes representing the twelve months in the Torre dell' Aquila at Trento,[3] which are approximately ten years older.

The disposition of the figures in Paul's calendar pictures is loose. In certain miniatures they do not face the centre, but are turned towards the edges of the picture. This device gives these paintings an occasional note and the character of a setting, emphasizing that they represent only an arbitrary selection of the many occupations of men during any one month.

---

[1] *Cf.* F. Winkler, *Burlington Mag.* LVI, 1930, p. 95, and O. Pächt, *Journal of the Warburg and Courtauld Institute* XIII, 1950, p. 43.
[2] According to Durrieu (*Les très riches heures du Duc de Berry*, Paris 1904) it is the city of Riom, capital of the duchy of Auvergne, another fief of the Duc de Berry.
[3] Published by K. Kurth, l.c.

11. Paul de Limbourg: *The Month of October.*
Chantilly, Musée Condé

In his rendering of the individual figures (*Fig.* 13, 36) Paul de Limbourg brings out the characteristic elements of their movements, in complete harmony with the 'international' style.

The first miniature (January) in the calendar portion is the only one of which the scene is laid indoors. In the second decade of the fifteenth century French miniature–painting introduced a new type of interior design, differing considerably from the Italian.

We find an echo of the Trecento type of interior in a pen–drawing of a manuscript now in the Bibliothèque Nationale, Paris (MS. Franç. 166). To judge by the completeness of the execution, it must have been conceived as a finished work. This drawing by a Franco–Flemish painter (*Fig.* 24) represents St. Jerome in his Study, an edifice resembling a tabernacle,[1] embellished with numerous little gables, turrets and carvings, the front wall being omitted. We see here approximately the same spatial construction[2], as in the left panel of Pietro Lorenzetti's triptych of 1340 in the Opera del Duomo at Siena, showing the birth of the Holy Virgin. In the pen–drawing the Saint, who is turning over the pages of a bulky volume, is placed right in the corner of the room.

The bookshelf behind him serves to emphasize the atmosphere of a study[3], while an elaborately decorated prie-dieu in the right half of the picture maintains the balance to the Saint's figure. In this room everything is in its proper place.

The religious character is emphasized by the dove whispering inspiration into the Saint's ear and by the choir-like niche piercing the rear wall and containing an altar of the Holy Cross.

The type of interior found in this drawing is still close to that created by Giotto, but in another manuscript of the Franco-Flemish school produced about the same time, i.e. about 1415, we find a new conception (*Fig.* 12). The illuminator, sometimes identified with the 'Boucicaut Master', of a manuscript entitled 'Demandes faites par Charles VI avec les réponses de Pierre Salmon' in the library at Geneva (MS. Franç. 165) shows us three courtiers in the royal bedchamber conversing with the insane monarch (†1422). The interior consists mainly of blue curtains and hangings, all sprinkled with golden fleurs–de–lis. This kind of pattern is derived from those found in the ornamental backgrounds of

---

[1] Charles Sterling (*La peinture française, Les Primitifs*, Paris 1938, p. 68) was reminded by the architecture of the cathedral at Bourges and attributes the miniature tentatively to a Franco-Flemish workshop in that city. Neither the forms of the architecture nor the late Gothic practice of overloading it with ornamental figures support its attribution (by Durrieu) to Paul de Limbourg, whose conception was purer and who used clear architectural forms in the 'High Gothic' sense. One must take into consideration that the Limbourg brothers were not the only artists in Northern France who painted miniatures during the second decade and that only the style of that decade is discernible in the drawing. Nevertheless, Paul probably knew this composition and may have made use of its construction for a smaller miniature in the 'Belles Heures du Duc de Berry' (now in the Edmond Rothschild collection), reducing the dimensions and altering certain details (*c.f.* Durrieu in *Gazette des Beaux-Arts*, 1906). A model-sketch of the architecture, now in the Boymans Museum, Rotterdam (*cf.* P. Wescher, *Phoebus*, I, p. 33 f.), was used by the master of the 'Heures de Rohan' (G. Ring, *op. cit.*, No. 88) as the basis for the architectural border of a miniature of the Virgin in the 'Cambridge Hours'.

[2] *cf.* F. Horb, *Das Innenraumbild des späten Mittelalters*, Leipzig and Zürich, n.d.

[3] The extent to which this solution is bound up with the period is shown by a comparison with the miniature of the same subject in the 'Heures du Maréchal de Boucicaut'; the arrangement of the composition is the same, despite the presence of an ornamented background we look into the study in the same way and there is the same effort to render spiritual activity by means of a careful reproduction of the milieu with its accessories resembling those of a still-life.

THE VIRGIN MARY. Detail from Plate 62. Before the latest restoration.

14. Miniature from the Book of Hours of the Maréchal
de Boucicaut: *The Murder of St. Thomas à Becket.*
Paris, Musée Jacquemart-André

calendar miniatures testifies to a striving after a spatial solution which will show clearly the relative positions of parts of a building before or behind one another. These efforts become still more evident in the scenes from the Gospels in the second part. In the miniature of the Presentation in the Temple the lavishly decorated setting with the protagonists is taken direct from Taddeo Gaddi's fresco in Santa Croce at Florence, including even the details, or with more probability, from a work dependent on this fresco, such as the beautiful drawing in the Louvre. In the miniature of Christ bearing the Cross (*Fig.* 27) we have a particularly clear example of the threefold task which the artist assigns to the architecture, viz. to decorate, to stress the grouping of the figures and to produce an effect of space. The scheme of composition, which is old, was given a stamp of its own in Siena and found its classic expression in Simone Martini's little picture now in the Louvre. In two respects, however, Paul de Limbourg surpasses Simone Martini—in the homogeneous direction of movement of the cortège and in the rendering of the view over the town. By erecting a huge city gate reminiscent of a triumphal arch, the artist provides an aperture through which we see a line of houses, four or five stories high and only slightly abbreviated. This spatial image is the only point of contact between Paul de Limbourg's settings and those of Altichiero and Avanzo (*Fig.* 26).

The regulating function, provided in the miniatures with architectural backgrounds by the buildings represented, is assumed in the scenes set in the open country by masses of figures, which with their free symmetry, e.g. in the miniature of the Adoration of the Magi (*Fig.* 34), counterbalance one another. This highly artistic composition is most eminently suited to the inner significance of the episode.

The three types of setting used by the Limbourg brothers for the calendar pictures are employed again very aptly in the main portion of the book. Tranquil and simple compositions, even when they contain masses of figures, have primitive landscape settings such as are found in the 'Livre de la chasse'. The animated miniatures of complicated construction, on the other hand, such as the Adoration of the Magi (*Fig.* 34), have the richer, more advanced settings of the type found in the 'Heures du Maréchal de Boucicaut'. In the background of Paul de Limbourg's Epiphany we see walls, roofs and towers of a city standing out against the sky, in all probability representing some actual place, since in the preceding miniature, showing the Three Kings on their way to Bethlehem, the Sainte-Chapelle and Notre-Dame de Paris are clearly recognizable. A relationship to Ambrogio Lorenzetti's fresco of 1339, showing the 'Ager Senensis', in the Palazzo Pubblico at Siena, can be safely assumed. Just as original and as significant for the future as the landscape in the October picture (*Fig.* 11) is the rendering of nature in a miniature of the second part, showing St. Michael battling with the Devil (*Fig.* 45). Beneath this scene, which takes place in the sky, we see, in front of the inclined plane of the open sea dotted with ships,[1] a view of Mont-Saint-Michel (Normandy), showing not only the church and the monastery, but also the town with its little houses rising one above the other on the steep long slopes of the hill.[2]

[1] This inclined plane behind a view of a town proves, among other things, that the artists of the second decade had not yet completely abandoned the spatial construction of the late Trecento.
[2] This is no more based on an exact drawing made from nature, than is the grisaille miniature, painted about half a century later, of Mont-Saint-Michel in the 'Miracles de Notre-Dame' (Paris, B.N., MS. Franç. 9199; reproduced in catalogue of exhibition 'Les plus beaux manuscrits', 1937, *Pl.* XII). In 1415 the reproduction from memory, not of one detail, but of the whole aspect of a given place, was in itself an artistic feat.

between the living courtiers and the horsemen woven into the tapestry, so that it is only the way in which the tapestry is hung across the corner that enables us to recognize it for what it is. Paul de Limbourg covers the table with gold and silver plates and bowls, apparently placed there at random. The cutting of the figures by the edges of the picture gives sharp emphasis to the fact that only a portion of the room is visible. A similarly designed room, narrow and shut off only by a side wall, is found in the miniature depicting the murder of Thomas à Becket in the 'Heures du Maréchal de Boucicaut' (*Fig.* 14). So far as I know this is the first time that an interior (and moreover in approximately correct dimensional ratio to the figures) is shown in such a way that, despite a few insufficiencies due to foreshortening, we are given the impression that it is a reproduction of a portion of a real building.

The very arrangement of the buildings in the

12. Franco-Flemish Miniaturist, about 1415: *King Charles VI conversing with Pierre Salmon.* Geneva, Library

[1]The motive is not quite unique. We find the window (this time closed) in the back wall of the dedicatory miniature, stylistically only slightly later, of the 'Poésies de Christine de Pisan', a manuscript (British Museum, Harley 4431) illuminated for Isabella of Bavaria, wife of Charles VI (reproduced in Martin, *op. cit.*, *Pl.* 87).

[2]Jacquemart de Hesdin's 'Marriage at Cana' in the 'Grandes Heures' (Paris, B.N., Lat. 919) contains the immediate forerunner of this type of setting, though the outside of the building is represented; the inside has the pure 'box' room with ceiling, floor and two side walls, and the table placed parallel to the pictorial plane as a 'repoussoir'; the table with its dishes and glasses is rendered, though in an abbreviated manner, with the fidelity of a still-life.

fourteenth–century French manuscripts and even the Limbourg brothers did not disdain to use it on occasion. But the painter here transfers the patterns of the archaic background in earlier miniatures to the materials in the room, which are so beautifully gathered up and foreshortened that we get a very good idea of the appearance of the room. In addition, the artist gives us in the rear wall a very realistic reproduction of an open double window.[1]

We find a very similar setting in the calendar picture for January (*Fig.* 13) in the Chantilly book of hours. Here we look into an interior of which we can see the rear wall, one of the side walls, the floor and the ceiling.[2] Paul de Limbourg dispenses with the lines leading sharply into depth used by the painter of the miniature we have just discussed (*Fig.* 12). Paul's chief means of foreshortening is the overlapping of the three groups of figures disposed parallel to the pictorial plane. As the body-colour of miniature-painting does not permit a material characterization of the surfaces, there is no essential difference in effect

13. Paul de Limbourg: *The Month of January.* Chantilly, Musée Condé

B

14. Miniature from the Book of Hours of the Maréchal
de Boucicaut: *The Murder of St. Thomas à Becket.*
Paris, Musée Jacquemart-André

calendar miniatures testifies to a striving after a spatial solution which will show clearly the relative positions of parts of a building before or behind one another. These efforts become still more evident in the scenes from the Gospels in the second part. In the miniature of the Presentation in the Temple the lavishly decorated setting with the protagonists is taken direct from Taddeo Gaddi's fresco in Santa Croce at Florence, including even the details, or with more probability, from a work dependent on this fresco, such as the beautiful drawing in the Louvre. In the miniature of Christ bearing the Cross (*Fig. 27*) we have a particularly clear example of the threefold task which the artist assigns to the architecture, viz. to decorate, to stress the grouping of the figures and to produce an effect of space. The scheme of composition, which is old, was given a stamp of its own in Siena and found its classic expression in Simone Martini's little picture now in the Louvre. In two respects, however, Paul de Limbourg surpasses Simone Martini—in the homogeneous direction of movement of the cortège and in the rendering of the view over the town. By erecting a huge city gate reminiscent of a triumphal arch, the artist provides an aperture through which we see a line of houses, four or five stories high and only slightly abbreviated. This spatial image is the only point of contact between Paul de Limbourg's settings and those of Altichiero and Avanzo (*Fig. 26*).

The regulating function, provided in the miniatures with architectural backgrounds by the buildings represented, is assumed in the scenes set in the open country by masses of figures, which with their free symmetry, e.g. in the miniature of the Adoration of the Magi (*Fig. 34*), counterbalance one another. This highly artistic composition is most eminently suited to the inner significance of the episode.

The three types of setting used by the Limbourg brothers for the calendar pictures are employed again very aptly in the main portion of the book. Tranquil and simple compositions, even when they contain masses of figures, have primitive landscape settings such as are found in the 'Livre de la chasse'. The animated miniatures of complicated construction, on the other hand, such as the Adoration of the Magi (*Fig. 34*), have the richer, more advanced settings of the type found in the 'Heures du Maréchal de Boucicaut'. In the background of Paul de Limbourg's Epiphany we see walls, roofs and towers of a city standing out against the sky, in all probability representing some actual place, since in the preceding miniature, showing the Three Kings on their way to Bethlehem, the Sainte–Chapelle and Notre-Dame de Paris are clearly recognizable. A relationship to Ambrogio Lorenzetti's fresco of 1339, showing the 'Ager Senensis', in the Palazzo Pubblico at Siena, can be safely assumed. Just as original and as significant for the future as the landscape in the October picture (*Fig. 11*) is the rendering of nature in a miniature of the second part, showing St. Michael battling with the Devil (*Fig. 45*). Beneath this scene, which takes place in the sky, we see, in front of the inclined plane of the open sea dotted with ships,[1] a view of Mont-Saint-Michel (Normandy), showing not only the church and the monastery, but also the town with its little houses rising one above the other on the steep long slopes of the hill.[2]

---

[1] This inclined plane behind a view of a town proves, among other things, that the artists of the second decade had not yet completely abandoned the spatial construction of the late Trecento.

[2] This is no more based on an exact drawing made from nature, than is the grisaille miniature, painted about half a century later, of Mont-Saint-Michel in the 'Miracles de Notre-Dame' (Paris, B.N., MS. Franç. 9199; reproduced in catalogue of exhibition 'Les plus beaux manuscrits', 1937, *Pl.* XII). In 1415 the reproduction from memory, not of one detail, but of the whole aspect of a given place, was in itself an artistic feat.

Surprising, too, is the originality of invention in compositions not derived from Italian models. Here we see clearly the beginnings of a loosening of the iconographic conservatism of mediaeval art. Let us take, for example, the miniature of the Betrayal of Christ (*Fig.* 15). The figures, which, in furtherance of the desire to create a nocturnal effect, are all painted in dark-blue or brown tones shading into grey, stand out against the star-studded sky. The stars, the haloes, the torches and the lanterns and their reflections are heightened with gold. Contrary to the iconographic usage of the time, the version of the subject is taken, not from one of the three synoptic Gospels, but from the programmatic Gospel of St. John. It illustrates the sixth verse of the eighteenth chapter: 'As soon as he had said unto them, I am he, they went backwards and fell to the ground.' This last triumph of the Saviour before his Passion, which St. John records in this one sentence, is transformed into a visual picture of astonishing impressiveness. Paul de Limbourg, therefore, did not think only of external sumptuousness and naturalness of the representation; he was also concerned with rendering the inner significance of the episode.

The narrative art of the calendar pictures is found again in the miniatures of the second part, despite the greater severity of compositional structure.[1] This can be seen in the numerous decorative accessories not required by the theme. One need only consider the masterly rendering of the leopards in the miniature of the Epiphany (*Fig.* 34), suggesting Lombard models. Even more than in the 'Livre de la chasse' (*Fig.* 8) we see the predilection for narrative naturalistic motives, which in French miniature-painting of the fourteenth century were confined to the marginal 'droleries', but are now set free to appear in the scene itself.

The style of the figures in the second part of the 'Très riches Heures' is, on the whole, the same as that of the calendar pictures. The oriental character of many of the costumes is also to be found occasionally in the works of Simone Martini, the two Lorenzetti and their followers, and in several French miniatures from the beginning of the fifteenth century, *e.g.*, in the 'Merveilles du monde' in the Bibliothèque Nationale at Paris (MS. Franç. 2810). Nowhere else, however, does it appear in such overwhelming profusion. Expressive gestures, such as the prostration of the foremost king in the Adoration of the Magi (*Fig.* 34), heighten the effect produced by the oriental costumes.

15. Paul de Limbourg: *The Betrayal of Christ*.
Chantilly, Musée Condé

The versatility of the Limbourg brothers in the rendering of the human form becomes apparent if we study their representations of the nude. A famous example is the highly original miniature of the terrestrial paradise with its four consecutive scenes. The nudes are characterized above all by their movements. The Gothic feeling expressed in their outlines[2] is in perfect harmony with the second phase of the 'international' style, which, be it noted, lasted longer in Italy than it did in the Low Countries, so that we find the nearest parallels to this mode of depicting the nude in the works of a Pisanello or a Giovanni di Paolo. Far more important for the development of the nude is the miniature between the calendar and the second part of the Chantilly book of hours. It represents the 'anatomical' man, seen

[1]To gain a full understanding of this art it is necessary to study, not only the miniatures, but the pages as a whole (*Figs.* 43, 45) with their borders, their heads, animals and flowers. These ornamental portions frequently serve to mitigate the all too strict symmetry of the pictorial construction and elsewhere have a harmonizing effect on the composition.

[2]Julius von Schlosser (*Jahrb. der kunsth. Sammlungen*, XVIII, Vienna 1897, p. 55) rightly stresses the fact that Paul de Limbourg was not influenced by the forms of antique art, although he used an antique motive for the kneeling Adam in the Fall of Man.

from the front and from behind, in the Zodiac (*Fig.* 43).[1] The modelling of the body is an improvement on that of the little figures in the miniature of the terrestrial paradise and reveals close observation of the human form, though without individualization.

The discovery of the diversity of the world found its first artistic echo in the Chantilly book of hours. Two picture cycles, the calendar and the illustrations to the Bible, give the painters an opportunity of expressing this diversity in a variety of themes. The totality of these book-illuminations is thus imbued with a cosmic character. In the various miniatures the new feeling for nature and traditional idealization exist side by side.

The 'Très riches Heures du Duc de Berry' is not only the most comprehensive and significant, but also by far the most advanced work of the Limbourg brothers. Immediately afterwards, miniature-painting, from the point of view of historical development, came to a standstill, which lasted in the Netherlands until the 1430's and in France until just before 1450.

The Franco-Flemish style of the second decade of the fifteenth century, which finds its purest expression in the Chantilly book of hours, can also be discerned in a few panel-paintings. We may safely assume that the works we know are but a small portion of those which originally existed. Two tendencies can be observed in them—one retrospective (French), destined to die out, and the other modern (Franco-Flemish), which leads us to the art of the brothers van Eyck.

The retrospective tendency permits a timid penetration of 'naturalistic' ideas only in the details. It is represented by a painting in the Louvre, monumental in its effect, of the Holy Trinity, the Last Communion of St. Denis and his martyrdom.[2] This important work has a clear stylistic relationship to panel-paintings in the idealistic manner dating from the early years of the century—paintings still closely linked with the Parisian tradition of the late fourteenth century. The modelling of the human form, however, has reached approximately the same stage of development as that of the Man in the Zodiac Circle (*Fig.* 43).

As for the second, more modern tendency, so few works have been preserved that we are compelled to resort to drawings made from lost pictures. Two pen-drawings, on either side of the sheet, now in the Städel Institute at Frankfurt-on-Main, are of special value in this connection. The discrepancy between carefully executed portions and others which are only roughly sketched in shows us that these are not designs for a picture, but that a first-class artist has copied from three panels with his pen what seemed to him to be important, namely figures and architectural elements. Instructive above all is the reverse (*Fig.* 16),[3] on which, as in a sketchbook, two groups in the same style, which can hardly have been taken from the same work, are placed side by side. The main group must certainly have originated from a panel or a wall-painting, for the comparatively large size of the sheet of paper and above all the careful, detailed drawing of figures and architecture seem to exclude the possibility that the original can have been a miniature. A number of spectators clad in fantastic costumes—they are probably Old Testament personages—is standing inside a round building, into which we look through two arches. We do not know what these men and women are gazing at so intently. The main theme of the lost picture has obviously been omitted and here we have probably only the right extremity of a composition. In the upper left-hand corner is a group of four men in sharply

---

[1]Harry Bober (*Journal of the Warburg and Courtauld Institute*, XI, 1948), who deals at length with the iconographic interpretation and derivation of this miniature, calls it 'Zodiac Man and Vein Man in Zodiac Circle'.

[2]The painting is usually identified with the altar-piece showing scenes from the life of St. Denis which, according to the conventional hypothesis, was begun by the court painter to the Duke of Burgundy, Jean Malouel (probably an uncle of the Limbourg brothers), for the Chartreuse de Champmol at Dijon and finished after his death in 1415 by Henri Bellechose.

    Against this identification one might adduce the complete uniformity of all stylistic features (pictorial structure, treatment of details and manner of painting), which makes the collaboration of two artists rather unlikely. Despite the retrospective conception, it is difficult to believe that the advanced method of grouping and moulding the bodies is due to an artist of Broederlam's generation, still rooted in the tendencies of the fourteenth century, such as Malouel must have been. Grete Ring (No. 54) draws attention to the fact that all we know is that in 1398 five altar-pieces (representing what subjects?) were commissioned for the Chartreuse de Champmol and that in 1416 Henri Bellechose purchased at Dijon colours for 'ung tableau de la Vie St. Denis'. But St. Denis was revered throughout France. Since the provenance of the picture cannot be traced back beyond the nineteenth century and since the Bartholomey collection, from which it came, was merely, according to the Louvre catalogue, assembled in Burgundy, the conventional hypothesis falls to the ground. There is only one point in favour of Burgundy as the place of origin of this picture, namely that the large tondo of the Pietà in the Louvre (Ring, No. 53), similar in style, though painted by another hand, which has the arms of the Duke of Burgundy on the back and must therefore have been commissioned by Jean sans Peur, is not Flemish in style. But it might very well have been painted by an artist of the Parisian school or by some other Northern French painter.

[3]On the recto of the page, too, the draughtsman was concerned mainly with copying the figures of a composition and has taken only one small Trecento tree from the setting of his model. The subject is the Tiburtine Sibyl conjuring up for the Emperor Augustus a vision of the Holy Virgin, who appears in the sky on the sickle of the moon. The style of the figures and draperies, and the simple and noble pose of the former, conform, like those of the figures on the verso of the page, with those of the miniatures in the Chantilly book of hours.

differentiated costumes, sketched in the same style as the group in the temple scene. Only the upper part of their bodies is visible and they appear to be seated.

The style of the lost original of a biblical Scene in a Temple (*Fig.* 16) must have been at the same stage of development as that of the Limbourg brothers. A link between the two artists is their striving to form compact groups, but the panel-painter was evidently more concerned with achieving a greater differentiation of the figures. Still more interesting is the architecture, the forms of which are derived from late Romanesque art, and which is overladen with figure decorations[1]. Since, so far as we can perceive, architectural forms in Franco-Flemish painting were previously derived either from Italian Trecento art or from French Gothic, this is a new feature. The dark shadows in the background of the interior and in the round niches seem to denote that in the lost original the artist aimed at a certain effect of light and shade.

Only a few years ago an important original work illustrating the same stage of development was discovered. This is a small altar-piece, which appeared in London during the recent war and eventually passed to the collection of Count Seilern. A number of scholars (e.g. L. Burchard, O. Pächt, Grete Ring, E. Schilling) claim that it is an early work of the Master of Flémalle, whom we can, with reasonable probability, identify as Robert Campin, active at Tournai from 1406 to 1444. As long ago as 1910 Ernst Heidrich dated round about 1420 the earliest works of this artist known to him. Charles de Tolnay later drew attention to the fact that one of the creators of the Ghent altar-piece must have been acquainted with an important work by this master. The newly-discovered triptych is stylistically older than the works hitherto accepted by scholars as being by Robert Campin.[2]

The triptych[3] consists of three scenes, terminating in a gold ground with plaster ornaments (vine tendrils). Each of the three pictures (*Fig.* 21) has an independent composition, even the size of the figures being different in each case. An idealistic style still prevails, but numerous realistic motives can be observed on the wing-panels. The centre compartment, showing the Entombment, is characterized by a strictly balanced, symmetrical arrangement developing mainly in the flat, a type of composition already known to us from the reliefs on Jacques Baerze's altar-piece in Dijon, which, like the representations on the 'Parement de Narbonne', are also disposed in arched niches. The landscape setting of Campin's wing-panels is, like Broederlam's, conceived as an inclined plane and the rendering of the individual motives (such as the very summarily indicated plants) of which it is composed shows but little advance on the style of about 1400 (*Fig.* 8). On the left panel in the foreground kneels the donor, apparently a burgher, with a scroll. In the background we see the hill of Golgotha, with the thieves already on the crosses, while a ladder is still leaning against the unoccupied Cross of Christ. The very animated and expressive figures of the thieves and the enlivenment of the scene by the insertion of a cheerful little dog represent stylistic parallels to the art of the Limbourg brothers. This also applies to the

16. Franco-Flemish School, about 1415: *Scene from the Old Testament.* Pen drawing. Frankfurt-on-Main, Städel Institute

[1]On the use of Romanesque architectural forms in Franco-Flemish and old Netherlandish painting, see Panofsky, *Art Bulletin*, XVII, 1935, note 28.

[2]The only work attributed (by Friedländer) to the Master of Flémalle which shows a style even more archaic than that of the Seilern triptych is the Virgin on the Turf-bank, in the closed garden (now in Berlin), which may date from about 1410. No matter whether it is an original early work by the Master of Flémalle or a school production derived from some lost painting, this little picture is an effective answer to any chronological doubts as to the identification of the artist as Robert Campin, that is to say a painter born about 1380 who in 1406 was already active as a master.

The Seilern triptych also refutes F. Winkler's theory (*Der Meister von Flémalle und Rogier van der Weyden*, Strasburg, 1913 and *Thieme-Becker* XXXVII, 1950), who tries to establish the preliminary stages of Robert Campin's style in the above-mentioned Trinity picture with St. Denis in the Louvre and in unknown lost works of the art at the Burgundian court.

[3]The whole triptych is reproduced in *Pantheon*, XVII, 1944, p. 31, where it is described as 'after Robert Campin'.

sumptuous, many-coloured and fantastic robes of the watchers by the Tomb on the right-hand panel, which shows the Resurrection (*Fig. 21*). As in the Chantilly book of hours, breaks in the masses of the folds, especially at the points where the garments touch the ground, show that in Flanders the end of the 'international' style is imminent. This stylistic feature enables us to date the triptych from the second decade of the fifteenth century.[1]

The works of the second decade are distinguished by the profusion of their narrative art, characteristic of the second phase of the 'international' style on both sides of the Alps, although it is not possible to establish the existence of relations between contemporary Italian and Franco-Flemish painting. The lyrico-sentimental note, however, which we frequently find at this time in Italy and Germany is rarely encountered in Flanders or Burgundy, or at the Duke of Berry's court. Great strides are made, especially in the rendering of the setting, whereas the observation of nature is limited in the main to a few recordings from memory. The intimate character so typical of fourteenth-century French art is almost everywhere preserved and is blended with a new delight in the imaginative rendering of the sacred stories.

3. *Robert Campin's Second Period*

Abᴏᴜᴛ 1420 the Master of Flémalle, who in all probability is identical with Robert Campin, enters upon a new stylistic phase, to which belong the most important of his works from the point of view of historical development. With these panel-paintings the artist definitely abandons the paths of the 'international' style. A symptom of this is the abrupt disappearance of the gold ground. A new, purely Flemish art now comes into being. The separation of Netherlandish art from that of France is now complete.

In a painting by Robert Campin in the Prado, Madrid (*Fig.* 17), only certain motives are reminiscent of Broederlam's wing-panels in Dijon (*Figs.* 1, 2). Two consecutive scenes are represented —the Choice of the Bridegroom and the Nuptials of the Virgin. Here, too, on the left side of the picture the exterior and interior of the Temple are shown simultaneously and the artist is no more successful than was the Sienese painter Duccio a century earlier in his effort to give perspective credibility to the overlapping of the round pillars by the figures. In the structure and in the fantastic embellishment of this round Romanesque building we also note a marked similarity to the temple in the Frankfurt drawing (*Fig.* 16), though the space is wider and therefore closer to nature. In the rendering of the cathedral portal on the right, which like many buildings in the second part of the Chantilly book of hours is set at an angle, the elaborate architectural decoration is artistically far ahead of that found in the works of the Limbourg brothers. Nevertheless, despite the profusion of individual motives, this portal is not intended to be taken as real. Its ultimate purpose is merely to give a symbolic emphasis to the scene.

The artist has made rapid progress since he painted the Seilern triptych. The relief-like style of the centre compartment of the latter altar-piece has been abandoned. In each of the two halves of the Prado picture, as in the Entombment, the foremost figures are seen from behind; in the left half they stand at some distance from the edge of the picture, but in the more important scene on the right they are so close to it that the edge cuts the robe of the foremost figure. The purpose of these figures seen from behind is to avoid giving the impression of a deliberate posing of the group. The illusion of depth is heightened by the well-foreshortened cathedral portal in the right half of the picture. It is in process of construction and is meant to symbolize the New Testament, whereas the Romanesque Temple in the left half is a symbol of the Old.[2] Particularly noteworthy are the

---

[1]The lost original of the Virgin in the Apse, preserved only in the form of copies (New York, etc.), must have been executed almost at the same time as the centre panel of the Seilern triptych, *i.e.* after the Virgin on the Turf-bank in Berlin. The picture showing God the Father with the body of Christ and four Angels, likewise preserved only in copies, must, to judge from the far more plastic modelling and the broken style of the folds, be of later date than the Seilern Entombment and even, in my opinion, than the Trinity in Leningrad, which Kurt Bauch (*Pantheon*, XVII, 1944, p. 37, note 1) believes to be the more recent version. His theory that the Louvain copy may be the counterpart of the original of the Virgin in the Apse seems to me to be contradicted by the complete lack of spaciousness.

The numerous copies of lost paintings of the Master of Flémalle certainly increase our knowledge of his artistic activity, but they also obscure the lines of his development. In each single case—we are here referring only to a few—we must first consider: (*a*) whether the original was really a work of the master's and not merely that of a follower, and (*b*) whether the copyist, whose achievement may have encouraged other copyists, followed the original faithfully without adding or omitting anything.

[2]See Panofsky's article in *Art Bulletin*, XVII, 1935, and Tolnay's book: *Le maître de Flémalle et les frères van Eyck*, Brussels 1938.

embellishment of the windows with paintings on glass and the decoration of the frontons, the intrados and the jamb with reliefs and of the lintel of the doorway with sculptures. In contrast to the purely decorative sculptures on the round building in the Frankfurt drawing, the choice of subjects is here in direct symbolical relationship to the whole. These symbols serve to emphasize the truths of the Christian faith represented and thus to preserve the religious significance of the picture. The style, however, has become realistic. The movements of the figures, with their rich, multi-coloured and fantastic attire, are more vigorous and more complicated than in the works of the Limbourg brothers. To quote the words of Jacob Burckhardt, we can perceive the striving 'nach all-bezeichnender Deutlichkeit' (to achieve a clarity signifying everything). This can be seen, for example, in the presence of numerous ugly heads. Only the gentle figure of the Virgin is in deliberate contrast to her surroundings.

In the landscape, although the buildings leave little room for it, three novelties strike the eye. First, there is a low horizon, the level of which, however, is not uniform, but is set a little higher or lower, according to the space available for the landscape. Still more surprising is, secondly, the vivid and natural cloudy sky. And lastly, each of the three landscapes displays a faithful rendering of simple and unpretending scenery.

From the art historian's point of view the importance of the back of the Madrid wing-panel (*Fig. 54*) is almost equal to that of the front. It contains the oldest grisaille figures to be found in a panel-painting. This method of painting, as is well known, owes its origin to Giotto, who used it for his socle frescoes of Virtues and Vices in the Arena Chapel at Padua. Since the Master of Flémalle, in contrast to Broederlam and the Limbourg brothers, does not reveal any trace of direct contact with Italian art, we must consider this to be a monumentalized transformation of the little stone figures crowning the capitals in Broederlam's Annunciation (*Fig. 1*). Robert Campin's grisaille figures are set in niches, closed at the top and bevelled at the sides.[1] In these niches the painted stone figures of St. James the Great and St. Clare stand on slightly over-foreshortened socles. There is still an echo here of Claus Sluter's powerful monumental style but the figures are at the same time given a naturalistic interpretation by the light falling from the top right-hand corner and casting strong shadows. Characteristic is the instantaneous note given to the figure of St. James by the apparently abrupt suspension of movement. This reminds us of the hasty movements of some of the 'pleureurs' on the tomb of Duke Philip the Bold in Dijon, which Campin probably knew. On both sides of the Prado wing we find a number of new stylistic problems, towards the solution of which not only Robert Campin, but also Hubert and the youthful Jan van Eyck were striving at about the same time. If we wish to trace the origin of this new style, it is advisable to follow the development of the oldest of the three artists, Robert Campin, until we can be certain that his art was not influenced by that of the brothers van Eyck.

The works of this second period of the Master of Flémalle present a very varied aspect. The artist does not adhere to any particular scheme of composition, but adapts his construction to each individual task. We are thus only partially able to arrange the works of this period in a definite chronological sequence.

The art of Robert Campin reveals hardly any affinity with that of the Limbourg brothers. The question thus arises, whether the artist was not influenced by some other painter whose style was more advanced than Broederlam's. We are surprised by the iconographic and compositional relationship between a number of Campin's conceptions—some of which have been preserved in their original form,

17. Robert Campin: *The Choice of the Bridegroom; the Nuptials of the Virgin*. Madrid, Prado

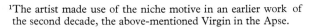

[1] The artist made use of the niche motive in an earlier work of the second decade, the above-mentioned Virgin in the Apse.

18. Robert Campin: *The Nativity*. Dijon, Musée

while others can be reconstructed from copies, either faithful or free—and the miniatures in the 'Heures du Maréchal de Boucicaut'.[1]

But the connection between the style of Robert Campin and that of the 'Heures du Maréchal de Boucicaut', the painter of which, like Campin, was not directly influenced by Italian art, does not consist solely in iconographic and compositional coincidences. Campin's rendering of landscape is also akin to that of the miniature-painter. The left wing of the Seilern triptych already contains undulating hills overlapping one another. The affinity is still more noticeable in the picture of the Nativity at Dijon (*Fig.* 18). Here we find an artistic device which occurs for the first time in the book of hours at the Musée Jacquemart-André. By means of a systematic elaboration of the lateral coulisses, the Master of Flémalle contrives to give the setting a consequential progression into depth, from the foremost

[1]In most cases, when we try to establish an influence exercised by a miniaturist on a panel-painter, we can only assume that the latter was acquainted with the models, methods of composition and stylistic peculiarities of the miniature school concerned.
The following features of Robert Campin or one of his immediate followers are derived from compositions in the manuscript at the Musée Jacquemart-André in Paris:

(a) The spatial setting of the Annunciation in the Prado, entirely in his style, by one of his followers (*Fig.* 23 ; *cf* p. 20, note 2).

(b) The construction of the St. George on horseback in Lady Mason's collection, which is by the hand of the youthful Rogier van der Weyden, but is apparently a true copy of a lost original dating from his teacher's second period.

(c) The composition of a lost Visitation, which can be reconstructed from the well-known versions, based on it, by the Master of Flémalle's two most important pupils, Rogier van der Weyden (in Turin and Lützschena) and Jacques Daret (in Berlin).

(d) The compositional design of a painting from Robert Campin's last period, executed after 1430, the Virgin on a bank of clouds at Aix-en-Provence, in which the artist adopts the fundamental elements of the construction of the David miniature in the 'Heures du Maréchal de Boucicaut' (*Fig.* 10).

19. Robert Campin:
The Ingelbrecht Altarpiece.
Brussels, Heirs of Princesse de Mérode

plane to the horizon. The road traversing the landscape, which we can also see in the left wing of the Seilern triptych, is here so boldly drawn in serpentine lines that it serves to heighten the effect of depth. But above all it is the Boucicaut master's background landscapes (*Fig.* 9) that Campin appropriates, showing, however, the motives in approximately correct proportions. For the first time we are offered a background landscape which produces the impression of being a whole. The many progressive features by far outweigh the few conventional elements (such as the formation of the rocks on the left). In the right-hand part of the section of landscape (*Fig.* 48) there is nothing reminding us of stenographic symbols. Here each motive is conceived and rendered as an optical entity.

In his presentation of the interior the Master of Flémalle achieves even more than he does in his rendering of landscape. We see this in the celebrated little altar-piece belonging to the Princesse de Mérode (*Fig.* 19), the armorial bearings on which show that it was commissioned by a member of the Ingelbrecht family of Malines. This is the oldest panel-painting that has come down to us in which the interiors filled with objects of everyday use are reproduced with real fidelity to nature.

In the centre panel, showing the Annunciation, the interior has the same box-like character[1] as the niches on the back of the Madrid painting (*Fig.* 54). On the left wing, with the kneeling donors, the scene is laid in the open air, in a little walled garden in front of the house. The link with the centre panel is provided by the steps leading up to the Virgin's chamber and by the door of the room opening outwards. Although the idea of bringing the centre compartment and the wing-panels into a spatial relationship is not carried to its logical conclusion, since the right wing, showing St. Joseph, has an independent construction of its own, this nevertheless represents an important novelty, which was soon taken up by other artists.

Three motives of the spatial image, the foreshortened fire-place, the timber ceiling and the box-like room, on the right wing, shut off on one side only, also go back to Italian Trecento painting. These three motives we find together, in similar design, in Pietro Lorenzetti's fresco of the Last Supper (*Fig.* 20) in the lower church at Assisi. As there is no reason to suppose that Robert Campin visited Italy, we may assume that there was some link, now lost, between the fresco and the Ingelbrecht triptych.

In the rear wall of the centre compartment Robert Campin gives us the same window with half-opened shutters that we have already seen in the miniature of the conversation between Charles VI

and Pierre Salmon (*Fig.* 12). In the Virgin's room the panes of the windows are closed, in order not to divert the spectator's eye from the action, but on the right wing-panel they are wide open. Through them we see—for the first time—a view of a Flemish town, peopled with little figures. Although we cannot assume any connection, the treatment of nature is very similar to that found in Paul de Limbourg's miniature of Mont-Saint-Michel (*Fig.* 45).[2] Robert Campin tried to give animation to the scene by showing Nazareth in the form of a fifteenth-century Flemish town.

Equally surprising, as Tolnay rightly stresses, is the treatment of light. The interior on the right wing-panel is seen (only at the back, not in the foreground where the figure is sitting) against the light streaming in through the window. So far as we know, this is the first instance of light being conceived as an artistic problem.[3]

This altar-piece (*Fig.* 19) was commissioned by a burgher of Malines, and the milieu and the furniture of the two interiors are such as would be found in the house of a well-to-do burgher. The contrast to the courtly art of the Limbourg brothers is evident. The occasional note, which in the Chantilly book of hours is found only in the secular pictures of the months, now becomes perceptible in a religious painting. The hand-towel by the lavatory niche is hanging from its stand as if it had only just been used. If St. Joseph is shown

20. Pietro Lorenzetti:
The Last Supper
(Detail). Assisi.

---

[1] This 'box room,' but with the exterior architecture indicated, is already found in the miniature of the Marriage at Cana in the 'Grandes Heures du Duc de Berry' (Paris, B.N., Lat. 919) by Jacquemart de Hesdin, as well as in various miniatures in the 'Heures du Maréchal de Boucicaut' (*e.g.* the Pentecost).

[2] The art of Robert Campin, which developed out of that of the master of the 'Heures du Maréchal de Boucicaut', reveals so little affinity with that of Paul de Limbourg that this can hardly be the result of a direct contact. We must not overlook the fact that at the time when Paul, who in age was probably not far removed from Campin, created his masterpiece, the Tournai master had already been working for some years in that Flemish city.

[3] For the use of colour in the Ingelbrecht Altarpiece *cf.* Chapter VII, 1.

making mouse-traps,[1] that is in deference to an old tradition of representing him employed upon some everyday task, a tradition followed by Melchior Broederlam (*Fig. 2*) and before him by the Hamburg master Bertram. That which in their case, however, produced a mildly comical effect, here strikes us as being meant quite seriously. The atmosphere of a burgher's house pervading the whole picture is deliberately heightened by means of this contemplative image of a craftsman at work. The fact that he is wearing his Sunday best instead of a workman's blouse is probably due to a desire to prevent the picture from descending to the manner of genre-painting.

The new treatment of the spatial setting seen in this work[2] is also found in the construction of a Madonna panel, now lost, which has come down to us only in the form of a drawing made from it, now in the Louvre (*Fig. 56*). To judge by the consequential foreshortening of the chamber and the greater freedom in the moulding of the figures of donors (their coats of arms are shown above the doors opening outwards), the lost original of this drawing must have been executed after the Ingelbrecht altar-piece.

In the Dijon Nativity the idealistic character of the Gospel story is stressed by means of scrolls and symbols. The symbols themselves, however, are quite realistically rendered, in exactly the same way as in the Ingelbrecht altar-piece. Thus the half-decayed rafters of the hut beneath the crumbling layer of clay and the torn-out bolt of the door seem to denote that the edifice of the Old Testament is about to collapse. The bad state of the hut has the same meaning as the broken rod of the blind 'synagogue' which the Master of Flémalle inserted on one side of the throne of God the Father in the little picture of the Trinity at Leningrad.[3] These symbols are particularly necessary in the centre compartment of the Ingelbrecht altar-piece in order to emphasize the import of the Gospel truth and to form a contrast to the realistic rendering of a room in a contemporary Flemish burgher's house. They thus provide a kind of compensation for the abandonment of the idealistic style.

Advanced though the works of Robert Campin's second period may appear, nevertheless the idealistic rendering of the sacred figures is not the only traditional element. There is yet another stylistic feature which can be compared with the Seilern triptych and has even some connection with the art of Melchior Broederlam, that is to say with the 'international' style, which might also be termed the style of beautiful colours. Campin's light and varied, but not complicated colouring is certainly more differentiated than that of the panel-paintings of Broederlam and his followers—works executed in another technique do not come into question for purposes of comparison—but it is based on a similar principle. True, the Master of Flémalle was already acquainted with some forms of colour-differentiation—he heightens, in the Dijon Nativity (*Fig. 18*), green with yellow, crimson with white, yellow with lilac—but he characterizes the substance of the surface, when depicting wood, straw, hair, far more with the aid of draughtsmanship than with that of colour.[4]

The style of Robert Campin's second period bears witness to a profound change in the conception of art. The supreme aim seems now to be faithful observation of nature in every detail. Only sacred personages, such as the Virgin and angels, have a claim to be endowed with beauty and charm; everything else must above all be characterized. Fidelity of reproduction is insisted upon, not only for the figures of the protagonists of the scene, but also for the setting, for all vegetation and animals and for all inanimate objects. In many cases symbols are employed in order to preserve the idealistic

[1] Huizinga (*Herbst des Mittelalters*, 5th German edition, 1930, p. 446, note 1) emphasizes that the mouse-trap may have a symbolic meaning and quotes the following saying of Petrus Lombardus: 'God set a mouse-trap for the Devil and baited it with the human flesh of Christ'.

[2] Robert Campin's treatment of space does not suddenly supplant the older method derived from the Trecento, which, as in the Prado wing-panel (*Fig. 17*), shows both the interior and the exterior of a building at the same time. One of the most interesting examples of the survival of the old form, to which Rogier van der Weyden returned to a certain extent about 1440, is a picture of the Annunciation (*Fig. 23*) likewise in the Prado. Here the new idea of depicting the Virgin in her chamber is blended with the old conception, which gives the room a temple-like character. This blending is emphasized in a curious fashion by the fact that beneath the arches of the church nave we see an open cupboard containing all kinds of utensils for daily use.

The figure of the Virgin in the Prado Annunciation is copied, with alterations hardly worth mentioning, from that in the Ingelbrecht altar-piece, from which the motive of the bench placed obliquely behind the figure is also taken. As long ago as 1913 Friedrich Winkler for this reason rightly rejected the hypothesis that this is a work of the Master of Flémalle. Campin's inventiveness was always fresh and original, so that in his works we may expect variants of a motive, but not mere repetitions. On the other hand, the rich exterior architecture as well as the figure of God the Father in the 'gloria' of angels and the cloudy sky are so completely in the master's style that we are bound to ask ourselves whether the painter of the Prado Annunciation did not take these motives from some other lost work by Campin.

[3] Like its counterpart, the Virgin by the fireplace (*Fig. 51*), this little picture shows that realistic form of setting and idealistic delineation of the figures which are characteristic of the religious pictures of the master's second period.

[4] *Cf.* Chapter VII, 1.

character of the scene. The style of all these works is a painter's style, which in the master's third period is replaced by a plastic style, vigorously modelled, very strongly characterized figures being rendered with a somewhat earthy ponderousness.[1]

4. Summary

THE development of Flemish painting from Broederlam's wing-panels to the works of Robert Campin's second period covers a span of about thirty years. The whole of this period is characterized by the dual efforts of artists, on the one hand to perfect themselves in the reproduction of nature, and on the other, not to sacrifice the idealism of the representation.

In these thirty years of artistic activity the exclusiveness so characteristic of fourteenth-century French art remains. Until towards the end of the fifteenth century the number of artists shows only a very small increase. There was no broad expansion of production such as took place in Germany and Italy even during the fourteenth century. The highest standards of execution continue to be demanded in Flanders as well. When, instead of princes and dukes, burghers become the artists' patrons, the milieu represented is occasionally altered, but not the method of representation, which remains exclusive, that is to say aristocratic.

Noteworthy, too, is a second significant characteristic of this artistic production. A number of considerable achievements in the reproduction of nature appears simultaneously in the works of various artists. Such innovations were the necessary result of an intensive study of the surrounding world. Let us take one example out of many. One of the greatest achievements of Robert Campin is held to be the motive, in all probability created by him, of a realistic view of a town through an open window. This motive occurs for the first time in the Ingelbrecht altar-piece (*Fig.* 19) and is repeated— each time with a different view, with or without landscape background—in the pictures of the Madonna in Leningrad (*Fig.* 51) and London (*Fig.* 46).[2] We have seen that two miniaturists anticipated his use of each of the two components that go to make up this motive—an open window realistically depicted (*Fig.* 12) and a characteristic rendering of a view over a town (*Fig.* 45). This shows that in the evaluation of artistic achievement we must consider, not the degree of novelty of the individual components of a motive, but the new manner in which they are combined, not the originality of the idea itself, but the originality and mastership of its execution.

This consideration involves another. We are very seldom in a position to trace the course of development in all its details. In most cases we do not know what work first suggested the new idea to the artist. On the other hand, we are usually able to perceive quite clearly the stylistic tendency from which the suggestion is derived; in other words the growth of the individual idea is often shrouded in darkness and will probably continue to remain obscure, but the formation of a style can be followed with relative clarity and exactitude.

During the 1420's, there is a change in this respect, too. The artistic personality of the particular painter suddenly acquires a plastic roundness and an individual stamp, which it has hitherto been impossible to discern. The works of Robert Campin's second period display a richness and a variety not previously encountered to the same degree. A new type of artist has arisen. An individual method of representation replaces the typical. If no other Flemish works but those of Robert Campin had been preserved from this decade of the century, we could describe him as a leading master. But as it happens, the works of his most fruitful and, as regards historical development, most important period are found side by side with those of a second artist and are overshadowed by those of a third and greater painter.

---

[1]In the first works of this third period, *e.g.* in the fragment showing one of the Two Thieves on the Cross at Frankfurt am Main, the material characterization of the surfaces shows hardly any advance on the Dijon Nativity and is mostly limited to the metallic portions (*cf.* Chapter VII, 1). In fact, as can be noticed in numerous German paintings executed in the realistic manner, the effect of steel, copper, etc., was easiest to bring out when the late mediaeval tempera technique was used.

[2]This was probably also varied in the original of the Louvre drawing (*Fig.* 56). There is another view of a town in the version, now in the National Gallery, London, of a composition of Robert Campin's second period showing the Death of the Virgin, the original of which has been lost.

The London fragment of a picture of the Holy Virgin belongs to Campin's third period, which is distinguished by very firm plastic modelling of figures realistically conceived. The realism of Campin's rendering of landscape, interior and still-life is now extended to the figure of the Virgin as well.

1. *The Lives of the Two Brothers*

OF Hubert van Eyck—who is assumed, probably correctly, though we have no proof, to have been the elder of the two brothers—we know very little. In 1425 the magistrates of Ghent paid him for two designs for a painting and we know that in the same year a sculpture of St. Anthony forming part of an altar-piece was in his workshop, probably waiting to be painted.[1] He died on 18th September, 1426[2], and left unfinished an altar-piece which we call the Ghent altar-piece. The inscription on the frame of this polyptych, which was added by his brother, who finished the work in 1432, or at all events was placed there with his consent, describes Hubert as the greatest (painter) of all times—'maior quo nemo repertus'[3].

We know considerably more about the younger of the two brothers, Jan or Johannes. Contemporary documents tell us that for some years, in any case from 24th October 1422 (the date of the first payment recorded), he worked as an artist for John of Bavaria, Count of Holland (†1425), in the count's castle at The Hague. On 19th May 1425 he was appointed court painter and 'varlet de chambre' to Duke Philip the Good of Burgundy. We have evidence that after that date he made long secret journeys on behalf of the Duke and that he was active for two years in Lille (until 1428) and visited Tournai. From 19th October 1428 until Christmas 1429 he was on the journey to Portugal, having been sent to King John I as a member of a ducal mission in order that he might make a portrait of the King's daughter, Princess Isabella, for whose hand the Duke was suing. At the request of the wealthy Ghent burgher Jodocus Vyd, Jan then undertook to complete the altar-piece left unfinished by his brother and he must have worked on this task during 1430 and 1431, when he was living in Bruges. On 6th May 1432 the work was finished and was installed in one of the ambulatory chapels of St. Bavon in Ghent. After this Jan continued to reside in Bruges. We hear of visits to his workshop by the Burgomaster in 1432 and by the Duke in 1433. On the occasion of a christening in 1434 the Duke presented him with six silver cups. In a letter to his council in Lille, written in 1435, the Duke complains that he cannot find another painter equally to his taste or of such proficiency in his art and science.

We also learn that in the same year Jan was paid for painting and gilding six statues and their tabernacles, intended for the front of the town hall in Bruges. In 1436 he was again sent on some secret business by the Duke. On 9th July 1441 his 'burial fees' were entered in the registers of the church of St. Donatian at Bruges.

We do not know for certain whence the brothers van Eyck came. According to a statement dating from the second half of the sixteenth century they were natives of Maaseyck near Maastricht, but various Belgian scholars claim that Maastricht itself was their home town. Nor do we know when they were born. From the documentary evidence, which begins in the 1420's, and from the style of

---

[1]The sources of information on Hubert and Jan van Eyck will be found in W. H. James Weale, *Hubert and Jan van Eyck*, London and New York 1908, and also in *The van Eycks* by W. H. James Weale with the co-operation of Maurice W. Brockwell, London and New York 1912.

[2]The dispute as to the authenticity of Hubert van Eyck's tombstone (*cf.* J. Duverger: *Het grafschrift van Hubrecht van Eyck*; *Verhandelingen v. de Konikl. vlaamsche Akademie voor Wettenschappen, Letteren en Schoone Kunsten*, 1945, Antwerp and Utrecht) appears to be of local interest only, as the ill-preserved object does not allow of any conclusion as to his art or his character.

[3]Two passages in this inscription—'major quo nemo repertus', in reference to an artist no other work by whom is attested by contemporaries, and 'arte secundus', in reference to the greatest European painter of the fifteenth century—have been the source of constant difficulty to scholars of the nineteenth and twentieth centuries, so that a tendency to reduce Hubert's share in the Ghent altar-piece has never quite disappeared.

Emile Renders, a Bruges art collector who was anxious to prove that the 'greatest painter of all times' was Jan, active in Bruges, and not Hubert, working at Ghent, put forward the theory that the inscription is a forgery, perpetrated about 1620(!) out of local patriotism (in honour of a man who was notoriously not of Ghent origin!). He propounded this theory energetically in three books. It would be unnecessary to mention this theory, had not M. J. Friedländer (in *Altniederländische Malerei* XIV)—the only serious scholar, as far as I know, to have done so—welcomed this assumption with a sigh of relief ('aufatmend begrüsst'), his relief being due to the fact that Renders was encouraged by, and supported, Friedländer's elimination of Hubert from the history of art (*Altniederländische Malerei* I), an idea which originated with K. Voll (*Die Werke des Jan van Eyck*, Strasbourg 1900, and *Altniederländische Malerei*, Leipzig 1906).
On the authenticity of the inscription, see J. Duverger, *loc. cit.*

those works of theirs that have been preserved, we can see that there is no reason to place the date of their birth much before 1400. Nor is there any reason to think that their ages differed by more than a few years.[1]

2. *The Works of Hubert van Eyck before the Ghent Altar-piece*

THE few panel-paintings which, on stylistic grounds,[2] can be attributed to Hubert van Eyck, or at all events are creations of his mind, reveal a clearly defined personality and show that, like Robert Campin, he stood at a decisive point of general development.

In the picture of the Three Maries at the Sepulchre (*Pls.* 1–6), now in the van Beuningen collection at Vierhouten, the figures are set in a spacious landscape, which plays, however, a more important role than has hitherto been the case. Rocky masses and the empty sarcophagus divide the picture into foreground and middle distance. The personages of the Gospel story are distributed about the foreground in a fairly symmetrical manner.

It seems probable that the artist was acquainted with the right wing (the Resurrection; *Fig.* 21) of Robert Campin's early triptych, now in the Seilern collection, London (or with some similar work which has since been lost). In Campin's wing and in Hubert's picture the manner in which the figures are set back from the foreground is the same. The richly attired watchers in Campin's wing-panel, grouped in cramped attitudes around the sarcophagus, are the forerunners of Hubert van Eyck's watchers at the Tomb (*Fig.* 22), but the Ghent painter makes the movements looser and less tense, thus rendering the figures more lifelike.[3] In the figures of the three Maries we notice that attention is paid to idealistic effect. The Angel and the three female figures are completely absorbed in their tasks: the reverent visit to the Tomb and the delivery of a divine message. The movements are as unobtrusive as those of most of the figures painted by the Limbourg brothers (*Figs.* 11, 13); the arms are held close to the bodies and the hands are often concealed. When, however, the artist

[1]None of the attempts to identify a portrait of either Jan or Hubert has met with success (recent literature: Aurelio Minghetti, *L'Arte*, 1940, XI. N.S. p. 36 and E. Schenk, *Zeitschrift für Kunst* III, 1949).
[2]See my article: *The Ghent Altar-piece* in *The Art Quarterly*, Detroit, Spring and Summer 1950.
[3]Huizinga (*op. cit.*, p. 448) cites as parallels the St. Joseph in Broederlam's Flight into Egypt (*Fig.* 2) and some of Paul de Limbourg's figures. The transition as here seen from the genrelike to the bizarre and the burlesque he calls the 'Breugel element in art about 1400'.

21. Robert Campin:
The Resurrection.
London, Count Seilern

22. Hubert van Eyck: *The Three Maries at the Sepulchre* (after the latest restoration).
Cat. No. 2. Vierhouten, Van Beuningen Collection

makes up his mind to give us an eloquent gesture, as in the case of the kneeling woman, it is rendered with emphasis.

Only in details, and especially in the rendering of the steel weapons of offence and defence, is Hubert van Eyck at pains to give material characterization to the surfaces of things. The general colour-scheme is darker than we are accustomed to seeing in the works of artists from Broederlam to Campin and the rich colours have a greater luminosity.

Hubert van Eyck has in common with the style of the second decade of the century the proportions of the figures to the format, the shifting back of the principal persons towards the second plane, the setting, still conceived as an inclined plane, and the rendering of landscape, in which, however, we do not find those individual features which are so striking in Robert Campin's Nativity (*Fig.* 18). In this way an idealistic note is preserved in the rendering of nature as well and the symbolical element is less prominent. Only on the left, behind the rocks, do we catch a glimpse of the sun, as in the Dijon picture.[1] Obviously both Campin and Hubert van Eyck were anxious to give animation to the existing setting by the insertion of details.

An enrichment by means of motives drawn from nature is already discernible in the foreground, where various plants are rendered in such a way that they can be identified with botanical accuracy, though the artist limits himself to what is indispensable to the characterization of the plants. In the bushes behind the sarcophagus every leaf is still visible, but in the middle distance, which contains some delightful motives obviously based on observation of nature, the reproduction becomes more sketchy. This is particularly noticeable on the slope of the hill (*Pl.* 6) leading up to the castle on the right. Some of these details, for example the cypresses, reveal a knowledge of southern climes. There is a parallel to the art of the Limbourg brothers in the way in which buildings, large and given in considerable detail, are placed on the horizon, but they are here products of the artist's fantasy. This city of Jerusalem is not realistically depicted or peopled with little figures like the Master of Flémalle's views of Flemish towns. Behind Jerusalem, forming a kind of background, the summits of a range of mountains appear, but without the intervening valleys. Despite all the naturalistic motives, the cumulative type of landscape setting prevalent during the second decade (cf., for example, *Fig.* 9) still survives. The artist does not yet aim at achieving uniform effect in a distant panorama, such as is found in the Dijon Nativity (*Fig.* 48).

The Vierhouten picture seems to have been, not an isolated panel, but the left wing of a larger work—a diptych or polyptych. In the course of the last cleaning traces of rays were discovered on the right edge of the picture (*Fig.* 22) towards the bottom and these must obviously have emanated from a neighbouring compartment (an Ascension, Pentecost or Coronation of the Virgin ?).

No less important than the Vierhouten picture is a second composition—an Annunciation (*Pls.* 7–8) now in the Metropolitan Museum, New York. Erwin Panofsky was the first critic to recognize the stylistic stage of development of this painting and to publish it as a work of Hubert van Eyck,[2] whose style can be discerned in the whole composition.

As the horizon of this Annunciation is higher than the top edge of the picture, it seems probable that the painting (and also the lost original, if one existed) was at one time higher. The possibility exists that the figure of God the Father was depicted in the upper left-hand corner and was the source of the main ray falling upon the face of the Virgin. We may conceive this God the Father to have been similar to that in the Madrid Annunciation (*Fig.* 23), painted by a follower of Robert Campin.[3]

The relationship between figures and architecture in the New York picture is the same as in Robert Campin's panel of the Nuptials of the Virgin in Madrid (*Fig.* 17). We see part of a church façade, the size of which is almost in the correct ratio to that of the figures. The landscape, too, is like an excerpt

---

[1] E. Panofsky (*The Art Bulletin*, XVII, 1935) draws attention to the fact that the light falls consistently from the right. He believes that the sun motive is a reference to the Resurrection of Christ.

[2] I myself have not seen the original and consequently know nothing of its state of conservation. I am therefore not in a position to give an opinion as to the hand that painted it.

[3] *Cf.* p. 20, note 2. Beenken (*The Art Bulletin*, XIX, 1937, p. 220 f.) rejected the attribution to Hubert van Eyck and returned the work to Petrus Christus on the basis of a faulty reconstruction of the vanishing lines, which in parts cannot be applied to the objects in the picture. His statements are therefore of little value as proofs of authorship. He goes on to say: 'The Petrus Christus panel, therefore, probably derives from a lost original and, like Panofsky, I should be inclined to believe from a pictorial conception of Hubert van Eyck'. Considering the execution of the landscape details by means of a good photograph, we are reminded of the bushes on the second plane on the left side of the Adoration of the Lamb (*Pl.* 17). The design of the landscape (*Pl.* 7) cannot be due to Petrus Christus, for he invariably used schematic landscape settings without any independent elaboration of the details.

23. Follower of Robert Campin: *The Annunciation.*
Madrid, Prado

from nature and contributes to the charm of atmosphere more than that of the Three Maries at the Sepulchre. The wall and the hedge of rose-bushes provide a line of demarcation between the foreground and the middle distance. As in the Three Maries, the various plants and trees, among which we again find a few cypresses, are so accurately rendered that we can give them their botanical names. The masonry, too, is drawn with great attention to detail.

In contrast to Robert Campin's Ingelbrecht altar-piece (*Fig.* 19), the general conception of the theme is purely idealistic. The Virgin is seen standing in the open doorway of a cathedral. The inscription on the tiles of the threshold hails her as the Queen of Heaven. As regards general effect, only the outside of the building is important. Panofsky pointed out that this Gothic church with a Gothic portal shows Romanesque forms in the narrow strip on the right edge of the picture (*i.e.* on the Virgin's left) and deduced from this that the two halves of the building symbolize the Old and the New Testaments.

In the Three Maries at the Sepulchre, a picture which can hardly have been painted before 1420, and in the composition of the New York Annunciation, which, to judge by its style, may have been designed a few years later, we have works of an artist imbued with all the new ideas evolved in art during the preceding thirty years. In the epical manner of presentation, in the silhouette effects of the figures and in the rich, but not obtrusive rendering of details, we are reminded of the art of the Limbourg brothers. In view of the difference of technique between illumination and panel-painting we cannot assume any direct contact, but it seems probable that there also existed panel-paintings in the style of Paul de Limbourg which have since been lost, but which Hubert van Eyck may have seen. He also seems to have known works of the Master of Flémalle's second period, but he cannot be held to have been a pupil of Campin's, since his colouristic execution is quite different from that of the Tournai master. As regards the latter's second period, reciprocal influences cannot be established. As the reproduction of worldly elements in Hubert's compositions plays only a minor part, he appears less revolutionary than Campin. A definite characterization of the master's work will, however, be possible only after we have considered the Ghent altar-piece.

3. *The Early Works of Jan van Eyck*

In the works which Jan van Eyck painted before 1430 he already displays an independent individuality. I begin with what I think is one of his earliest compositions, a work usually held to be by the hand of Petrus Christus. This is the dark-coloured, beautifully painted little picture of St. Jerome in his Study (*Pl.* 9), now in the museum at Detroit. Every single detail—the moulding of the head and hands, the rendering of the richly ornamented and carved furniture, the still-life elements—can be found again in authenticated works of Jan van Eyck. Even the shape of the lion is so closely akin to that of the somewhat stylized brass and stone lions in later paintings (*Pls.* 122, 126) that it seems to me certain that at least the conception of the picture must be due to Jan.[1]

The room in this picture is constructed in the simplest manner. A forerunner of this type of setting

[1]As I have not seen this painting since 1927—at that time I considered the assumption reasonable that we have here to do with an early work of Jan's (*Belvedere*, 1927, p. 82)—I am not in a position to give a definite opinion as to the executing hand. If it was really painted by the much coarser hand of Petrus Christus, then the latter, whose usual practice was to simplify Jan's style, must here have made a faithful copy, without essential alterations, of an early work of the master's which has since been lost.

is to be found in the already mentioned drawing of the same subject (*Fig. 24*). Jan must have seen this drawing or some other composition derived from it, for the left side of the picture with the window above the Saint's head is very similar (*Fig. 25*) and this can hardly be due to chance. Very characteristic is the way in which Jan cuts his motive out of the older composition and then proceeds to enrich it. The novelty consists first of all in the lifelikeness of the Saint's figure and in the neat and simple rendering of all the objects which surround him and fill his cell, but which are nowhere rendered summarily, as they are in Paul de Limbourg's miniature for the month of January (*Fig. 13*); secondly, in the fact that the faithful reproduction of inanimate objects, despite the absence of the dove whispering inspiration to the Saint, does not divert our attention from the figure; and thirdly, in the uniform character of the whole. St. Jerome is obviously immersed in his studies and his absorption is expressed by his attitude and also by the intimate atmosphere of the study and the pose of the lion, very similar to that of the lion in Dürer's famous engraving.

An even closer connection with the art of the second decade is shown by a work which is certainly an original—the little masterpiece of the Virgin in the Church (*Pl. 10*), now in the museum at Berlin. This is a typical early work of a youthful genius who has grown out of tradition and who in his aims, and above all in his pursuit of those aims, has left all his contemporaries far behind him. Here we look into the nave of a High Gothic cathedral, in which the Virgin, wearing the crown of the Queen of Heaven, is standing with the Child in her arms. She is conceived as the patroness of the church.[1] The disproportion between the size of the figure and the dimensions of the church is thus deliberate.[2]

The Child in his Mother's arms stretches out a caressing hand towards her, a motive popular in Franco-Flemish art about 1400. The pose of the Virgin, with the upper part of the body drawn back, the robe with its high girdle and the bold sweep of the voluminous mantle, stamp this figure as one

---

[1]Panofsky (*The Art Bulletin*, XVII, 1935, note 72) speaks of a 'quasi-visionary apparition of superhuman grandeur' and corroborates his opinion by a reference to Rogier van der Weyden's panel-painting of the Seven Sacraments in the Antwerp gallery, the architectural setting of which is borrowed from Jan van Eyck's Virgin in the Church. It is, in fact, true that in the centre panel of the triptych the ratio of size between the Crucifix and the church interior is similar.

[2]Since, in the works of Robert Campin and later in those of Jan van Eyck's mature period, such one-sided interiors were usually designed when a counterpart was planned, it seems possible that what has been preserved is only the left half of a diptych. The Berlin Virgin in the Church was copied twice—in 1499 (Antwerp Museum) and at the beginning of the sixteenth century (Rome, Galleria Doria)—and in each case it appears as the left half of a diptych. In both cases the right portion contains a portrait of the donor, in the first case alone in a secular interior in Campin's style and in the second together with a patron saint in a landscape.

24. Franco-Flemish Miniature-Painter: *St. Jerome in his Study*. Pen drawing. Paris, Bibliothèque Nationale

25. Jan van Eyck (original?): *St. Jerome in his Study*. Cat. No. 5. Detroit, Institute of Arts

26. Altichieri and Avanzo: *The Presentation.*   Padua, Oratorio di San Giorgio
27. Paul de Limbourg: *Christ bearing the Cross.*   Chantilly, Musée Condé
28. Jan van Eyck: *The Virgin in the Church.*   Cat. No. 4.   Berlin, Deutsches Museum

of the latest versions of the theme of the 'beautiful Madonna', which is characteristic of the artistic conception of the 'international' style outside Italy.

If we compare Jan's Queen of Heaven with Hubert's women standing by the Tomb of Christ (*Pl.* 2) or with the Virgin of the New York Annunciation (*Pl.* 8), the stylistic relationship becomes as clear as the individual differences. The more marked characterization of the Virgin in the Church is evident. How much richer in details is the robe and how much more exuberantly and capriciously the mantle is wrapped around it!

The figure at once attracts the eye, but it does not conceal any essential element in the structure of the church interior. Architecture and figure exist side by side.

The construction of the interior shows an adherence to tradition, for it can be traced back ultimately to the architectural settings of Altichiero and Avanzo in Padua. If we cover up the exterior architecture of the fresco of the Presentation in the Oratorio di San Giorgio (*Fig.* 26), we arrive at the source of this type of spatial construction, in which only one lateral wall is shown. Jan van Eyck obviously took this from the style of the Limbourg brothers. In the miniature of the Bearing of the Cross in Chantilly (*Fig.* 27), the eye of the spectator is led into depth through the very high city gate and past a long row of many-storied houses. In the Berlin painting the semicircular top of the picture (*Fig.* 28) is substituted for the gateway. It seems evident that Jan must have adopted an already existing and highly developed scheme of setting. Paul de Limbourg would probably have composed a church interior in a similar way, but the forms would have been quite different. In one essential point the rendering of space in this picture marks an advance on the art of the Limbourg brothers. Owing to the foreshortening based on a vanishing point lying within the picture, the spectator is also included in it. The vanishing lines of the floor emphasize strongly that here a subjective sector of the interior is shown.[1] Apart from this fact, the novelty lies in the execution.

In the architecture of the Berlin picture we are surprised by the meticulous attention given to every detail of the interior, from the tiles of the paving to the panes of the windows. The construction of the interior is not yet homogeneous, for the choir has a higher vanishing point than the nave; this is peculiarly noticeable if we follow the lines of the dwarf arcade beneath the windows.

This painting is ahead of all other church interiors painted before it. Two facts prove this. True, Hubert van Eyck was the first to paint an imaginable church façade (*Pl.* 8), but he showed only a portion of it and left it to the spectator to complete the impression. Here, the whole interior of a cathedral is shown, with a short flight of steps leading up to the choir behind a rood-screen, the

---

[1] This is clearly expounded by Panofsky in his article: *Die Perspective als "symbolische Form"* (*Vorträge der Bibliothek Warburg*, 1924–25, p. 317, note 52).

C

29. Miniature from the Book of Hours of the Maréchal
de Boucicaut: *St. Francis receiving the Stigmata.*
Paris, Musée Jacquemart-André

ambulatory, the transept and the three-aisled nave, all in such detail that it creates the illusion that this is an actually existing building.

Still more important than this is the second fact, the masterly handling of light. In the Ingelbrecht altar-piece (*Fig.* 19) the effect is based on the contrast between the lighted portions of the rooms and those which are in shadow. The rendering of the direct effect of the sun's rays did not yet form part of the problem. In the Virgin in the Church we find something new. As regards the lighting, the artist not only makes use of transitional half-tones and distinguishes the brightly lighted portions from those lying in semi-obscurity, but he also paints large patches of sunlight on the paving. This treatment of light was possible only as a result of the refinement of his technique, which enabled him to give correct values to everything that can possibly be reproduced by means of painting.

We are thus witnessing the birth of modern painting. This is the decisive moment when modern artistic practice breaks away from mediaeval art. We must remember in this connection that Vasari[1] praised Jan van Eyck not only as the inventor of oil-painting, an achievement which he corroborated with an anecdote, but also used the beautiful expression: 'La nuova invenzione del colorito'. Michelangelo's pupil did not just mean a new medium, but also something spiritual, when he spoke of a new invention in colouring. And in fact, from now on panel-painting takes the foremost place, ahead of mural-painting and book-illumination, which were unable to produce effects even remotely approaching these. For the tendency towards mere illumination, noticeable in panel-paintings, too, and to a certain extent even in the Master of Flémalle's (*Fig.* 18), the new technique substitutes a painting tendency. Jan insists that a panel-painting shall be really painted and that colour shall be its essential element. The task of colour is to give characterization to the surfaces of things, to distinguish clearly between the brilliant and the dull, between the smooth and the rough, the hard and the soft, and it also has to bring before our eyes all the gradations of light.

Here we touch one of the essential problems of our subject. Attempts have often been made to confute the old notion that Jan van Eyck was the founder of oil-painting by drawing attention to the fact that as early as the fourteenth century Cenino Cenini, and even before him the Byzantine monks on Mount Athos, were acquainted with recipes in which oil was used as a medium. But was there not perhaps some truth in Vasari's assertion that Jan van Eyck was the inventor of a new technique? In the elucidation of this question the chief difficulty seems to me to be the fact that the modern experts on technique—painters, restorers and chemists—have not yet managed to reach agreement, in the course of their controversies based mainly on empirical grounds, as to when one can speak of tempera painting and when of oil painting. If an artist like Vasari was really thinking only of the medium, which he could certainly not have examined himself, it seems permissible to suppose that he would have expressed himself differently. By using the words 'invenzione del colorito' he probably wanted to convey that something more than a technical novelty had been created. In the few works of Jan van Eyck which he had seen he must have noticed that the substantial effects of things were reproduced for the first time in a most impressive manner with the aid of an intensely luminous colouring. Moreover, it is probably true to say that Jan's efforts to achieve fidelity to nature in the

[1]In the Vita of Antonello da Messina.   He uses almost the same words as Facius did in 1456: 'multa de colorum proprietatibus invenisse'.

reproduction of every detail led him on to new technical experiments, and not *vice versa*, as the anecdote related by Vasari would lead one to suppose.

The new technique was connected with the evolution of art at the beginning of the fifteenth century, which paid far more attention to the reproduction of nature than the Gothic period did. But not until the works of Jan van Eyck, from the early Berlin Virgin in the Church to his last paintings, do we find this new, intensely luminous colouring, differentiating in a manner hitherto unknown and rendering in a most convincing way the effects of materials and the phenomena of light. Neither in the works of the Master of Flémalle's second period nor in those which I believe can be rightly attributed to Hubert van Eyck do we find more than tentative efforts to achieve what is found to such an astonishing degree in the Berlin picture of the Virgin. If we compare Jan's painting with the most advanced products of Italian art at that time, we see at once what this means. The anecdote ascribing the invention of oil painting to Jan must therefore be understood symbolically, that is: he was the first to grasp all the possibilities offered by the new technique.

In another sense, too, the Berlin Virgin is symptomatic of Jan van Eyck's art. The religious character of the work is completely and unequivocally preserved. Natural though the movements of the Child are, there is not the slightest doubt as to his divinity. Here we have before us the very essence of Jan van Eyck's art. On the one hand (in form, colouring and lighting effects) this art ensures the utmost fidelity in the reproduction, down to the last detail, of all the things of this world, and on the other hand it conveys an unmistakable feeling that through this reproduction the Creator Himself is praised. It is true, that the Virgin is clad in worldly garments, which are reproduced in masterly fashion, and that she appears natural in poise and gesture, but she has the same grave solemnity, the same gracious expression, the same sweetness of emotion that we find during the golden age of late mediaeval art in the 'international' style. The church itself, in which we see no human

30. After Jan van Eyck: *St. Francis receiving the Stigmata. cf.* Cat. No. 6. Turin, Galleria Sabauda

beings but only angels, is not a resort of worshippers, but the abode of God upon earth. The flooding of the interior with light enhances this impression.

Whereas the Berlin Virgin in the Church appears to us to be the masterpiece of a young genius treading new paths, another early work by Jan van Eyck, the Stigmatization of St. Francis (*Pl.* 13), now in the Johnson collection at Philadelphia, still has an experimental character, clearly discernible in the faulty proportions of the Saint's figure, with its too short arms and its too long shanks, and also in the body of the sleeping monk. The cross-legged posture of the latter is so unusual that the painter who made the copy of it now in Turin (*Fig.* 30) misunderstood it.[1] Both figures are in *front* of the landscape rather than *in* it. The affinity of this landscape to Hubert's landscape style, as seen in the Three Maries at the Sepulchre, cannot be denied; it evokes the feeling that it has been assembled out of separate motives. It is, however, true that these motives, in particular the rocks, are more powerfully modelled in light and shade than those in Hubert's painting and reveal a close observation of nature. In the distance we see a river valley peopled with tiny figures. The background is thus not merely indicated as it is in Hubert's Three Maries, but is a careful spatial reproduction of mountains and valleys and also the principal factor in conveying the illusion of depth.

The composition has none of the dramatic power that Giotto gave to his version of the theme in his fresco in Santa Croce at Florence. Nor do we find in Jan van Eyck's little picture any trace of the passionate ecstasy of the Saint which we see in the 'Heures du Maréchal de Boucicaut' (*Fig.* 29). Equally curious is the fact that Jan does not, as other artists usually do, treat the sleeping friar as a secondary personage, relegated to a corner of the picture, but co-ordinates him with the Saint. Jan's rather conventionally conceived figure of the Saint is similar to those of kneeling donors in devotional pictures and this grave, ceremonial pose deprives the painting of the character of a picture of action, giving it that of a 'situation' picture.

In contrast to this type of 'situation' picture, we find a dramatic method of presentation in the only two scenes from the Passion due to Jan's inspiration that have come down to us. Two miniatures in the 'Heures de Turin' (*Figs.* 31, 33) are derived from lost paintings by Jan van Eyck which would seem to have been executed before the Ghent altar-piece. They represent the Agony in the Garden and the Crucifixion. That the originals of these miniatures were painted at a fairly early date can be deduced above all from the spatial image, which still contains obvious reminiscences of Hubert's inclined plane. The dramatic force of these compositions, which are at the same stage of development as the little picture of St. Francis, proves that the purely descriptive character of the Stigmatization is not due to any placidity in the painter's temperament, but is deliberate.

That the two miniatures are not, as Hulin assumed, by Jan's own hand becomes clear if we consider the originals, now preserved in the Museo Civico at Turin. They were painted by a miniaturist who also contributed works of his own invention (Hulin's group 'J') to this book of hours. We shall speak of him again in Chapter VII, 2. In his own contributions, such as the initial showing the Flagellation and the border miniature of the Bearing of the Cross (both of them underneath the miniature of the Agony in the Garden, *Fig.* 33), the artist appears as an imitator of Jan's art. On occasions he does not hesitate to borrow movable pieces of scenery from the art of the second decade, but elsewhere (*e.g.* in the border miniature of the Prophet Jonah; *Fig.* 32) he contrives to produce a remarkably homogeneous picture. If we compare the manner in which the light-grey rocks and the trees are painted in the miniature of the Agony in the Garden (*Fig.* 33) with the rendering of the same objects in the border miniatures showing the sacrifice of Isaac (*Fig.* 31) and the Prophet Jonah (*Fig.* 32), the identity of the hand becomes evident.

In the miniature of the Agony in the Garden (*Pl.* 12) we are at once struck by the block-like figures of the sleeping Disciples in their gay attire. The forcefulness of the heads is very close to that of the heads of the Hermits in the Ghent altar-piece. We perceive an individualization far in advance of that of Hubert's Watchers by the Tomb, who merely represent different types. The steel-grey figure of Christ is so isolated in the middle of the scene that the loneliness and anguish of the Saviour are vividly stressed. The not-quite-convincing attitude of Christ and the green landscape, put together out of separate motives and extending into the blue distance only in the right half of the picture, are very close to the little Stigmatization of St. Francis in Philadelphia (*Pl.* 13).

---

[1] He overlooked the fact that the left foot is shown with the sole turned upwards, so that in the copy the figure seems to have two right feet.

31. Page from the 'Heures de Turin', *The Crucifixion*, after Jan van Eyck (Cat. No. 34)
Abraham's Sacrifice, by a follower of Jan van Eyck. Turin, Museo Civico

32. Follower of Jan van Eyck: Marginal miniature from the 'Heures de Turin',
Jonah emerging from the jaws of the Whale. Cat. No. 60. Turin, Museo Civico

In the miniature of the Agony in the Garden (*Pl.* 12) we may safely assume that there are minor divergences from the lost van Eyck original. The gaily attired soldiers must certainly have been less conventionally modelled than they are in the miniature. Much that is merely indicated in the latter, *e.g.* the fence, must differ from the execution of the original to the same extent that the sketchy, unsubstantial rocks behind the Disciples differ from the stony mass, plastically moulded in light and shade and really painted, in the Philadelphia panel (*Pl.* 13).

In the miniature of the Crucifixion (*Fig.* 31) we can see exactly what alterations and simplifications the miniaturist made when copying Jan's lost picture, for we possess a fifteenth-century Flemish copy (now at the Cà d'Oro in Venice) of the original which in some details is richer and in which several motives omitted from the miniature are also in Jan van Eyck's manner. We can thus gain a relatively clear idea of the appearance of the original. The painter who made this copy (*Pl.* 11) followed the plan of the original more faithfully, but the miniaturist (*Fig.* 31) comes nearer to the spirit of Jan van Eyck's art. Not only does he simplify the view of the town with its bright-coloured roofs and the green terrain in the foreground and reduce the number of accessory figures, but, following the art of the Chief Master (see Chapter VII) of this book of hours, he renders even more delicate the figure of Christ. On the other hand, the panel-painter who copied the lost picture abbreviated the landscape and suppressed its effect of depth.

In the composition of the Crucifixion Jan van Eyck has chosen to represent the moment when, after the death of the Saviour, His enemies have left Golgotha and only the Virgin and St. John remain at the foot of the Cross. The Holy Women who have also remained behind are separated from the Virgin and relegated to the middle distance. This was probably done for iconographic reasons. He wanted to develop one of two traditional themes out of the second. He shows the transition from the action of the Crucifixion to the 'situation' of Christ on the Cross between the Virgin and St. John. This procedure, which in its way is unique, shows us how carefully Jan van Eyck reflected upon every subject he had to represent.

In this composition, in which the figures are brilliantly characterized and their movements expressively rendered, there is nothing traditional, no imitation of Italian art, nothing of the style of the Limbourg brothers. The novel spaciousness of the composition is also striking. The eye is led from Golgotha down into the valley and thence over the lofty buildings of Jerusalem to the distant mountains. The city itself is shown on rising ground—the one solitary reminiscence of the inclined plane. The little clouds in the sky remind us of the Stigmatization of St. Francis in the Johnson collection. Against this sky rises the lonely body of the Saviour, sharply modelled and following the shape of the Cross. The figure of St. John is given the strongest accentuation of feeling. The grief expressed by his gesture is echoed in the movements of the arms of the foremost mourning woman.

We thus possess, partly in their original form and partly in the form of copies, five compositions by Jan van Eyck,[1] which in style are older than the portions of the Ghent altar-piece that he himself

[1] Hulin de Loo attributed two more miniatures (from the burnt portion of the 'Heures de Turin') to Jan van Eyck. Of these two compositions the one showing God the Father in an open tent, enthroned and surrounded by angels (Durrieu XIII), is most certainly the earlier work.

designed. These early works, dating from the third decade and most of them from the latter part of it, show occasional isolated links with the style of the second decade, *i.e.* with that of the Limbourg brothers. The fact that in these works we can discern no link with the art of Robert Campin may be due to the chance selection of works that have been preserved. Jan's starting-point would appear to have been essentially the art of Hubert van Eyck, which he followed in the designing of his landscapes and in the modelling of his figures.

It is still connected with the 'international style' and, as regards the angelic figures, with Hubert's art (*cf.* Tolnay l.c.). The sharp and broken lines in the system of folds may be due to the copyist's inclination towards modern forms. The relation to Hubert's style does not exclude the possibility of an unknown designer.

The second miniature, a Lamentation (Durrieu XXIX), is very closely akin to Jan's manner about 1430, especially in the types, the folds and the landscape. The lack of expression in the female countenances, the conventional composition and the faulty fore-shortening of the body of Christ do not allow me to think that it is an exact copy. We can do no more than suppose that the miniaturist used a picture by Jan, now lost, and made alterations.

There is at least one miniature (Durrieu XXVIII) from the 'Heures de Turin' in the Louvre, a rigid composition, showing Christ and the Holy Virgin kneeling before God the Father (*cf.* Panofsky in Festschrift für M. J. Friedländer, Leipzig, 1927, p. 293), which F. Winkler and Tolnay derive from a lost work by Jan. I can only find that the construction is in the style of the third decade.

33. After Jan van Eyck: *The Agony in the Garden*. Cat. No. 33.
Follower of Jan van Eyck: *The Flagellation*. Turin, Museo Civico

CHAPTER III: THE GHENT ALTAR-PIECE

I. *The Theme*

THE Ghent altar-piece is the most comprehensive work produced in France or the Netherlands during the fifteenth century. It is a polyptych with movable wings painted on both sides and the central portion, the so-called shrine, is also painted, not carved. Each of the wings, as well as the centre portion, consists of several pictures. The individual compositions are not independent, as is the case in other altar-pieces of the period composed in tiers, but form groups which in significance and form are closely interrelated.

When the wings are opened (*Pl.* 14), we see that the pictures are arranged in two tiers and that there is a definite contrast between the upper and the lower row. In the upper we see only a few figures, which in themselves almost fill the scene, but in the lower we find numerous figures placed in extensive landscape settings. In this we have a survival of a mediaeval idea according to which the relative size of the figures was determined by their importance.[1] For this same reason the figures in the heavenly sphere have no settings, whereas the multitude of human beings in the earthly sphere, together with the extent and diversity of the landscape, is intended to demonstrate that what is depicted symbolizes the whole world. By his choice of motives the artist emphasizes that the world he depicts is not our present world full of evil, sorrow and labour, but a world which has once again become a paradise.[2] An eschatological theme is represented—the adoration of Christ in eternity. We see before us a beautiful garden. Nowhere are there any traces of the lowly activities of mankind. The buildings in this paradise are not mere huts or dwellings, but great cities with cathedrals and belfries and mighty castles—symbols of spiritual and worldly power.

The middle picture in the lower row is the focal point of the whole representation (*Pls.* 15–42). Before our eyes is a picture of All the Saints. Christ appears in the symbolical form of the Lamb, while the Holy Ghost hovers above the scene in the shape of a dove, but in the upper row (*Pl.* 14) the figure of God the Father, completing the Trinity, is visible *in persona*.[3] The paving, with its vigorous colouring,[4] at once catches the spectator's eye and leads it to the divine figure. All the paintings inside the altar-piece have a thematic relationship and form an integral whole, from which it would not be possible to omit a single component part. Without the Trinity, the Virgin Mary and St. John the Baptist a picture of All the Saints is unthinkable, but a glorification of salvation also requires some reference to the ultimate reason for its necessity—the Fall of Adam and Eve.[5]

When the wings are closed we also see two tiers of pictures (*Pl.* 85), but the compartments of the upper row are further subdivided horizontally by the frame, thus forming a third tier. The exterior lacks the thematic unity of the interior. Between the pictures of the two upper and those of the lowest row there is no direct relationship of subject.

The main representation is in the middle row of the three, the Annunciation. The texts around the Prophets and Sibyls in the topmost row all refer to the coming of the Messiah. The two upper tiers thus show the beginnings of salvation, to the glorification of which the interior of the altar-piece is dedicated.

The two St. Johns in the lowest row have no connection with the Annunciation; thematically they only refer to the inside of the altar-piece, the Baptist as bearer of the symbolic Lamb and the

---

[1]*Cf.* Georges Hulin de Loo, *Annuaire des Musées royaux de Beaux-Arts de Belgique*, 1940–41.

[2]Tolnay's theory (*Le maître de Flémalle et les frères van Eyck*, Brussels 1939) that the heavenly vision was transplanted to earth, is accepted by H. Sedelmayr (*Die Enstehung der Kathedrale*, Zürich 1950, p. 490 f.).

[3]Towards the end of the Middle Ages we occasionally find other instances of the countenance of God the Father being shown as youthful and resembling the type of Christ. As examples of this I would mention the Annunciation by Bernardo Daddi in the Louvre; the Baptism of Christ by Niccolò di Pietro Gerini in the National Gallery, London; Charonton's Coronation of the Virgin at Villeneuve-lès-Avignon; Jean Fouquet's Holy Trinity in the book of hours of Etienne Chevalier, and the left wing of the triptych of the Garden of Delights showing the Creation of Eve (now in the Prado, Madrid) by Hieronymus Bosch.

[4]The copies of the compartments of St. Mary and St. John, painted by Michiel Coxie for Philip II of Spain between 1557 and 1559, now in Munich, show only coloured tiles without the gold lines which now separate the tiles of the originals.

[5]R. Günther (*Die Bilder des Genter und des Isenheimer Alters*, I, in 'Studien über christliche Denkmäler', edited by Joh. Ficker, new series, No. 15, Leipzig 1923, p. 32) quotes a sermon by Honorius of Autun, De omnibus sanctis, in which Adam and Eve appear among the Prophets as types (sic) of Christ and the Church.

Evangelist as author of the Apocalypse, from which the text inscribed on the Well of the Water of Life below the altar of the Lamb is taken. On either side kneel Jodocus Vyd, at whose request the altar-piece was completed, and his wife Isabella Borluut.

The Ghent altar-piece is the oldest Franco-Flemish work we know that bears a signature. It runs along the lower margins of the frames on the outside, is in Latin and tells us[1] that Hubertus Eyck, the greatest painter ever known ('maior quo nemo repertus') began the work and Johannes, the second in art ('arte secundus'), completed it at the request of Jodocus Vyd on the 6th (16th?) May 1432.

2. Hubert's Share

A CLOSE critical examination of the style of all the compartments of this altar-piece clearly reveals that we have before us the work of two different artists.[2] A comparison with the authenticated works of Jan van Eyck corroborates this statement. As there are no plausible grounds for mistrusting the assertions made by the inscription on the frame, we are able to identify the older style as Hubert's. To him we owe the basic elements in the construction of the inner compartments. It is obvious that at the time of Hubert's death much was still unfinished in those portions which he had designed and that much had been little more than sketched in, so that Jan had to complete many portions.

To Hubert's design belong the main portions of the inside, i.e. the composition of the Adoration of the Mystic Lamb, the figures of God the Father, the Virgin and the Baptist, and probably, as E. Heidrich and G. Hulin assumed, the fundamental idea of the Angels singing and making music.

The main picture of the Adoration of the Lamb (Pls. 15–42) shows a broad tract of landscape stretching almost to the top edge of the compartment. The scene of the action is still conceived entirely as an inclined plane with symmetrically arranged groups. In particular, in the case of the kneeling Angels in the centre (Pl. 16) we note how they seem almost to be gliding off the plane. In the four groups the standing figures (Pls. 18, 19, 22, 23) are so crowded together that very few of them have room to display movement. In most cases the heads of the kneeling Prophets (Pls. 20, 32, 34) and also those of the bearded Apostles (Pls. 21, 29, 31) differ from each other only in their age and in the dressing of their hair and beards; in other words they are conceived not as individuals but as types. The Angels (Pls. 24, 27) and the Holy Maidens (Pls. 22, 25) too are modelled after one type. The treatment of the draperies is heavy, the play of the folds is restricted to a few motives and the contours of the figures are sharply accentuated. The ground is covered by a smooth carpet of green, dotted with different kinds of plants like the flowers strewn about a tapestry (Pl. 36). They can be identified with botanical accuracy, but seem to be reminiscences of a painter who has absorbed the essentials of their forms rather than reproductions after nature. They are still nearly in the same stage of development as the Italian ' Herbal Illustrations ' from the first years of the century.[3] The figures in the second plane are not yet correctly proportioned to the trees rising behind them. No characterization of the surfaces of materials is achieved either in the kneeling figures (Pls. 16, 20, 21) or in the two groups in the rear (Pls. 18, 22). The buildings in the right half of the picture (Pls. 40, 41) form a direct termination of the upper limit of the inclined plane.

If we compare a vertical section (Fig. 35) of the Adoration of the Lamb with one of Paul de Limbourg's multi-figured compositions, for example the miniature of the Adoration of the Magi in Chantilly (Fig. 34), we see in both cases the same arrangement of the setting as an inclined plane dominated by the buildings of a city, and a similar loose, rhythmical distribution of crowded groups, while within these groups there is the same assimilation of the individual faces to one basic type, together with the same preference for depicting the heads in profile.

The figures in the Adoration of the Lamb have in common with the religious compositions of the Limbourg brothers the wholly idealistic conception, but in their costumes the oriental note is lacking. The fanciful form of certain of the head-coverings (Pls. 19, 20) is the only parallel to the exaggeration of costume details found in the works of Robert Campin (Fig. 17). As a result of this idealistic style, the symbols are barely emphasized, unless, like the Lamb, the Dove or the Well of the Water of Life,

[1]Cf. p. 22, note 3, For the other inscriptions on the Ghent altar-piece see Chapter IV, 3.
[2]Cf. the detailed demonstration of this in my article: *The Ghent Altar-piece of Hubert and Jan van Eyck*, in *The Art Quarterly*, Spring and Summer, Detroit, 1950.
[3]Published by O. Pächt, *Journal of the Warburg and Courtauld Institute*, XIII, 1950.

34. Paul de Limbourg: *The Adoration of the Magi.*
Chantilly, Musée Condé

35. Hubert van Eyck: *Detail from the Adoration
of the Lamb.* Cat. No. 1. Ghent, St. Bavon

they constitute the substantial and formal centre of the picture. The buildings of the Gothic town,
receive the full effect of the rays of the Holy Ghost (*Pl.* 40), the towers of the Romanesque town are
only touched by the rays (*Pl.* 41), a motive which is given as little importance as the juxtaposition of
the two styles in the building of the New York Annunciation (*Pl.* 8). Their purpose is to provide a
reminder of the Old Testament in the right half of the picture, as is done by the two foremost groups
of kneeling Prophets and standing Patriarchs in the left half.

Not only the design, but also a large part of the execution of the Adoration of the Lamb can be
attributed in the main to Hubert van Eyck, namely the centre of the picture with the altar (*Pl.* 16),
the well (*Pl.* 26), the grassy slope (*Pl.* 36), parts of the Holy Maidens and of the Holy Martyrs (*Pls.* 18,
22, 23), the Holy Bishops and the kneeling Angels, Prophets and Apostles (*Pls.* 20, 21). The forms
are still hard and rather arid. Only the last glazes are by Jan.

In the five compartments of the upper row, we are first of all struck by the fact that the floor on
which the figures stand or sit is shown as if we were looking down on it. The figures themselves are
massive and relatively simple. In the three middle panels the whole of the design (*Pls.* 60, 62, 63),
even including the majority of the details, would appear to be due to Hubert. In the two pictures of
Angels (*Pls.* 72, 73) also, the fundamental design, *i.e.* the construction of the figures, may be Hubert's.
The designer gave the standing Angels dimensions notably smaller than those of the seated figures in
the middle compartments.

The outside of the Ghent altar-piece is less homogeneous than has been maintained. Here, too,
a break in style can be determined. The ceiling of the four pictures in the middle row (*Pls.* 86, 87)
is seen slightly from below, but the floors definitely from above (more so, in fact, than the floors of
the lowest row). In the creation of the spatial image, the designer of the Annunciation scenes has
paid no attention to the spectator's viewpoint. The figures of the Angel and the Virgin in the
Annunciation fill the picture almost to the same extent as do the three figures of the upper centre
panels, so that the space behind them seems to be merely additional. The general aspect of the figures
is simple. The accumulation of folds where the Angel's flowing mantle touches the floor still resembles

those of the draperies of the foremost kneeling Prophets who worship the Lamb. The head of the Angel, with the metal band, surmounted by a cross, which keeps his hair in place, and with the crossed neckcloth (*Pl.* 92), is of the same type as that of the Angel in the Three Maries (*Pl.* 3).

The two wing-panels of the Annunciation showing the Angel and the Virgin form the backs of the compartments of Angels singing and making music. We must assume that the spatial image of the two Annunciation panels was designed in its main lines by Hubert and that Jan afterwards completed them (and, in fact, made considerable additions). Moreover, that the designer wished to set the Annunciation scenes in a room as far as possible unfurnished, is proved by the fact that, contrary to the normal iconographic usage of the period the lily in a vase is omitted and in its stead a stem of lilies is placed in the Archangel Gabriel's hand.

One quite unique feature is the fact that here the two panels containing the figures of the Annunciation (*Pls.* 86, 87), to be found on the outsides of so many altar-pieces, are not adjacent to each other. The artist must have had some definite reason for this. Even a very simply executed box-shaped room—the elder brother did not shun undecorated details—needed a continuation on the two narrow panels in the centre.

The parts of the Adoration of the Lamb painted by Hubert (*Pls.* 16, 18, 20, 21, 22) are everywhere at the same stage of stylistic development as the Three Maries at the Sepulchre (*Pls.* 1–6). Acquaintance with the style of Paul de Limbourg enlarges the sphere from which Hubert's art takes its origin. On the other hand, neither in the parts of the Ghent altar-piece probably executed by Hubert nor in those which he merely designed do we find any influence of the works of Robert Campin. Hubert's art ran parallel to the realistic style of Campin's second period. When we compare the first draft of the Annunciation in the Ghent altar-piece (*Pls.* 86, 87) with the Ingelbrecht triptych (*Fig.* 19), we see Hubert's monumental figures dominating the picture, instead of Campin's delicately intimate forms subordinated to the setting, and consequently, instead of a too lavishly furnished room, an almost empty apartment with a weighty ceiling.

3. *Jan's Share*

THE change of style in the Ghent altar-piece is already manifest in the absolutely unique fact that in a work consisting of tiers of panels, the widths of compartments standing immediately above one another do not coincide, so that on the wings we find wider compartments below narrower and *vice versa* (*Pls.* 14, 85). This change of format must have been undertaken in the lower row, for the three centre compartments of equal width in the upper row make any other division of the wings impossible, whereas in the lower row, with its one large centre panel, it would have been possible to divide each wing into one wider picture nearer the centre and one narrower one outside.[1] The reason for this change of format becomes clear when we examine the wing pictures of the inside designed by Jan van Eyck.

The four lower wing-panels (*Pls.* 44–59) represent a continuation of the theme of the Adoration of the Lamb, in that the hosts of saints are hastening to the paradisal garden in order to take part in the act of worship. Here the ground is no longer turf, but earth, yet here too we find precious stones strewn among the stones of the fields to emphasize the paradisal character of the scene. Above all, Jan has altered the spatial image. Instead of an inclined plane terminating in a narrow strip of distant panorama, we find three grounds sharply differentiated by their colouring (*Pls.* 44-45)—brown and grey for the foremost plane, green for the landscape and blue for the distant mountains.

For the sake of the general effect, Jan had to keep the top of the inclined plane more or less as it was, but he transformed it into mountain slopes which, as the valley in the extreme right-hand panel (*Pl.* 45) shows, are considerably higher than the line of the horizon. This new spatial image, however, made it impossible for him to dispose two groups on two planes one above the other, as Hubert had done. He needed a separate picture for each of his four groups and it was therefore a natural consequence that he should decide to have four wing-panels of equal width instead of two wide and two narrow panels.

---

[1]This combination of wings, consisting of a wide and a narrow one, is also found elsewhere in Franco-Flemish art, *e.g.* in the altar-piece of the Virgin (Ring, *op. cit.*, No. 22) and the so-called 'Retable de Thouzon' (Ring, *op. cit.*, No. 34), both in the Louvre.

In his arrangement of the groups of horsemen in several ranks one behind the other, in the less crowded disposition of the riders and in the rendering of the horses' movements and trappings (*Fig.* 37), we can clearly discern a return to the style found in its most advanced form in the calendar miniatures of the Limbourg brothers (*Fig.* 36), who, as regards historical development, were far ahead of the panel-painters of the second decade. Even if it were not the arrangement of the cavalcade in the Chantilly book of hours, Jan must have had in mind some similar representation by Paul when he designed the wing-panels of the Just Judges and the Warriors of Christ (*Pl.* 44).

Jan van Eyck, however, wanted not only to substitute a more natural scene for the traditional one, but also to achieve a more homogeneous aspect in the whole of the inside of the altar-piece. This he succeeded in doing most effectively by his choice of colours, a choice which probably coincides with Hubert's original intentions. The prevailing colour of the whole composition is the glowing red in the draperies of God the Father, which is taken up again by the covering of the altar of the Lamb and distributed all over the picture in strong, separate accents, being again and again opposed to its complementary colour, the green of the vegetation. This red is also used on the wings, in the mantles of the Just Judges, in the banners, crosses and staffs of the Warriors of Christ and in the mantle of St. Christopher.

As it is obvious that portions of the centre compartment, especially towards the lateral edges, were unfinished when Hubert died, Jan must at least have had to deal with the fashioning of the details. He did not alter the design, but he probably made additions. We may thus assume that in the group of the Holy Martyrs (*Pl.* 23) most of the figural ornaments on the croziers and buckles are his work. But above all he differentiated the faces in the two groups of standing figures on either side and also, perhaps, some of the countenances of the Holy Confessors (*Pl.* 18). We have only to compare a head like that of the bald patriarch in the front row on the left (*Pl.* 28) with the heads of the kneeling Apostles (*Pl.* 29), or the countenance of one of the Popes, seen frontally, with the face of his neighbour seen in profile (*Pl.* 33), in order to perceive the difference, despite the outward similarity of form, between typical and individualistic representation. We note the same difference if we compare the free play of the folds of the Patriarchs' mantles (*Pl.* 19) with the conventional forms of the

36. Paul de Limbourg: *The Month of May.*
Chantilly, Musée Condé

37. Jan van Eyck: *The Warriors of Christ.*
Cat. No. 1. Ghent, St. Bavon

draperies of the Holy Bishops (*Pl.* 18). Moreover, the run of the folds in the draperies of the Holy Maidens (*Pl.* 22) is still reminiscent of Hubert's Three Maries (*Pl.* 2), though the foremost figures, at least, in this large group (*Pl.* 25) may have been revised by Jan, so that, despite the fact that the types are the same, the St. Barbara and the Saint standing on her left have richer, more complicated garments based on contrasts in colour, in addition to which their whole appearance is more differentiated. Their heads, too, with their more animated charm, differ from the similar faces of the Angels kneeling round the altar and of the other Maidens. In the next figure, St. Dorothy (*Pl.* 22), we see the same light colouring as in the rest of Hubert's figures in this group.

A similar enrichment can be seen in the landscape portions. In the middle distance the hand of the artist who finished the work gives us all the enchantment of luxuriant, flowering gardens with rose-bushes and vines (*Pl.* 17), irises, lilies and peonies (*Pl.* 37), enhances the beauty of the indigenous vegetation by adding a fig tree, an orange tree (*Pl.* 42) and a palm (*Pl.* 18) and provides a distant view of chains of hills clearly arranged one behind the other in the middle of the picture (*Fig.* 49) and on the left above the Confessors (*Pl.* 18). He may also have added details such as the blossoming fruit tree to the wood which formed part of Hubert's design (*Pl.* 39). In the distant landscapes Jan follows the method used by Hubert for the middle distance of the Three Maries at the Sepulchre (*Pl.* 6), but he surpasses the execution of the latter picture, which stylistically is on a level with those parts of the Adoration of the Lamb that were probably executed by Hubert. The view of the town on the left edge of the picture (*Pl.* 38), despite the detailed modelling of the houses which are piled one upon another so closely that no street or square is visible, still reminds us of Hubert's Jerusalem in the Three Maries, but the intimate landscape on the right edge (*Pl.* 42) is in every respect in harmony with the landscape motives on the wings (*Pls.* 43, 57). We must assume that Jan added many an assimilating glaze in order to make the difference of the execution less marked.

The wing-panels of Angels are slightly wider than the three centre compartments, their designer having given them narrower frames. The artist who finished the work could thus extend his wing-panels downwards and above all make them higher (*Pls.* 44, 45), thus leaving more room for the cloudy sky. The clouds, together with the flying birds, bring back to the foreground the eye of the spectator, which the landscape had led into depth.

The divergences of style in the pictures of the upper row on the inside of the altar-piece are almost more striking than in the lower row (*Pl.* 14). Next to the panels of Angels, in which the flooring is shown as if seen from above, we have the two panels containing Adam and Eve (*Pls.* 80–83), in which the niches, as well as the figures themselves, are shown as if seen from below. Here, therefore, the artist is taking into consideration the position of the spectator and this implies a conception of reality which Hubert was still far from possessing. Moreover, the sturdy stride of Adam and the firm stationary posture of Eve can only be assigned to Jan. For our common ancestors he chose dimensions lying between those of the centre figures and those of the Angels, thereby modifying the archaic hieratical stress which Hubert gave to rank by means of bodily dimensions.

Another important factor surprises us in this representation of the Fall—the two original sinners are placed in the upper row, in other words in the heavenly sphere. Jan van Eyck was well aware of the singularity of this position. He places them, like the donors, in dark niches, thus stressing the contrast to the natural sky in the panels of Angels and to the solemn hieratic heaven of the three centre compartments, conveyed by means of the religious texts in the semicircles[1] and the sacred symbols woven into the brocades.

These clear divergences of style in both form and content can only be explained as being due to a change of designer. Hubert probably planned to have two narrow outer and two wider inner wing-panels in the lower as well as in the upper row. It is also conceivable that he intended to place the four groups, which Jan distributes among the four wing-panels, on two planes in the two wider inner compartments, thus bringing the construction into line with that of the centre picture. The two external wing-panels in the lower row may have been destined for Adam and Eve, either alone or with a group of Patriarchs, as was the custom in pictures of Christ descending into Limbo. With Jan's distribution of the wings, however, there was no room for them in the lower row, which would

---

[1]The tops of the three pictures—above the brocades—were probably gilded. The copies of the Virgin and St. John, painted by Coxie, now in Munich, show, instead of profiled niches, only semi-circular lines without any modelling in light and shade. The spandrels of the originals of the three upper centre compartments are completely over-painted.

have been their proper place. Since Jodocus Vyd or his ecclesiastical adviser did not wish to omit the representation of the Fall, Jan inserted it in the upper row, stressing the contrast to the adjacent wing-panels by his very drastic rendering of the scenes from the story of Cain and Abel in the spandrels above (*Pl.* 84).[1]

In the upper portion of the picture, just as much as in the lower row, Jan was concerned with the harmony of the general aspect. He deliberately made his type of Adam (*Pl.* 82) resemble Hubert's type of the Eternal Father (*Pl.* 61) and his moulding of Eve's countenance (*Pl.* 83) resemble that of the Virgin Mary's (*Pl.* 64), the increased individualization of the forms being in harmony with the theme.

The execution of large parts of the upper row is Jan's. As there are some overpaintings in the compartments of God the Father, the Virgin and St. John, it is difficult to say what Hubert executed, but one can detect clear differences between the three centre pictures and the wing-panels of Angels. In finishing God the Father, the Virgin and the Baptist (*Pls.* 60–71), Jan seems to have adhered faithfully to Hubert's preliminary design and probably even retained his underpainting. Jan's invention can be detected only in the elaboration of some accessories, especially in the sceptre in God the Father's hand (*Pl.* 69) and perhaps also in the patterns of the brocades. On the other hand, in the wing-panels of Angels (*Pls.* 72–79) it is probable that he not only added the accessories—the decorated tiles of the flooring (*Pl.* 79), the music-desk, profusely embellished with figures and ornaments (*Pls.* 77, 78), the ornamental strips on the organ (*Pl.* 75), the frontlets, buckles and embroideries (*Pls.* 74–76)—but was responsible for the differentiation of the heads, especially of those in the foremost row of the left wing-panel (*Pl.* 74). Only Jan could have contrived to convey the difference between singers with high and those with low voices. The greater plasticity was possible only because of Jan's higher degree of technical ability. The hands of the Angel playing the organ are likewise Jan's. For all these reasons we may assume that these two panels were merely drafted by Hubert and not even, or only in parts, underpainted by him. Lastly, it seems probable that the natural pale-blue sky was Jan's idea.

In the colouring, Jan was at pains to attenuate the difference of style. Starting from the simple, very vigorous colouring of the centre compartments, he contrives in the wing-panels of Angels, by changing the background, by making the colours of the flooring less vigorous despite the more elaborate ornamentation and by adding dark tones, to achieve a transition to the panels on the extreme right and left, which, in quite a different respect, are kept as simple as the centre compartments, since in their case the light tone of the flesh stands out against the dark niches; the general effect is thus almost monochrome and this is heightened still more by the little grisailles.

In the Annunciation on the outside (*Pls.* 86, 87) Jan took over Hubert's construction of the interior and probably also the contours of the figures. In the works of the younger brother we find no interiors so bare, so simple and so devoid of ornamentation as the room in which the two figures kneel and none with so ponderous a ceiling, so low that the figures would be unable to stand upright.[2] In accordance with his temperament Jan endeavoured to enrich the original project as much as possible.

The two narrow compartments in the middle (*Pls.* 86, 87) are the backs of the Adam and Eve panels designed entirely by Jan. It is unlikely, but not to be excluded, that the elder artist began the settings on the backs of these narrow panels. It was at all events a remarkable solution not to give these panels any thematic significance of their own, but to make them merely an extension of the area in which the action of the Annunciation scenes takes place. Tolnay

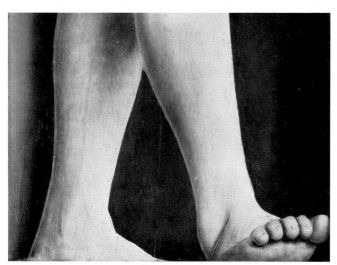

38. Jan van Eyck: *The Feet of Adam*. Cat. No. 1.
Ghent, St. Bavon

[1] Originally, Hubert may have intended to place other angels in these narrow panels. It is possible that the Angels singing and making music were to have been continued here. On the other hand he may also have intended to show the Archangels, who are invoked in the Litany of All Saints, the plan of which coincides in many respects with that of the inside of the Ghent altar-piece.
[2] The ceiling in the wedding portrait of Arnolfini and his wife, and even more that of the Annunciation picture in Washington are high up above the heads of the figures.

thinks that Jan was inspired by Robert Campin's Ingelbrecht altar-piece (*Fig.* 19), choosing two motives for the decoration of this portion of a room, on the right the niche with the washing bowl, which as a symbol of the Virgin Mary is naturally enclosed within a Gothic framework, and the towel hung neatly, with almost pedantic exactitude, on its rack,[1] and on the left a view through a double window over the city of Nazareth peopled with little figures. It is characteristic of Jan's artistic taste that in Hubert's very simple, bare room he inserts, not an ordinary framed window such as might be found in any burgher's house and such as the Master of Flémalle painted, but a Romanesque twin arch, supported in the middle by a marble column. Through this aperture in the left-hand centre panel the eye is led still further into depth. To obviate a one-sided effect, Jan introduced two other twin-arched windows behind the Virgin and the Angel, thereby extending the view into two other apartments, which in their turn have twin-arched windows affording views over the town. Hubert's simple room is thus transformed into the hall of a palace, with a recessed centre and projecting wings. Jan leaves the two back rooms empty, except for stone window-seats, but he embellishes the windows opening on to the town with Gothic tracery and gives animation to the interiors—an idea which could only have occurred to him—by means of the play of sunlight. It seems quite conceivable that the Romanesque forms of the front room and the Gothic forms of those at the back may be allusions to the Old and New Testaments, as are Hubert's views of towns in the main picture (*Pls.* 40, 41) and the architectural forms of the cathedral, Romanesque to the left of the Virgin and Gothic to her right, in the New York Annunciation (*Pl.* 8). This seems to be corroborated by the fact that on the window-seat in the room behind the Virgin (*Pl.* 93) we see a wine-bottle, *i.e.* a symbol of the Eucharist.

We have no idea what Hubert intended to depict in the spaces above the Annunciation, which from the beginning were destined to contain detached pictures. The four pictures in the top row (*Pl.* 85) are creations of Jan's, this being proved not only by the fact that the four figures are shown as if seen from below, but also by the nice differentiation of shapes and the individualization of the faces. Above all, the countenances of the Erythraean Sibyl and the Prophet Micah (*Pls.* 90, 91) are masterpieces of psychology. To Jan's design also belong the four figures in the bottom row (*Pls.* 100, 101). In the tense poise of the two donors there is a clear affinity to Claus Sluter's portrait figures on the portal of the Chartreuse de Champmol. Jan van Eyck is obviously at pains (*Fig.* 40) to rival the full plastic effect achieved by the great sculptor (*Fig.* 39). The trifoliate tops of the niches closely enframing the figures (*Fig.* 42) are similar to those found on Sluter's tomb of Philip the Bold (*Fig.* 41). Jan's treatment of the folds—almost thirty years after Sluter's death—is more massive and heavy, so that the bodies beneath the draperies are hardly perceptible. The artist here evolved a special style of draperies, a style of vigorous ponderousness which is not found elsewhere in his work. In his imitation of carved stone figures and in the manner in which these are placed on hexagonal bases in the niches, Robert Campin on the back of the Madrid wing-panels (*Fig.* 54) anticipates Jan van Eyck. The manner in which the problem is solved, however, is different. The Master of Flémalle lays particularly strong emphasis on the effect of light and shade and even, in order to give greater prominence to the cast shadow, brings the head and upper part of the body of the male figure out of the main axis of the niche towards the source of light, thus achieving an instantaneous effect, whereas Jan stresses above all the stone nature of the figures and therefore, in this case, does not allow the lighting to achieve an effect of its own. He draws the attention of the spectator to the complete roundness of the forms and in head and beard conveys the impression of stonemason's work (*Pl.* 99).

On the outside of the altar-piece Jan followed the then prevailing co-ordinating principle for altar-pieces arranged in tiers. The single figures are isolated without regard to their relationship to the neighbouring figures. In all the outside pictures a great variety can be observed. On the one hand we have grisaille figures, figures in white and others in coloured draperies, and on the other hand figures depicted in living-rooms, figures in an architectural stone-frame and others in simply brick-masoned niches with large, fluttering scrolls.

It was, therefore, impossible for Jan to formulate a basic colour scheme, the preservation of which in the general aspect of the inside of the altar-piece is so much to his credit. As is proper for the outside of an altar-piece, he limits himself to simple and relatively pale colour effects. The question

---

[1] Jan seems to have thought that only an obviously unused towel was a fitting symbol of virginal purity, not one hung carelessly over a towel-rail, as in Campin's Ingelbrecht altar-piece (*Fig.* 19).

39. Claus Sluter: *Duke Philip the Bold of Burgundy*.
Chartreuse de Champmol

40. Jan van Eyck: *Jodocus Vyd*. Cat. No. 1.
Ghent, St. Bavon

still remains, however, whether the pure white in the draperies of the Angel and the Virgin has not a causal relationship to the grisaille figures in the lower row.

4. *Jan's New Style*

THE parts of the Ghent altar-piece designed by Jan reveal four important new features as compared with those for which Hubert made the preliminary drawings. These new features are: (1) a more intensive observation of nature; (2) a homogeneous spatial image; (3) a more marked concentration; and (4) greater individualization.

The intensive representation of nature in Jan van Eyck's work can only be described as cosmic. Even in rendering details he strove to do justice to the whole of Creation. Every component part, whether direct, *i.e.* something provided by Nature herself, or indirect, *i.e.* something fashioned by the hand of man, must be conceived in its very essence. At one and the same time the artist shows us how the part in itself forms an entity and how, in the place where it belongs, it is subordinated to

41. Claus Sluter and Claes de Werve: *Two Mourners from the Tomb of Duke Philip the Bold*. Dijon, Musée

42. Jan van Eyck: *St. John the Evangelist*. Cat. No. 1. Ghent, St. Bavon

a higher entity. Jan carefully elaborates every leaf that Hubert would only have sketched in, and every single fruit (*Pls.* 42, 56), but at the same time he gives us the characteristic general appearance of the tree and the play of light amidst its foliage (*Pl.* 57).

This cosmic feeling can be seen at its clearest in those panels which for reasons easily understandable enjoyed the greatest celebrity in the fifteenth and sixteenth centuries, namely the pictures of the Fall. The fidelity to nature here displayed is something entirely new, something to which we find no parallel, not even in antique painting. The greatness of this achievement becomes evident when we consider the cursory manner in which nudes had hitherto been painted in late mediæval art and when we compare, say, Paul de Limbourg's miniature of the 'Man in the Zodiac' in the Chantilly book of hours (*Fig.* 43) with the figures of Adam (*Fig.* 44) and Eve in Ghent (the only point of affinity being the ideal of the beauty of the female body with the protruding belly). The difference is most striking in the figure of Adam. Jan follows every line of the body (*Pl.* 80), renders its hairy portions with meticulous exactitude and draws a chromatic distinction, not only between the male and the female body, but also between the lowered hand, in which the blood circulates more freely and which is therefore darker, and the raised hand which is lighter. Jan would never have shown his nudes, so true to nature in every detail, in Hubert's false perspective. This admirable fidelity to nature is all the more convincing because the figures appear to the eye of the spectator in the correct foreshortening, that is to say as if seen from below (*Fig.* 38). Thus the reason becomes clear why Jan, for all his reverence for his brother's memory, was compelled to discard Hubert's perspective.

In the portraits of the donors on the outside (*Pls.* 100–103) the simple motive of the inflowing light frees the figures from their isolation in the niches and provides a link between them and the outside world.

In the Ghent altar-piece we can best study Jan's homogeneous spatial image if we examine his landscape setting in the four wing-panels (*Pls.* 44, 45) of the Adoration of the Lamb. Jan van Eyck was the first to break away from that inclined plane to which Robert Campin and Hubert van Eyck had still remained faithful. We now see for the first time a consequential treatment of depth. In the construction of the interior (*Pls.* 86, 87), the back rooms of the Annunciation scene likewise represent an improvement on Campin's art. In painting north of the Alps they are the first interiors which are drawn in nearly correct perspective.

Similarly, the more marked concentration which distinguishes the wings designed by Jan (*Pls.* 44, 45) from Hubert's centre compartment of the Adoration of the Lamb (*Pl.* 15), may be described as a personal characteristic of the more progressive of the two brothers. In Hubert's picture only the middle groups are turned towards the focal point of the picture, the Lamb; the outer groups do not even glance at the object of general worship. Their presence thus serves merely to give greater richness and solemnity to the scene. The groups on the wings, on the other hand, are not only far more closely integrated with the landscapes in which they move, but are also in every way in direct

D

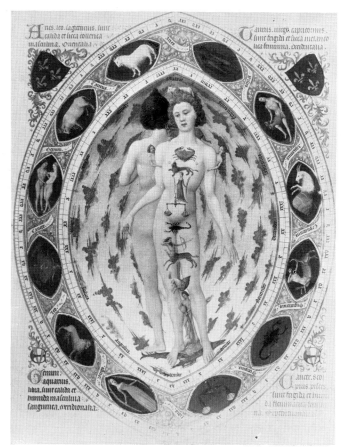

relationship to the altar of the Lamb in the centre compartment. In every one of these figures we see clearly how they are striving towards a goal. Thus, while the main panel remains a picture of situation, the eagerness with which the groups on the wings press forward towards the Lamb clearly shows that we have before us four pictures of action. We have already seen that in his Stigmatization of St. Francis (*Pl.* 13) Jan gave the scene a character of situation in order to underline the religious significance. If he here goes to the opposite extreme, this must be due to his desire to achieve concentration of effect. By showing the groups on the wing-panels advancing vigorously towards a visible goal, this goal is emphasized and the whole attention of the spectator is drawn back again to the Lamb.

43. Paul de Limbourg: *The Man in the Zodiac Circle*. Chantilly, Musée Condé
44. Jan van Eyck: *Adam*. Cat. No. 1. Ghent, St. Bavon

The fourth mark of Jan van Eyck's art is the individualization of the figures. It will suffice if we mention a single example. Despite the remodelling of so many heads by Jan, it has not occurred to anybody to seek living models for any of the faces in the centre compartment, whereas repeated endeavours have been made to identify as portraits the most prominent heads among the Just Judges (*Pl.* 46) for no other reason than that of their lifelikeness and their direct connection with the spectator.[1]

The Ghent altar-piece confirms the conclusions we were able to draw from Jan's previous works concerning the derivation of his style. As regards conformation and technique, the parts painted by him show a marked affinity to Hubert's style. In the horsemen we see a fresh return to the stylistic level of the Limbourg brothers. The manner in which Jan completed the Annunciation scene seems to bear witness to his knowledge of Robert Campin's Ingelbrecht altar-piece, two motives of which we find also in the Annunciation panels at Ghent.

It is, however, precisely when we compare these motives that we become aware of the difference. We have already seen how Robert Campin combined two motives created by miniaturists of the second decade (cf. *Figs.* 12 and 45) to form a new one, that of a view through a window over a town, and how at the same time he varied it in many respects. Surprising though Paul de Limbourg's view of a town (*Fig.* 45) may appear at a first glance, and even more so Robert Campin's (*Fig.* 46), nevertheless, when we compare them with the view from a window in the Ghent altar-piece we see how many conventional and summary elements they still retain. The window in the London painting of the Virgin in her chamber opens on to a town, the houses of which produce the effect of delightfully carved and painted toys. Only Jan's view of a town (*Fig.* 47), seen from above, gives us the very atmosphere of a Flemish street. The main difference does not lie in the falseness or correctness of the perspective, but in the conventionalism of the one and the faithful reproduction of nature in the other. Jan's keen eye is not

---

[1]That attempts have been made since the sixteenth century to identify the fourth judge in the left compartment (*Pl.* 46) as a self-portrait of Jan, is due to the fact that his attire is relatively fashionable and also that his face is turned towards the spectator, though this is also true of one of the bearded Hermits. In these groups Jan strives to achieve the utmost individualization of every single figure and he consequently differentiates them not only by their features and styles of beard, but also by different turnings of the heads.

content with approximations; it seizes upon the fundamentals of every phenomenon. A comparison between the figures of donors in the Ingelbrecht altar-piece (*Fig.* 64) and the portraits of Jodocus Vyd and his wife (*Pls.* 100, 101) is instructive. Campin imbues his donors with a pronounced expression of awkwardness. This genre-like note emphasizes the difference of rank and thus impairs the religious effect of the picture, whereas Jan's donors preserve their dignity in the proximity of the sacred figures as worthily as do Claus Sluter's Duke and Duchess (*Fig.* 39).

A comparison between the two painters is, however, important chiefly because it allows us to determine the exact date of the birth of the new painting. In all the groups on the wing-panels hastening to worship the Lamb, notwithstanding their multiplicity, we see none of that vehemence, bordering almost on the comical, which characterizes Campin's suitors for the hand of Mary or the high priest and his followers (*Fig.* 17). This vehemence was a legacy of the 'international' style. And we find the same difference in the reproduction

45. Paul de Limbourg: *St. Michael*. Chantilly, Musée Condé

of nature as we do in the conception. Here we perceive clearly that Jan was the first to take the decisive step and to cross the dividing line between mediaeval art and that of modern times. Let us place a reproduction of the distant landscape at the back of Campin's Nativity (*Fig.* 48) beside a photograph of the background of the centre compartment of the Ghent altar-piece (*Fig.* 49). The

46. Robert Campin: *Detail from the Madonna in her Chamber*. London, National Gallery

47. Jan van Eyck: *Detail from the Annunciation*. Cat. No. 1. Ghent, St. Bavon

48. Robert Campin: *Detail from the Nativity*. Dijon, Musée

49. Jan van Eyck: *Detail from the Adoration of the Lamb*.   Cat. No. 1. Ghent, St. Bavon

Master of Flémalle seems to have relied entirely on his fantasy in the drawing of his landscape, but Jan van Eyck, despite the traditional rendering of the rays emanating from the Holy Ghost, seems to have taken his scenery straight from nature. Above all, however, we note that the background landscape of the Dijon picture was first drawn and then coloured. It produces an effect of being 'constructed', whereas that of the Adoration of the Lamb is painted with transitions and 'valeurs', and seems real.[1]

Jan's stupendous rendering of nature, whatever portion of the Ghent altar-piece we may choose to examine, proclaims a strong desire to sing the praises of creation to the glory of the Creator. In this the artist is following his brother's example.

5. *The Significance of the Ghent Altar-Piece*

A. *The Significance of Hubert's Share*

THE importance of Hubert van Eyck's contribution to the development of modern painting[2] is to be found primarily in his share in the Ghent altar-piece, but not, however, in the execution, and not even so very much in his original design, that is to say in the creation of new pictorial ideas, but rather in the fact that he set himself new aims.

For us Hubert van Eyck is above all the artist who conceived a grandiose plan, even though he was able to realize only part of it. The very idea of building up an altar-piece in two tiers of pictures not co-ordinated with each other, but subordinated one to the other, and of giving each of the two tiers a structural unity of its own, is so new and revolutionary that its creator deserves the highest credit for it. Here we have the beginning of a new development which was to continue throughout two centuries of Netherlandish painting and reached its culminating achievement with Rubens' altar-piece of St. Ildefonso.

Before the Ghent altar-piece Franco-Flemish painting never succeeded in producing figures which could vie in monumentality with those in its centre panels. And who before Hubert attempted to create a composition like the Adoration of the Lamb, to include so many figures, or to give such spaciousness to the settings?

The curious inscription on the Ghent altar-piece, which describes as second in his art the greatest and most significant painter produced by Europe in the fifteenth century and gives the victor's palm of peerlessness to another, must have been worded with Jan's consent. This can hardly be another example of the boastful language so frequently found on the epitaphs placed on tombs; it is far more likely that it was intended primarily as a homage to the greatness of the idea, an exaltation of the first man who tackled that idea, of its 'inventor', as he would have been called a century later. But it may mean something more.

The Ghent altar-piece was begun at a time when a completely new conception of art was arising, in that same important decade during which epoch-making novelties were being experimented in Florence, in sculpture, architecture and painting. The end of mediaeval art had come, of that art which always retained a remnant of a merely indicative tendency, a tendency to leave things unsaid. From now on everything must be clear, everything depicted as if it really existed, even if the object to be represented were a symbol, such as the Lamb (*Pl.* 16). On the other hand, the grandiosity of this new realism was used, not for worldly purposes, but for the glorification of God. The highest praise was to be given to Him by depicting the beauty of His Creation. The secularization of conception was a danger which many great artists of the time had not contrived to escape. Here, however, was an aim which, for the first time in art, strove to render unto Caesar the things which are Caesar's and unto God the things that are God's, or in other words to depict nature as faithfully and as clearly as possible without sacrificing any part of the lofty idealism of mediaeval art, and always to make it clear that this involved representing the truth of salvation, instead of merely reproducing faithfully some chance event which might also have a secular significance. This new postulate, that faithfulness to nature

---

[1] *Cf.* Chapter VIII.

[2] To compare one brother with the other, would be to do an injustice to the one who died first, for the interval of approximately four years which elapsed between Hubert's death and the time when Jan resumed work on the altar-piece, was a stimulating period of rapid artistic development, so that these years gave the survivor a notable advantage.

must be combined with idealism of representation, is found for the first time in the Ghent altar-piece. Thus the inscription is something more than an expression of brotherly affection. If we take into consideration the general condition of art in 1432 and Hubert's new aims, we see that there was justification for those laudatory words: 'Maior quo nemo repertus'—'greater than any other painter known'.

B. *The Significance of Jan's Share*

WHILE the significance which Hubert's share conferred upon the Ghent altar-piece appears to be more or less circumscribed, the question of the new element in Jan's contribution requires careful definition.

It is conceivable that any artist who after Hubert van Eyck strove to realize his ideal of combining fidelity to nature with the transcendental, even though he might have succeeded in carrying Hubert's beginnings to the height of perfection, would have been proclaimed by Hubert's admirers to be his successor, i.e. as the second in painting ('arte secundus').

However important it may appear that Hubert van Eyck in the Ghent altar-piece was the first to stipulate that the reproduction of the things of this world should be made subservient to the glorification of those of the next and that it was thus impossible for him to be content, as was Robert Campin, with the introduction of symbols, in order to help the theologically initiate to disregard the apparently secular aspect of the picture, the fact remains that such an aim cannot be achieved unless the idealism of the representation is beyond all doubt and unless, moreover, the faithfulness of the reproduction of nature approaches the highest degree of perfection.

In the Ghent altar-piece Jan achieved this aim with the means of his century. This is already noticeable in those parts of the work for which a collaboration of the two artists may be assumed, that is to say when Jan executed a design by Hubert. Take, for example, the devotion displayed by the Angels in their singing and music-making (*Pls.* 74-76). Here every detail lives and the fact that they are performing a hymn in praise of the Lamb is beyond all doubt.

But far more interesting for us are those portions of the work which owe their existence to Jan alone.

The donors (*Pls.* 100-103), with their genuine self-content, are the most lifelike portrayals created by any artist down to that time—even when we discuss the works of Jan van Eyck from a scholarly point of view an accumulation of superlatives is justifiable—they are masterpieces of psychology. And yet what an expression of devotion and piety! The devotion of Jodocus is self-contained. This is a man whose thoughts elsewhere are evidently concerned with the things of this world, but who here in the church contrives to achieve an absolute concentration on spiritual things. The religiousness of the woman differs from that of her husband. It may be that it has its roots deeper within her and that it has more influence on her actions, but in the presence of her husband she does not fall into the same absorption, for even in church she cannot refrain from glancing across at him to see what he is doing.

Then, take the representation of the Fall (*Pls.* 80-83). There is no action, and therefore there is no serpent. Leaf and fruit—the first is not, as usual, a fig-leaf and the latter, oddly enough, is a lemon —are mere attributes. The figures themselves are representative, like those of God the Father, the Virgin and St. John the Baptist; they are there to remind us of the original sin. What psychological mastery lies here in the differentiation of the sexes! Adam is the simpler, the franker of the two as he gazes out upon the world. Eve's gaze is turned thoughtfully inwards. How clearly we realize that the initiative was hers and feel at the same time the fatality of her action, which cannot be explained as due to mere sensuality or curiosity!

The same inner strength is found among the groups hastening to worship the Lamb. I will cite only a few examples. The concentrated earnestness of the mail-clad leader of the Warriors of Christ (*Pl.* 47), full of assurance but devoid of fanaticism, and the almost gleeful sense of superiority in the faces of some of the Just Judges (*Pl.* 46). The passion, the religious zeal expressed by individual heads among the Holy Hermits (*Pls.* 52, 54), heightened (in the first and fourth from the left) almost to the point of insanity, must certainly have been the inspiration of Hugo van der Goes when he painted his Death of the Virgin (now in the Bruges Museum). But with Jan van Eyck we find, in immediate proximity to these faces filled with wild passion, others (e.g. the bald-headed hermit or the two female hermits) expressing blissful resignation to their self-chosen lot. And lastly the beatitude of the Holy Pilgrims (*Pl.* 53), the simple souls, the meek in spirit, led by the giant Christopher (*Pl.* 55), from whose countenance charitableness radiates just as distinction does from the features of the bearded man behind him. None of the groups is reduced to a common denominator; everywhere the variety of the human species is displayed. This magnificent portrayal of human forms goes hand in hand with careful taste in the reproduction of their clothing, their armour and jewellery (*Pls.* 46, 47, 49), and is continued in the splendid rendering of animals, among which I will mention only the wildly neighing horse (*Pl.* 51).

All this skill in the rendering of human figures would not suffice to produce the delightful harmony of effect, if they were not set in the midst of most enchanting landscapes, every detail of which is closely studied, from the stony ground to the sandy sloping paths (*Pl.* 57) and the grass-covered tops of the rocks (*Pl.* 48). The general aspect is constructed out of these accurately observed details in an apparently arbitrary manner, for the various pictures are not intended to be naturalistic sections of scenery, but 'world landscapes', giving a synthetized idea of the beauties of the earth. Jan van Eyck is attracted not only by the details of vegetation and by the individual growth, but also by the juxtaposition of plants in nature, the darkness of forests (*Pls.* 56, 57) and the charm of sloping meadows, and he knows how to bring out the gradations between objects seen from close at hand, in which every leaf is clearly delineated, and those seen in the far distance, of which only the silhouettes are recognizable. His finest achievement is perhaps the rendering of distant scenes, whether it be a grandiose Alpine landscape (*Pl.* 50), extended far into depth by means of the most delicate shading of the surfaces or by successions of silhouette-like summits, or a marshy valley landscape bounded by the buildings of a small town and by a gentle chain of hills (*Pl.* 59). Thus he conveys to us in the highest degree the impression of Elysian fields.

The portions painted by Jan himself after his own designs prove that a reproduction really true to nature does not by any means result in a naturalistic style, but can be blended with an idealistic conception of the theme which does justice to its inner content. The idealistic effect of the Ghent altar-piece is due, not only to the elimination of all ordinary, or even fortuitous elements, but above all to the dignified gravity of the presentation, which is in perfect harmony with the significance of the theme. Just as it is quite clear that the landscape motives, in their choice and arrangement, have a paradisal character, so, too, not the slightest doubt is left as to the idealistic purpose of the cavalcade of the Just Judges and the Warriors of Christ, or of the procession of Hermits and Pilgrims. These wing-panels are the first paintings in which a religious subject is presented in such a way that the spiritual character is preserved in its entirety, and this is done without resorting to summary stylization. Although every detail appears as if really seen and drawn from nature, we are never for a moment allowed to forget the transcendental significance of the work.

CHAPTER IV: THE RELIGIOUS PAINTINGS OF JAN VAN EYCK'S MATURE PERIOD

I. *The Characteristics of Style*

JAN VAN EYCK'S mature period, during which he displayed complete mastery of his art, begins with his share in the Ghent altar-piece. The other works are for the most part devoid of action.[1] We should be able to form a clearer idea of the scope of his art if the painting of St. George, acquired in 1445 by Alfonso V and showing the Saint slaying the Dragon, had been preserved.

Of the compositions which Jan painted, or at all events finished, after 1432 five are signed and dated,[2] the respective dates being 1433, 1434, 1436, 1437 and 1439. One might think that, on the basis of stylistic criteria, it would be easy to assign dates to the undated pictures, one of which is a work of the highest importance, but curiously enough this is not the case. All scholars who have attempted to do it, have reached different conclusions, in some cases varying very widely.[3] As there can be no doubt that all these works were executed by the same artist who designed them, the difficulty of establishing a completely satisfactory line of development gives food for thought. We have to reckon with two possibilities. The first is that the artist, because of the time which the nature of his technique required, worked on several pictures at the same time and occasionally postponed the completion of one or the other of them. In this case the date would merely tell us when the picture was finished,[4] but not when it was begun, though in the case of quite small paintings, such as those dated 1437 and 1439, a long

50. After Jan van Eyck: *Jael and Sisera*. Cat. No. 49.
Drawing. Brunswick, Museum

---

[1]The one exception is a composition preserved only in the form of a drawing made from it, now in Brunswick—Jael and Sisera (*Fig.* 50)—which M. J. Friedländer rightly believes to be connected with the art of Jan van Eyck, though he describes it as the work of a pupil. Everything in the main group gives the impression of having been designed by Jan. The vividness of the narrative reminds us most strongly of the two grisaille groups above the Adam and Eve (*Pl.* 84). One could very well imagine that the group was designed for a painted sculpture and that it was intended to serve as an Old Testament parallel for the enrichment of a picture of the Virgin, in order to remind the spectator that the Virgin annihilated the Devil in the same way as Jael slew Sisera and Judith Holophernes. A pupil may have copied this group and amplified it into a spatial construction, in doing which he did not keep literally to the text of the Book of Judges, where the incident takes place inside a hut and not in front of a tent. Perhaps the whole of the background was copied from some other work.

[2]It may be assumed that many of the lost frames, but apparently not all of them (the preserved original frames of the Dresden triptych are undated), bore dates. Only in the case of the Melbourne Madonna of 1433 is the signature on the picture itself, for which reason it has often been assumed that it is not authentic, but copied from the lost frame. Nevertheless, in the Tymotheos portrait of 1432, the earliest work of the artist's bearing his signature, the motto is on the panel itself, though it is true that it is on the stone sill forming the foot of the picture. In subsequent pictures the signature is invariably on the frame. The appearance of van Eyck's name in a prominent position in the Arnolfini wedding portrait has another significamce.

[3]The recently published book by Th. Musper (*Untersuchungen zu Rogier van der Weyden und Jan van Eyck*, Stuttgart) merely adds to the confusion already existing.

[4]In the signatures the formula of creation (*fecit* or *actum*) alternates with that of completion (*complevit* or *completum*). In one case Jan employed both of them together. The wording does not permit of any deduction as to the time of commencement.

interval between the beginning and the completion of these works seems rather unlikely. The second possibility thus appears to be the more probable of the two, namely that Jan van Eyck, who about 1430 had reached the zenith of his artistic ability, from then on adapted every aspect of his art, which he had mastered completely, on the one hand to his subject and on the other to the size of the picture.

All Jan's mature compositions have the following peculiarities in common. With very few exceptions, the starting-point of the conception was obviously the spatial image. The presentation of the figures is so closely bound up with the setting that they form with it an integral whole. All the compositions are planned and carried out down to the last detail. We do not notice many of the details until we approach quite close to the picture.[1] When, however, we stand at that distance which is necessary if we wish to obtain a comprehensive view of the composition at one glance, the details do not emerge and we are thus able to grasp clearly the fundamental problems of the construction. Symmetrical arrangement is the basic condition as regards both setting and figures. In the colouring, too, there is a careful balancing of shades. In well-preserved pictures the very rich colours are deep, but never really dark.

A particular feature of old Flemish painting is the predilection for a small format, sometimes hardly larger than that of a miniature, a factor admirably suited to the essence of Jan's art. It is precisely the inanimate object, such as architectural details, furniture, utensils, fruits, etc., that loses some of its reality through the very reduced format, which idealizes it without robbing it of any of its artistic charm. The reason why this unusual fidelity to nature in the rendering of things never results in a realistic effect in the coarser sense of the term lies not only in the dignified pose of the figures or the careful choice of subjects, but is also partly due to this artistic device. The reduced dimensions have also a further advantage; the eye of the spectator glides automatically from one object to the next in the same field of vision, so that the meticulous rendering of the detail heightens the general artistic effect.

There is one other peculiarity in Jan's art which is due to the format. More than half of his religious paintings (and, of course, all his profane ones) are self-contained works, i.e. they do not form part of an altar-piece or of a diptych, but were, as is proved by the preserved frames, originally conceived as self-contained works of art, destined for domestic devotion. The portable picture seems to have originated from the 'international' style, for we find it in Franco-Flemish art as well as in German schools as early as 1400. In Jan van Eyck's œuvre, too, it appears at first in small format, but in due course he also painted self-contained pictures of relatively large dimensions, such as the Madonna with Canon van der Paele. The small detached pictures of the 'international' style are no more than casual productions, which never exhaust all the possibilities of the style, but in the last decade of Jan's activity the self-contained pictures occupy the more prominent place. They pave the way for the predominance of the self-contained painting, which did not become general until the days of Leonardo, Dürer and Giorgione.

2. *The Probable Course of Development*

THE first of Jan van Eyck's mature works are still connected by numerous threads to those of his youthful period. In the little Virgin (*Pl.* 104), now in the National Gallery at Melbourne, the connection is shown above all in the human figure. We have here before us a very delicately modelled Madonna whose body is almost completely concealed by the rich folds of her mantle. The peculiar turning of this figure is strongly reminiscent of the Berlin Virgin in the Church (*Pl.* 10). The unusual motive of the Child, now very fully modelled, turning over the pages of an illuminated prayer-book is, in itself, an illustrative motive, here used to heighten the atmosphere of pious devotion.

The picture shows us the Virgin in her chamber and thus belongs to that category of representations of the Virgin which we often find in the œuvre of the Master of Flémalle. The relationship of size between figure and setting is, in fact, similar to that found in Robert Campin's little painting of the same subject in Leningrad (*Fig.* 51), which forms one half of a diptych. Jan's little picture in Melbourne (*Fig.* 52) was obviously planned without a counterpart, for the interior is symmetrically

---

[1]As early as 1456 Bartholomeus Facius noted this: '.... si paulum ab ea discedas, videtur introrsus recedere et totos libros pandere, quorum capita modo appropinquanti appareant.'

51. Robert Campin: *The Madonna in her Chamber.*
Leningrad, Hermitage

52. Jan van Eyck: *The Madonna in her Chamber.* Cat. No. 7.
Melbourne

arranged. Instead of Campin's faulty foreshortening of the room itself and of individual articles of furniture, we have here an almost correct perspective rendering of the room,[1] which in part is calculated mathematically, but in the main is conceived visually.

The eye of the spectator is not, as it is in Campin's picture, led away from Mary through the open window into distance, but is caught by a sumptuous canopy, from which it is led back to the principal figure. The concentration of the subject is still further stressed by the inflowing sunlight (as in the early Berlin picture; *Pl.* 10), which casts its strongest rays on the countenance of the Mother and on the Child.

The undated triptych in the Dresden gallery (*Pls.* 105–107) is the only complete small altar-piece by Jan that has come down to us. The three pictures (*Fig.* 53) form a spatial whole. We are looking from the transept into the choir of a Romanesque church. The centre panel shows the nave of the choir, while the wings afford glimpses into the aisles. In the nave the Virgin is set back into depth; the two subsidiary figures, St. Michael, who is presenting the donor, and St. Catherine, stand in the foreground of the wing-panels. The construction of the centre panel seems to be a combination of the pictures in Melbourne (*Pl.* 104) and Berlin (*Pl.* 10). The setting is planned as if for a representation of the Virgin in her chamber, the interior being then enlarged into a church. The Virgin is here seated on the site of the altar. For the first time in a picture of this subject we see a building in the Romanesque style which, though it terminates in an unbroken wall like all Cistercian churches, has none of their severe formal language. The enrichment of the Romanesque architectural elements with Gothic details seems to be due solely to the desire to represent a church interior as profusely decorated as possible. This craving for ornamentation is likewise satisfied by the precious Italian brocade of the canopy and the beautiful oriental carpet, which is spread over

---

[1]On perspective in Jan van Eyck's works see Panofsky, *Die Perspektive als symbolische Form,* in *Vorträge der Bibliothek Warburg,* 1924–25, p. 281 f. and note 52.

53. Jan van Eyck: *The Dresden Altar-piece*. Cat. No. 8

the steps of the throne and partially conceals the decorated tiles of the paving.[1] The settings of the wing-panels are less sumptuous and their lines lead the eye back again to the centre panel. The only subsidiary motive in the whole altar-piece is an open window in the chapel behind St. Catherine, affording a view of a cluster of buildings forming part of a castle or a convent. The peaceful mountain landscape gives the effect of an excerpt from nature and may have been planned as the reproduction of some definite locality connected with the person of the donor.

The style of the figure of St. Catherine still shows a close relationship to that of the Virgin in the Berlin picture (*Pl.* 10). On the other hand, this Virgin enthroned is more compact than the 1433 Madonna (*Pl.* 104), the figure is more plastic, the draperies are heavier. The body of the Child is likewise a little fuller and sturdier. Only the Mother's hands have the same slender delicateness. The donor, unusually slender, is about to fold his hands in prayer—a transitory gesture like the shadow of a smile on the face of the Child.

In the treatment of light the Dresden triptych differs from the Berlin picture and the Madonna in Melbourne. In place of the inflowing sunlight we have everywhere a diffused lighting which harmonizes with the solemnity of the scene and with its character as a picture of situation.

When the wings are closed (*Pl.* 105), we see the grisaille figures of the Angel and the Virgin of the Annunciation, in two simple stone niches. They remind us less of the two St. Johns of the Ghent altar-piece than of the figures on the back of Robert Campin's wing-panel in Madrid (*Fig.* 54). As in the latter, the figures, unusually slender, owing to the narrow format (*Fig.* 55), and even the dove hovering above the Virgin, cast heavy shadows on the walls. As this little altar-piece must necessarily be viewed from close up, the figures do not need that firm plastic moulding of the draperies which distinguishes the saints in niches in the Ghent altar-piece.

The series of twelve pen-drawings of the Apostles in the Albertina at Vienna (*Pls.* 108–111), can most conveniently be inserted here. These are probably derived from lost originals by Jan van Eyck, probably drawn as models for statues. The delicacy of the moulding also shows that they may have been intended for small-sized plastic works, which were perhaps destined to adorn a carved or cast shrine. Apparently they were intended to be disposed in two rows, for six of the Apostles, the most eminent, are shown standing and six seated on low footstools. In each row three of the Apostles are

---

[1] This motive of the oriental knot carpet, later so popular in Netherlandish painting, here appears for the first time.

54. Robert Campin: *St. James the Great, St. Clare*. Madrid, Prado

turned towards the left and three towards the right, Peter and Paul being obviously intended as counterparts to each other. The formal stress is laid entirely on the draperies and on the heads. Immediately behind the figures a horizontal line indicates space. These Apostles are variants of the figures of Pilgrims, Hermits and Patriarchs (*Pls.* 19, 45) in the Ghent altar-piece,[1] but the Apostles show a more delicate, broken style, approaching that of the Dresden triptych. A simple but firm pathos speaks from these block-like figures.

It is particularly regrettable that of an altar-piece of relatively large dimensions only the left wing-panel, showing the Annunciation (*Pls.* 113-115), has been preserved. In this work, now in the National Gallery at Washington, Jan van Eyck's starting-point is likewise the spatial image.[2] He terminates the room at the top with a ceiling. Once again the scene is laid in the choir of a late

---

[1]That they were created somewhat later is proved by the St. John, a modification of the grisaille figure in Ghent (*Pl.* 101), this variant being so delicate that, as F. Winkler (*Jahrbuch der preussischen Kunstsammlungen*, Berlin 1916, p. 297 f.), who first introduced these drawings into the van Eyck literature, observed, there is no reason to suspect that it is due to a mere imitator. Certain weaknesses in the moulding of the hands and feet are probably the fault of the copyist.

[2]On Romanesque buildings in Jan van Eyck's paintings see Panofsy's article (*The Art Bulletin*, XVII, 1935, p. 449, note 28), in which he combats the opinion expressed by W. Körte (*Leipziger Dissertation*, 1930) that to an ever-increasing extent Jan was attracted to the Romanesque style from a purely artistic point of view. Panofsky advances the hypothesis that, in accordance with the idea of the heavenly Jerusalem, Romanesque forms were used by the artist 'for the visualization of a place where mortals are admitted to the presence of the Deity'. I suppose, however, that the young Jan was still following the notion prevalent in the second decade. In the Ghent altar-piece he used Romanesque forms only to symbolize the Old Testament. After 1432, however, the less familiar Romanesque interior must have seemed to him to be a suitable ambient for religious figures. He uses such interiors as settings not only for pictures of situation including donors, but also for Gospel scenes such as the Annunciation. Even the 'burgher' apartments in versions of the Virgin in her chamber are not always treated in a nondescript manner, as Panofsky asserted; window and niche in the Frankfurt version have semi-round Romanesque tops. (On the other hand, in the St. Barbara (*Pl.* 127), executed in 1437, the architecture of the tower is pure Gothic; in the picture in the Rothschild collection (*Pl.* 132) it is of late Gothic design with Romanesque details.)

55. Jan van Eyck: *Virgin of the Annunciation.*
Cat. No. 8. Dresden, Gemälde-Galerie

Romanesque basilica of Cistercian type with unbroken end-wall, the architectural forms of which, with the pointed arches, are akin to the transitional style. As the light enters the building mainly from high up on the right, it is less diffused than in the Dresden triptych and there are more strongly accentuated contrasts between the lighted and shaded portions. As regards furniture, besides the Virgin's prie-dieu, almost completely covered by her mantle and thus almost invisible, there is a low, empty stool in the foreground, serving as repoussoir and intersecting the traditional vase of lilies. As already mentioned, the figure of the kneeling Virgin has its forerunner, as regards both type of countenance and costume, in that of the Cumaean Sibyl of the Ghent altar-piece. The whole poise is less statuesque owing to the difference of task. There is little to be seen here of the animation and spiritual expressiveness of the Annunciation in the Ghent altar-piece. All action is suppressed and the construction and composition are entirely those of a picture of situation.

About the middle of the same decade we find two other instances of the representation of two figures of equal compositional value in a closed room, the works in question being, together with the Ghent altar-piece, the most important that Jan van Eyck painted. These are the wedding picture of Jan Arnolfini and his wife (*Pl.* 137) and the Virgin with the Chancellor Rolin (*Pl.* 116). Both are self-contained works, symmetrically constructed, so that comparisons with the composition of the Washington wing-panel are not always possible. For the wedding picture, painted in 1434, Jan once more uses the spatial image of the Melbourne Madonna, except that he terminates the room at the top, as in the wing-panel of the Annunciation (*Pl.* 113), with a flat ceiling.

In contrast with the closed, box-like room of the Arnolfini picture, the interior of the Virgin with the Chancellor Rolin (*Pls.* 116–119) is open not only at the top, but also at either side. This is due primarily to the problem which the artist set out to solve.

In defiance of the custom of the period, the Duke of Burgundy's powerful chancellor dispensed with the presence of Saints, whose task would have been to present him to the Virgin and the Child. The commission itself thus made the placing of the Virgin in the centre of the picture impracticable. The four Annunciation compartments of the Ghent altar-piece (*Pls.* 86, 87), designed by Hubert and enriched by Jan, must be considered as being virtually the preliminary stage of the construction of this picture. Jan's enrichment of another artist's pictorial design contained the germ of a new pictorial idea, which the painter now brought to full fruition. As in Ghent, the only possible solution was a composition empty in the middle, with the two figures counterbalancing each other on either side, but from the point of view of content greater stress had here to be laid on one of the two sides, since the difference between the human and the divine being, requiring a portrait-like delineation of the one and an idealized representation of the other, had to be brought out more strongly than in a centralized composition or in one containing subsidiary figures of Saints. Jan solved this problem in a masterly way by introducing a third element into the construction, namely the representation of Creation.

The scene is laid in the two-storied, profusely decorated main room of a Romanesque palace, to which columns and an arcade give an architectonic character. The open sides of this hall serve the dual purpose of emphasizing the width of the room and reducing the effect of depth. The solution whereby only part of the hall is shown, also makes it possible to bring the size of the figures into an approximately correct relationship with that of the architecture. There are only two pieces of furniture, the Virgin's chair and the chancellor's prie-dieu, the former being partly concealed by a bluish-gold cushion and the latter completely so by a blue cover edged with red, this being for chromatic reasons, and also, in all probability, to eliminate the impression of actuality which furniture inevitably evokes. The seated figure of the Virgin, wrapped in a red mantle, counterbalances the kneeling figure of the donor in his brownish-violet robe of gold brocade. The point of stress, however, is shifted by the presence behind the Virgin of a hovering Angel in a blue dress with multi-coloured wings, who holds the heavenly crown above her head. On the left side of the picture, in correspondence to the crown, we see the capital-reliefs above the chancellor's head, showing scenes from Genesis ranging from the expulsion from the Garden of Eden to the Drunkenness of Noah and thus symbolizing the entry of sin into the world. On the Virgin's knees sits the naked Child, blessing the chancellor, who kneels before him in a solemn, official attitude. Whereas the heads of the Virgin and the chancellor stand out against neutral mural surfaces, that of the Child is silhouetted against the innumerable details of the landscape, visible through the three openings of the arcade. Thus the Child becomes the chief figure and the landscape behind is brought into direct contact with him. The orb in his left hand characterizes him as the Creator of the world. The landscape is thus his Creation, to which the centre portion of the picture is dedicated. The view, which in the Annunciation panels of the Ghent altar-piece was merely an ornamental accessory, here acquires a primary significance.

Through the arcade (*Pl.* 119) we see first a flower-garden alive with birds and terminating in a crenellated wall.[1] The conception of the *hortulus conclusus*, found in so many pictures of the Virgin in the 'international' style, is thus present here too. To heighten the effect, two men, seen from behind and clad in elegant red and blue costumes, are standing by the wall, one of them leaning forward to look through a crenellation down into the valley. The view is, in fact, superb, the illusion being created that the palace stands on a hill. In order to be able to render the landscape in such detail, the artist, in contrast to his practice in the right wing of the Dresden triptych, had to give up the idea of having one viewpoint for both landscape and architecture. Jan van Eyck always attached more importance to the artistic effect than to strict accuracy in the naturalistic sense.

From the distant snow-covered mountains a broad river winds down towards the spectator. A bend to the left which it describes and which we can just see through the crenellation of the wall shows that it skirts the foot of the hill on which the palace stands. On the two banks linked by a bridge lies a populous town[2] with red and blue roofs; on the right, that is to say behind the Virgin, is the city with a Gothic cathedral and other churches and towers; on the left, behind the Chancellor, is a suburb with the church of some mendicant order and the courtyard of their convent. Numerous tiny figures people the bridge and the streets. An island in midstream is almost entirely occupied by a castle. The cultivated slopes of the hills with their bright green meadows and woods and yellowish fields are depicted with loving thoroughness. As in the landscapes on the wing-panels of the Ghent altar-piece, it is only in the far distance that the shapes of the mountains begin to dissolve into a bluish-white haze. Small though these details are, it is precisely in them that the strokes of the painter's pencil are clearly recognizable (Frontispiece).

The description in itself shows how carefully this landscape is composed. It cannot, therefore, be a faithful rendering of an existing place, for every detail fits perfectly into the whole picture. On the contrary, this landscape must be considered in the same way as the backgrounds of the Adoration of the Lamb, the aim in both cases being to depict the grandeur and beauty of Creation. In this case, however, we have before us not an earth which has once more become a paradise, or in other words an idealistic vision of the future such as we have in Ghent, but a reproduction of the present world. This section of landscape thus becomes the symbol of the whole country governed by the chancellor.

As regards the artistic effect produced by this scenery, it is significant that it appears to be completely bathed in light. The source of the light is not visible, but must be imagined as lying to the

---

[1] The practice of representing the Mother of God in a closed garden, one of the chief themes of the 'international' style, remained popular long after the disappearance of this style, not only in Germany, but also in the Netherlands, where it is found several times in works of Robert Campin's school.

[2] Several towns have been suggested as the original of this view (Maastricht, Liége, Lyon, Geneva, Autun), or at least one building in them (the tower of St. Martin in Utrecht). If Jan had been commissioned to depict a certain town, he would certainly have done it with no less fidelity than Paul de Limbourg. It is far more likely that the Chancellor would have insisted on some town dear to him being depicted, than that Jan should merely have reproduced his native place. That it is not Autun, the city for which the picture was probably destined, is proved by the fact that in Courtépée's *Description du Duché de Bourgogne* (1778) the town represented in the picture, which at that time was in the sacristy of Notre-Dame at Autun, is described as being Bruges (!), a city through which no river flows.

right of the picture, that is to say in the western portion of the town, since both the cathedral and the church of the Barefoot Friars are oriented towards the left. Only by comparison with the brilliant lighting of the landscape does the interior of the room appear to be immersed in twilight.

Soon after the completion of the Virgin with the Chancellor Rolin, a slight change becomes perceptible in Jan van Eyck's works. Whereas in the Louvre picture the seated figure of the Virgin, whose body disappears almost completely amidst the folds of her mantle, still has something of the fragile charm of the Melbourne Madonna (*Pl.* 104), two other paintings, the Virgin in her chamber, now in the Städel Institute at Frankfurt-on-Main, and the Virgin with Canon van der Paele, in the Museum at Bruges, show us a heavy, more massive type, for which the chief figure in the little Dresden triptych is already a preparation. In these works in Frankfurt and Bruges the spatial image plays a less important role.

The Madonna in her chamber at Frankfurt (*Pl.* 126) shows almost the same construction as the Melbourne picture. The interior is more restricted. To compensate for this greater stress is laid on the architecture, for here the round-arched window and the bull's eye have as their counterparts in the opposite wall a niche and a bull's eye of the same forms and dimensions. The throne is heightened by means of a podium. These motives give the picture a greater solemnity, and it was probably with a view to enhancing this still further that the inflowing rays of the sun were omitted. Instead of the illustrative, almost genre-like motive of the Child turning over the pages of a prayer-book, we here see the Virgin suckling the Child, a *Virgo lactans*. Erect and straight-backed, the Child sits upon its Mother's knees as if on top of a parapet.[1] Everything in the picture, the deep colour included, strives towards greater concentration. For the brocade canopy the artist chooses a pattern composed of smaller details which does not attract the eye so sharply. Every trace of the 'international' style, which was still recognizable in the Melbourne Madonna in the broad expanses of the folds and in the asymmetrical movement, has now disappeared. An unusually precise method of presentation is employed. Tolnay has rightly drawn attention to the geometrical element in this style, which confers upon the painting a monumental character.

In the Madonna with Canon van der Paele, now in the Museum at Bruges (*Pls.* 120–125), the forms perhaps stand out a little more clearly and more sharply. The original frame, bearing long inscriptions, also contains the artist's signature and two dates. The earlier, 1434, refers to the Canon's donation to the church of St. Donatian in Bruges and is therefore probably that of the year in which Jan was given the commission, while the later, 1436, is that of the completion of the work. The scene is laid in the semicircular sanctuary of a Romanesque church,[2] illuminated partly from above by the unseen windows of the nave and partly by the bull's-eye windows of the ambulatory with semicircular tops. Of the pillars dividing the sanctuary from the ambulatory with its groined vaulting several are partially or wholly concealed, but four are visible with only a few overlappings. Two of them enframe the Virgin's throne and the other two the whole composition. Immediately above the capitals of these two foremost pillars runs the top edge of the picture, coinciding with the top line of the canopy. The whole arrangement of the setting is therefore highly condensed.

Seen straight from the front, the Virgin upon her throne occupies the site of the altar. A carpet, just intersected by the fore-edge of the picture, leads the eye of the spectator straight towards her. The Child has his face turned towards the Canon, but at the same time is playing with a parrot. On the left of the throne stands the patron saint of the church, St. Donatian, with his attribute; on the right is the donor's patron saint, St. George. The latter has just arrived and raises his helmet in greeting while with his left hand he presents the grey-haired, kneeling Canon to the Mother of God (*Pl.* 120). To do this he is obliged—a motive producing a very direct effect—to let go of the shaft of his standard, and to prevent it falling, he supports it with his forearm and shoulder. The pleasing characteristics of the Child and St. George serve to attenuate the severity evoked by the tense construction and the rigid symmetry.

This picture belongs to the same category of representations as the lost painting of the Virgin by the Master of Flémalle, known to us only through the drawing made after it which is now in the

---

[1] Until well into the sixteenth century this composition was often copied in half-length pictures.

[2] G. J. Kern (*Die Grundzüge der linear-perspectivischen Darstellung in der Kunst der Gebrüder van Eyck und ihrer Schule*, Leipzig 1904) conjectured that the building was a round one. The plan which he draws of it is partly, as regards the ambulatory, arbitrary, and partly wrong—note the two centre windows. Kern's main argument in favour of a round building is that he does not know of the existence of any Romanesque choir with a pillar in the middle of the axis, but this does not seem to me relevant, for Jan did not copy the choir from a real building but invented it, constructing it without concern for historical accuracy, according to the needs of his figure composition.

56. After Robert Campin: *The Madonna with Donors and their Patron Saints*. Drawing. Paris, Louvre

Louvre (*Fig.* 56). But what in the latter appeared to be merely accidental, here acquires the greatest coherence (*Fig.* 57). We have before us a *sacra conversazione*, a type of picture known in Italy from the middle of the fourteenth century. In France and Flanders the source of these pictures showing donors being presented to the Madonna by their patron saints is to be found in panel-paintings and miniatures in the 'international' style—I will mention here only the diptych of King Richard II of England in the National Gallery, London, and the title-page miniatures of the 'Très belles heures du Duc de Berry' in Brussels. Campin seems to have been the first artist in the Netherlands to use a centralized construction for this theme and Jan now creates its classic form.

In his excellent analysis of this picture Tolnay points out that the donor is gazing into vacancy, unaware that the eyes of the Mother and Child are directed towards him. By means of this essentially mediaeval device, the whole scene is transformed into a vision conjured up before the spiritual eye of the Canon absorbed in contemplation.

This very well preserved picture, which in recent years has been cleaned in an admirable manner, is a coloured jewel of indescribable charm. In the harmony of the vigorous and glowing colours, in the sparkling of the precious stones, the gold, the armour and the flames of the candles, there lies a fabulous splendour upon which a shimmering diffused light is thrown. It needs rare skill to give the utmost clarity to individual details such as the ornamental capitals in the nave and the figured capitals in the ambulatory, and at the same time to build up the general construction so clearly and simply. We need only take as an example the juxtaposition of the dull-coloured pile carpet and the smooth gleaming material of the mantle (*Pl.* 121). The artist has employed all the devices of his art in his effort to achieve greater perfection, without allowing any of them to predominate over the others.

The construction of this picture is in direct continuation of the line leading from the Berlin Virgin in the Church (*Pl.* 10) to the Dresden triptych (*Pls.* 106–107).[1] The interior, visible up to the vaulted ceiling, of a Gothic cathedral (*Pl.* 10) becomes the choir, cut off by the edge of the picture, of a

---

[1]This fact seems to me to make it clear that Jan did not draw his inspiration from the Master of Flémalle's lost picture (*cf. Fig.* 56), but arrived at this solution on his own initiative, combining the three compartments of a triptych in one picture.

57. Jan van Eyck: *The Madonna with Canon van der Paele.* Cat. No. 13. Bruges, Museum

Romanesque church (*Fig.* 53) and this in its turn becomes a simple representation, extending to just above the vertices of the round arches, of an edifice which in its essence is a pure Romanesque sanctuary (*Fig.* 57). But above all, there is no longer any dualism of space and figures; the figures stand alone in the forefront of interest and the setting no longer has an independent existence of its own, but is so designed that, with its chapel-like narrowness, it just suffices to enframe the figures. It is given pictorial significance by means of the colouring, and still more by means of the light. The four bright windows give precise accents to the picture; by hinting at the outside world they fulfil the inner task of opposing it to the spiritual aloofness of the figures.

Two wing-panels now in the Thyssen collection at the Villa Favorita, near Lugano (*Pl.* 112), belong to the same period as the Madonna with Canon van der Paele. As in the Dresden triptych, the two figures of the Annunciation are executed in grisaille. To bring out the full plastic quality of the figures, Jan makes use of an illusionistic trick, a *trompe-l'œil* unusual before the days of mannerism. He creates the illusion of stone figures standing before a brown marble wall, so smoothly polished that they are mirrored in it. To heighten the impression still more, Jan imitates on the surface of the panel the strips of the frame, painted in greyish yellow tones, which he normally glued round his pictures. The general arrangement is essentially the same as in the Dresden picture, the main difference being the much sharper moulding of the forms in light and shade.

In the works which he created about the middle of the 1430's the full plasticity of Jan's forms reaches its culminating point. In this respect, these works are parallels to those, produced at a somewhat earlier date, of Robert Campin's third period of activity. The ideal of clear representation of form here reaches its zenith.

In his next painting Jan tackled a completely new problem, the combining of a single figure with the representation of an extensive landscape. This is the little picture of St. Barbara (*Pl.* 127), now in the Antwerp museum, which the master signed in full and dated 1437 on the lower edge of the glued-on frame. Despite the frame and the signature, however, what we see is merely the preliminary drawing on a chalk ground. Nevertheless it establishes every detail of the projected painting.

E

58. Miniature from the Book of Hours of the Duke of
Bedford: *The Tower of Babel*. London, British Museum

59. Jan van Eyck: *The Tower of St. Barbara (Detail)*. 1437.
Cat. No. 14. Antwerp, Museum

This little work is a picture of situation. When depicting the single saint, fifteenth-century artists generally made the standing figure the chief motive, putting the abbreviated attribute in the figure's arms, or relegating it to a modest position in the background. But in Jan van Eyck's work the huge tower dominates the whole picture, the human figure being subordinated to it in the composition. In order that the figure shall not overlap the doorway of the tower, the artist orients the latter at an angle of 45 degrees to the pictorial plane. According to the legend, Barbara's father caused a tower, or rather a keep, to be built in which he intended to confine his daughter. Jan shows us workmen erecting a profusely-decorated tower—the octagonal ground-plan excludes the possibility that the construction of a cathedral is planned—which, though it is an independent building, does not in any way suggest a keep. This curious enrichment of the subject[1] was evidently inspired by that passage in the legend which relates how, in the absence of her father, Barbara persuaded the workmen to make three windows, instead of two, these three windows symbolizing the Trinity. It is in deference to this symbol that Jan makes the tower dominate the picture.

A simple theme thus becomes a complicated one, which Jan unfolds before our eyes, together with a profusion of details. As in the lost painting of the Crucifixion (*Fig. 31, Pl. 11*), a horizontal fold in the ground divides the picture spatially into two parts, thus separating the landscape with the tower from the figure seen from close at hand. The hilly country is rendered in much the same way as the environs of the town in the Rolin Madonna. The second plane of the picture teems with life like Bruegel's great painting of the Tower of Babel, executed 126 years later, with busy workmen and idle spectators everywhere. It may be that when Jan designed this composition he was thinking of a representation of the Tower of Babel in the style of the Limbourg brothers. In any case we see a similar general composition and similar little genre figures in a version of this subject in the book of hours of the Duke of Bedford (*Fig. 58*),[2] which was illuminated between 1423 and 1430. As this

[1]There are other cases of St. Barbara's tower looking more like a church tower than a keep, but most artists overlooked the symbol of the Trinity.
[2]Ring, No. 18; London, British Museum, Add. Mss. 18850.

miniature, especially in the layout of the landscape, still adheres to the style of the second decade, it is possible that it may have been derived from a model created by one of the Limbourg brothers or a member of their school. Naturally in this case the tower completely dominates the scene. A comparison between the summary methods of the miniature and Jan's faithful reproduction of the human figures and landscape (*Fig.* 59) provides a striking proof of the scope and significance of his artistic achievement. The forms of his tower reveal a pure, rather sober Gothic, equivalent to the style of the fourteenth century. The abundance of details to be seen—even the pages of the prayer-book which the Saint is perusing contain a written text adorned with initials—is in harmony with the general style of the work.[1] The figure of St. Barbara reminds us more of the Virgin in the Washington Annunciation (*Pl.* 113), or even of the Madonna in Melbourne (*Pl.* 104), than of those in the works executed immediately before (*Pls.* 112, 120, 126). This, too, can be interpreted in two ways, either as an abandonment of the plastic style, for which the delicate late works of Robert Campin, such as the Werle wing-panels of 1438 in the Prado at Madrid, provide a parallel, or else as a supreme example of the adaptation of artistic skill to a particular task.

The extent to which, in Jan's mature works, the methods used were determined by the task the artist had to accomplish, becomes particularly evident if we study the little Madonna by the Fountain in Antwerp (*Pl.* 128), which according to the inscription on the frame was completed in 1439. Here again we find the closed garden, the *hortulus conclusus*. Owing to the absence of lines leading into depth, the effect is one of unusual simplicity. The glowing colouring, too, is not at all complicated. As so often occurs in Jan's works, the chief contrast is provided by the antithesis between blue and red in the draperies and the carpet, blending with the yellow and orange of the rainbow-winged angels and the yellow of the gold brocade to produce a harmonious effect. The theme is archaic, but not the style of the work, in which Jan, in deference to the subject and perhaps also to the smallness of the format, refrains from displaying his skill in the elaboration of landscape. The standing figure of the Virgin has a firm, statuesque poise, similar to that of the Madonna of the Annunciation in the Thyssen collection (*Pl.* 112). The sharp folds in the neck of the Child, whose movements are more vigorous than in previous pictures, are found repeatedly after the Rolin Madonna. The traditional character of the theme has thus had no influence whatever on the formal execution. It should be noted that in his last years Jan twice painted, with only a few insignificant variations, an even more hieratical motive, the countenance of Christ, seen directly *en face*, as King of Kings (*Pls.* 130, 131).[2]

The flat spatial image of the Madonna by a Fountain appears again in the Virgin with a Carthusian, now in the Rothschild collection, Paris (*Pl.* 132). Like the Rolin Madonna, it shows us a section of a hall open on all sides. In recent times some scholars have doubted whether this little painting is an authentic late work of Jan's. As it is many years since I had the opportunity of examining it closely, I am unable to express an opinion. If genuine, it would be the only work in which Jan made a copy of a motive he had used in an earlier picture. Though other details have been altered, the right portion of the landscape is, as regards the contours of the river-bank, copied exactly from the view of a town in the Rolin Madonna, whereas the left portion is an independent conception.

The centre panel[3] of the Maelbeke altar-piece (*Pl.* 129), which originally came from St. Martin near Ypres, shows sure signs of having at least been conceived by Jan. In the course of years it has undergone numerous restorations, so that it is now difficult to form an opinion as to many of its details. The style is of a grandiose simplicity. The artist shows us an open Romanesque hall, in which the donor kneels reverently before the Madonna. The vigorous arrangement of the folds of the Virgin's mantle gives the figure an unusually solemn effect. We find here a continuation of the style of the Angel of the Annunciation in the Thyssen collection (*Pl.* 112). Once again we perceive to how great an extent the size of the picture on the one hand, and the task on the other—instead of the *hortulus conclusus*, we here see the Virgin standing before the wide world—determined whether

---

[1] In the wing-panels of singing Angels in Ghent the writing on the slip of paper inserted in the music-book was not added until the final execution.

[2] Of the 1438 version, in which the light falls from the right, the Berlin gallery possesses a panel (*Pl.* 130) on the frame of which the signature appears in full, but the unusually dry and pedantic execution of the picture seems to point to its not being original. Of the second version dating from 1440 (the date on the Bruges copy), in which the light falls from the left, a panel from an English private collection (*Pl.* 131) was loaned in 1923 to the Mauritshuis at The Hague; its quality is superior to that of the Berlin picture.

[3] The unfinished wing-panels, each divided into two compartments each of them containing two symbols of the Virgin, in accordance with the *Defensorium beatae virginis*, were obviously added later. They reveal neither Jan's technique nor his method of composition.

the moulding should be more plastic or not, and whether the aspect of the figure should be monumental or intimate.

3. *The Religious Programmes*

IN a category of representation very suited to his art, namely that of pictures not especially intended to be narrations, but merely to awaken devotion, Jan's pictures of religious subjects have invariably a religious programme, to a far greater extent than is the case with his contemporaries. It is noteworthy that his art, which is pre-eminently clear, so often resorts to the spoken word. If we are to believe old reports, the lost original frame of one of his early pictures, the Virgin in the Church, bore an inscription addressed to the Virgin and the Child. It is understandable that the Ghent altar-piece, the pictorial representation of a great religious programme, should include numerous inscriptions. When, however, we see that in many other subsequent works executed for various secular and ecclesiastical patrons Jan made use of words to paraphrase the contents, it seems advisable to examine the inscriptions on the Ghent altar-piece more closely.

On the frames of the Ghent altar-piece it is only occasionally, when the subjects of the panels are quite obvious, *e.g.* the Angels or the Adam and Eve, that we find a short paraphrase; in most cases, however, there is a very concisely expressed explanation of the subject, telling us that the horsemen represented are the Just Judges or that the kneeling female figure is the Erythraean Sibyl. In the majority of cases the theological explanations and panegyrics are written on the pictures themselves. It may be assumed that this was a stipulation, made by whoever first commissioned the work, which Hubert van Eyck was bound to follow. Not only do the front of the altar of the Lamb and the parapet of the Well bear explanatory inscriptions with the appropriate biblical quotations, but we also find that the steps of the throne of God the Father and the semicircles above Him, the Virgin and the Baptist are covered with monumental characters praising the divine or saintly personage represented. Occasionally we also find the first words of a hymn on the seam of a mantle or on the boss of a shield.

On the outside of the wings there is a more sparing use of inscriptions.[1] One special peculiarity, which Jan afterwards repeated in the Washington picture (*Pl.* 113), is that in the Annunciation scene the angelic greeting is simply written on the surface of the panels, close to the Angel's mouth, so that it stretches out across architecture and sky. The Virgin's answer (as recorded by St. Luke) is shown in the same way near her head, but in this case the letters are upside-down, apparently in order to make it clear that the words are spoken by Mary and addressed to the Angel. This shows that the purpose of these inscriptions was not merely that they might be read by the spectator. On the contrary, they must have had some higher significance.

This delight in inscriptions as seen on the Ghent altar-piece persists in Jan's other mature works, but in the cases of which we have knowledge[2] he transferred them from the picture to the frame. We have no proof that other Flemish artists did likewise, since the original frames of nearly all the works of Campin, Daret, Rogier van der Weyden, Petrus Christus,[3] etc., have been lost. But it seems possible that it was precisely Jan's practice of placing inscriptions upon them that was responsible for so large a percentage of the original frames of his works being preserved. The hypothesis that this was a peculiar feature of Jan's art thus seems tenable.

In the Dresden triptych (*Fig.* 53) all four sides of the three frames are covered with verses running concentrically, these being quotations referring to the Virgin and hymns to St. Michael and St. Catherine. These inscriptions, too, are not merely intended to be read by the spectator, since those on the lower edges of the frames are upside-down. This practice is understandable in the case of small portraits—*cf.* that of Jan de Leeuw (*Pl.* 142)—which might be picked up by anyone who wished to examine them more closely, but it is difficult to explain when we find it followed on altar-pieces.

---

[1]The texts on the scrolls of the Prophets and Sibyls are probably intended to show that they are included in the picture on account of these prophetic words.

[2]The only exception is the Child in the Dresden triptych whose scroll bears words addressed to the spectator. On the other hand it is quite in accordance with the custom of the period to place an inscription on the seam of the Madonna's robe or on a canopy, or to adorn a suit of armour with a short text.

[3]The only original frame preserved is that of the 1449 Madonna by Petrus Christus, who followed Jan van Eyck's art very closely, at all events since 1446; the bottom strip of this frame bears the artist's signature, on the other three sides are the words of a hymn to the Virgin (Lugano, Thyssen Collection).

In such cases the purpose of the inscription must be to complete the meaning of the work, which it surrounds as with a magic band.[1]

The numerous symbols in Jan van Eyck's religious pictures serve the same purpose as the inscriptions on panel and frame. Examples are the references to the Fall (the apples in the window; *Fig.* 72) or to Salvation (*e.g.* the eucharistic symbols), the representation of parallel scenes from the Old Testament on the tiles of the floor and the wall in the Washington Annunciation, and those from Genesis illustrating the sins of mankind on the capitals above the head of Chancellor Rolin, or even the choice of the flowers growing in the gardens or of the birds walking about in them. Such symbols occur even in secular pictures, if they have any connection with religion (*e.g.* the solemnization of a wedding). They are all the more striking since Jan van Eyck's realistic representation, unlike Robert Campin's, needs no counterpoise, because it is imbued with a transcendental solemnity.

Undoubtedly this marked programmatic element in devotional pictures, this constant desire, discernible in every picture, to proclaim numerous aspects of the truth of salvation or at least to make symbolical allusion to them, is a thoroughly mediaeval trait, contrasting oddly with Jan's modern conception that painting should depict only what our eyes can see, with the utmost fidelity to nature. We may assume that with his inscriptions and symbols the artist was endeavouring to prove that his new, hitherto unthought-of reproduction of reality did not in any way signify a secularization of art, but that this perfected rendering of nature was nothing but a hymn in praise of the Creator. We thus find in Jan's work a peculiar, unique factor, which can only arise when a great pioneer in art sets himself a new task. The artistic conquest of the visible world which Jan perfected was achieved without detriment to the religious character of the works of art. What we have before us in his works is thus merely the fusion of the chief artistic tendencies of two epochs, of the Middle Ages and modern times.

---

[1]On the other hand in the case of the comparatively large Madonna with Canon van der Paele (*Pl.* 120), which was not intended for a private house, but for a church, three sides of the frame bear inscriptions referring to the holy personages represented, while the bottom strip (as in the case of the Ghent altar-piece, the St. Barbara of 1437, the Madonna by the Fountain, and various portraits) is reserved for the artist's signature.

CHAPTER V: JAN VAN EYCK'S PORTRAITS

1. *The Preliminary Phases*

ABOUT the year 1430 Jan van Eyck reached the first peak in the development of modern portrait-painting. His fidelity of reproduction is unsurpassed in the whole Occident. The path which led to this zenith of modern portraiture is not always clear but in its essentials it can be reconstructed, for the earliest stages, *i.e.* some of the first attempts made to the north of the Alps to make portrait-painting an independent branch of art, are known.

In Italy the efforts to create portraits begin as far back as the thirteenth century.[1] To the north of the Alps the Gothic era, too, witnessed a striving to achieve a representation of the human form corresponding to nature. This urge suffered a setback during the first half of the fourteenth century. Although the advent of Gothic had put an end to the irrationalism of early and high mediaeval art, there was no beginning of a great evolution in France such as we observe at the same time in Italy. The method of composing paintings in only two dimensions, which was prevalent in High Gothic art, did not allow any conquest of space. Thus the 'naturalistic' conception found no adequate field of activity and sought continually for outlets, which it found in the realistic rendering of details. Max Dvořák[2] undertook to explain the great transformation which began to take place, from about the middle of the fourteenth century, in the significance of fidelity to nature as regards the general content of artistic creations and which, in the first half of the fifteenth century, resulted in a complete transposition of the two fundamental tendencies of Gothic art, namely the 'idealistic' and the 'naturalistic'.

From the second half of the fourteenth century there have been preserved in France and other regions strongly influenced by French culture isolated works which stand at the beginning of a continuous line of development in the art of portrait-painting. We may justifiably assume that these oldest portraits known to us were among the earliest to be created.

The first of them is the approximately lifesize portrait of King John II of France, surnamed the Good, now in the Louvre (*Fig.* 60). It is authenticated by the contemporary inscription and apparently reproduces faithfully the ugly features of this monarch, who died in 1364. The second painted portrait which has come down to us from this period is also that of a ruler. It represents the Austrian Duke Rudolph IV the Founder, who died at the age of twenty-six in 1365, and is now preserved in the Diocesan Museum at Vienna (*Fig.* 61).[3] Likewise authenticated by the contemporary inscription on the original frame, it shows the person portrayed not as a private individual, but wearing his ducal crown. More important, however, is the fact that he is not shown in the traditional profile attitude—such as Giotto used for the founder of the Arena chapel in Padua, Enrico Scrovegni, or Simone Martini[4] for Robert d'Anjou (Naples)—but three-quarters turned. Whereas, stylistically, the portrait of the French king stands alone, the style of the portrait of the ' Archduke ' Rudolph is found again in the portrait heads, likewise crowned and similarly conceived, of Emperor Charles IV, his father-in-law, and of Wenceslas of Bohemia, his brother-in-law, in the votive picture of Bishop Očko of Vlasim,[5] now in the Rudolphinum at Prague. The stylistic affinity is unmistakable. To judge from the age of King Wenceslas, who was born in 1360, this epitaph must have been executed during the 1370's. The ' Archduke ' Rudolph portrait must have had forerunners in lost Bohemian portraits. A comparison with the paintings in Burg Karlstein and with the carved busts by Parler in Prague cathedral shows that in the Očko epitaph certain features of the Emperor Charles' countenance have been very individually observed. Moreover, that the painter was trying to create a likeness is

---

[1] *Cf.* the exhaustive article by H. Keller: *Die Entstehung des Bildnisses am Ende des Hochmittelalters*, in *Römisches Jahrbuch für Kunstgeschichte der Biblioteca Herziana*, III, 1939.

[2] *Kunstgeschichte als Geistesgeschichte*, Munich 1924, p. 119.

[3] *Cf.* J. Wilde in *Kirchenkunst*, Vienna 1934.

[4] Unfortunately no independent portrait by the Sienese painter is preserved. To judge from presumable copies, they were in profile attitude, too.

[5] *Cf.* Matejicek, *Gotische Malerei in Böhmen*, Prague 1939, No. 55. In the Očko votive picture the painter not only uses the three-quarters turned, but also gives a profile portrait of the Bishop.

60. French School, about 1360: *King John the Good.*
Paris, Louvre

61. Austrian School, about 1365: *Duke Rudolph the Founder.* Vienna, Diocesan Museum

shown by the marked difference between the faces of the rulers and that of the Bishop. This relative lifelikeness of the heads is an element of style linking the stylistic groups of paintings to which the votive picture belongs with contemporary French art. In view of the close relations existing between Charles IV and the French royal family—a relationship of blood, as well as of political and cultural bonds—it is quite possible that the stimulus for the new art of portraiture came from France. We must remember that a document dated 10th April 1380 has been preserved, according to which King Charles V's small study at the Hôtel St. Pol in Paris contained portraits of King John the Good, Charles V himself (when he was still Dauphin), King Edward III of England and the Emperor Charles IV.[1]

It is a remarkable fact that the only two painted works of self-contained portraiture preserved from the fourteenth century, the French portrait of King John the Good (*Fig.* 60) and the Austrian portrait, showing Bohemian influence, of 'Archduke' Rudolph (*Fig.* 61), are the prototypes of the two categories of portraits produced during the first half of the fifteenth century, namely the profile view and the three-quarters turned. Both categories have this in common, that they show the body including the shoulders, but without the hands.

Unfortunately, as regards paintings preserved, there now comes a gap and the development during the next fifty years after these two portraits can be followed only in miniature-painting and in sculpture, but not in cabinet-paintings. That such pictures not only existed, but were also considered by contemporaries to be real portraits, is proved by the fact that we have two reports which maintain the fiction that a royal bridegroom was induced by a portrait to sue for the hand of a princess whom he had never seen.[2]

From the reign of Charles V, the son and successor of John II, we find to an increasing degree that painters of historical or symbolical subjects strive to individualize the countenance of the king, or

[1]*Cf.* Ring, No. 1.
[2]It is in this way that the marriages of Charles VI of France with Isabeau of Bavaria (1385) and Richard II of England with Isabella of France (1396) are said to have been arranged. See Huizinga, *Herbst des Mittelalters* (German translation), 5th edition, p. 370 f.

sometimes those of other persons as well, *e.g.* that of the poet Guillaume de Machaut (†1377). At first the miniaturists, and likewise the draughtsman of the celebrated Parement de Narbonne, limit themselves to stressing a few outstanding features, such as a pointed nose or chin, but at the beginning of the fifteenth century princes, *e.g.* the Duke of Berry, are portrayed in such a manner that they are easily recognizable, in most cases still in profile, but sometimes, as on a page of the 'Heures de Turin' (destroyed by fire) three-quarters turned. For all the efforts to mark personal characteristics these portrayals of living personages in miniatures (*cf. Figs.* 12, 13) are still illustrations, in the sense that no attempt is made to achieve absolute lifelikeness, which was not demanded until about 1420, and then only in panel-paintings. Just before the beginning of the century, in the famous diptych now in the National Gallery, London, King Richard II of England is hardly more individualized than he would have been in a miniature. Similarly, in the celebrated picture of King Richard II enthroned, in Westminster Abbey, the features are still completely mediaeval in their assimilation to type. It is true that the kneeling princes in dedicatory miniatures painted after the beginning of the fifteenth century appear to be the immediate forerunners of the portraits of donors in the small panel-paintings of Robert Campin and Jan van Eyck, but this applies only to the structure of the composition, and not to the actual portrayal. These miniatures do not create the impression of being accomplished portraits, as is the case with monumental and funerary sculptures of the period.

Throughout the fourteenth century in France sculpture, and in particular monumental sculpture, occupied the leading place among the formative arts and it is therefore not surprising that the most expressive achievements in the sphere of portraiture at that time were carved in stone. These were still figures for the embellishment of churches. For this reason the magnificent standing figures of King Charles V and his wife Jeanne from the portal of St. Célestin, now in the Louvre, are still bound up with the tradition of cathedral sculpture. Despite all the individualistic details the figures still retain traces of idealization. Nowhere in France do we find any attempt to achieve, by means of an elaboration of ugly or even trivial features, that effect of lifelikeness to be seen not only in Northern Italian murals (*e.g.* Tommaso da Modena) or in Bohemian panel-painting, but also in Peter Parler's busts, which show the same degree of stylistic development, despite the fact that their creator must have had some knowledge of French art at the court of King Charles V.

With Claus Sluter a great artistic personality appears upon the stage. Full plastic conception of the figure and monumentality of effect (*Fig.* 39) distinguish his works from those of his contemporaries. But without belittling his own artistic achievement, we must not overlook the fact that an intensive production of stone statues of donors now began. If the magnificent, monumental figures of the kneeling Duke of Berry and his wife at Bourges seem, with the more block-like character of the self-contained figures, to be more bound up with tradition[1] than Sluter's donors, nevertheless here, too, a real individualization of the features is achieved. Even in the third decade of the sixteenth century they made so vivid an impression on that portrait-painter par excellence, Hans Holbein the Younger, that he copied them in drawings with the most scrupulous exactitude. The individualization peculiar to monumental sculpture in Burgundy and Northern France about 1400 is found again in smaller funerary sculptures, *e.g.* in the extremely natural movements of the figures of the goldsmith Jacques Isack and his wife (both of whom died in 1401), at the feet of the Mother of God on the votive relief in Tournai Cathedral (*Fig.* 63). This memorial is a typical creation of the 'international' style. Although these kneeling personages have not the vital strength of Sluter's figures of donors, the whole manner of portrayal makes it evident that Franco-Flemish sculpture of the first decade of the fifteenth century exercised a greater influence on Jan's new art of portraiture than did contemporary painting.

Painted panel-portraits, too, were produced by Franco-Flemish art during the first, and more especially during the second decade of the century, but unfortunately no important works from this period have come down to us. We can, however, draw conclusions from the copies made of portraits of contemporary princes. Two types can be distinguished, the same as those we encountered about 1360. One of the best examples of the first type[2] is the water-colour portrait of Louis II of Anjou

---

[1] *Cf.* Martin Weinberger, *The Journal of the Walters Art Gallery, Baltimore*, IX, 1946, p. 9.

[2] Ring, No. 63. J. M. Richter (*Burlington Magazine*, 1929) and B. Degenhart (*Pisanello*, Vienna 1940) assign to the French school the portrait of a lady in profile, previously attributed to Pisanello, in the National Gallery, Washington (Ring, No. 64). In sentiment and costume it is, in fact, closely akin to the female figures in the calendar miniatures at Chantilly or the portrait of the Duchess of Bedford (London, British Museum, Add. MSS. 18856). It may be assumed that the portrait was painted about, or shortly before, 1420.

(1377–1417) in the Bibliothèque Nationale, Paris, which in the elaboration and animation of the features represents an advance on the portrait of King John II (*Fig.* 60). Like the latter it is concise and shows only the head and shoulders without the hands. The second type can be reconstructed from a small, very fine copy in the museum at Antwerp (*Fig.* 62), which, however, was not painted before the middle of the 1430's. It represents the Duke of Burgundy, who was murdered in 1419, in half-length against a blue ground, with the hands resting on a barely indicated parapet covered with a piece of material adorned with coats of arms. A quite unique feature is that the parapet is not continued right across the picture, only a narrow portion of it being shown in front of the figure as a support for the hands. These hands, however, with their slender, delicately-nerved fingers and the thumb projecting at an angle, are very similar to the hands painted by Rogier van der Weyden.[1] This proves that the picture in Antwerp cannot have been painted during the lifetime of the Duke and makes it appear likely that the model was a bust-portrait without hands. We must therefore assume that a pupil or follower of Rogier copied an original dating from about 1415, adding the parapet and the hands. The marked, characteristic features of the Duke are objectively rendered. The copy in Antwerp is the work of a painter brought up in a manner richer in nuances.

62. Netherlandish School, about 1440: *Duke Jean sans Peur.* Cat. No. 68. Antwerp, Museum

Nevertheless, for all the emphasis laid on the features, we still have a survival of the concise and yet summary portraiture of the fourteenth century, which reproduces only the most important essentials of the subject.

It may be due to the fortuitous selection of pictures preserved, that the new portrait style which replaces the summary methods of the late fourteenth century manifests itself in donor portraits sooner than in works of independent portraiture. In the donor portrait on the left wing-panel of the Seilern triptych in London, the strict profile design (already fully developed in the Parement de Narbonne commissioned by Charles V) is abandoned. Here Robert Campin was obviously following, not miniature-painting, but the sculptures in Tournai which were constantly before his eyes. The pose of the head is halfway between profile and three-quarters turned, just as it is on the bas-relief of the goldsmith Isack and his wife (both of whom died in 1401; *Fig.* 63). In a later work (of Campin's second period), the left wing of the Ingelbrecht altar-piece (*Fig.* 19), we find a simplification of the draperies. The affinity with the sculptural solution is thus even more evident. There is no longer anything mediaeval in these donor effigies of the Master of Flémalle, which are neither abbreviated nor stylized.

The abundance of nuances in the modelling of the heads represents a definite advance in development compared with the portrait of Jean sans Peur (*Fig.* 62). The Master of Flémalle endows his figures with an intimate note; he even gives them—and this is something new, which in subsequent works, too, is found only in portraits of donors—a definite and instantaneous expression, in this case one of shyness. But if we compare Campin's Ingelbrecht (*Fig.* 64) with the donor (*Fig.* 65) in Jan van Eyck's Dresden triptych, we perceive at a first glance that real animation and complete

[1] *Cf.* Rogier van der Weyden's early female portrait in Berlin, and also the mature one in Washington. This observation is not new. In the descriptive Catalogue of Old Masters in the Museum at Antwerp (1905) we read: 'some think.... of Hubert van Eyck himself; others opine for Rogier, who, however, was not capable of working from nature.' The unsatisfactory proportions as between figures and format, caused by the addition of the hands and the sill, had already been noted in the nineteenth century and a restorer attempted to mitigate them by means of lateral additions. The lost original must be imagined as similar in format to the replica in the Limpurg-Stirum collection (reproduced in *Jahrb. d. preussischen Kunstsammlungen*, 1921, p. 73, *Fig.* 4), which shows only head and shoulders.

63. *Tomb of the Goldsmith Isack and his Wife.* Tournai, Cathedral
64. Robert Campin: *The Donor Ingelbrecht and his Wife.* Westerloo, Collection of Countess Mérode
65. Jan van Eyck: *Donor.* Cat. No. 8. Dresden, Gemälde Galerie

naturalness of effect are achieved only in the latter.[1] Noteworthy, too, is a second factor, the relationship of the donor in Dresden, as regards attitude, gesture and contour, to the Isack epitaph in Tournai (*Fig.* 63).[2] We thus see that the origins of Jan van Eyck's portraiture must be sought in sculpture rather than in painting. In a work of more intimate art like the Dresden triptych the relationship to a product of the Tournai style, the Isack epitaph, is significant, but in monumental works such as the figures of donors for the Ghent altar-piece Jan took as his model—in all probability consciously—the great portrait figures of Claus Sluter.

2. *Jan van Eyck's Self-contained Portraits*

NO portrait by Hubert van Eyck has come down to us and we do not know whether any ever existed. The earliest self-existent portraits by Jan that have been preserved were executed during the 1430's. Several of them are dated or can be dated with reasonable accuracy. This is an advantage, for not a single portrait by Robert Campin can be accurately dated. They merely represent parallels to Jan van Eyck's portraiture and no direct connection between the portrayals of the two artists can be established.

Of course, as the reason for his journey to Portugal proves,[3] Jan did paint portraits as early as the 1420's and the magnificent effigies of donors in the Ghent altar-piece with their experienced method of portraiture also prove that attempts in this field of art must have preceded them. The chance selection of works preserved shows us within Jan's activity a development running from bust-portraits to half-lengths and from uniaxial to biaxial portraits. We do not, however, know whether

[1]For the sake of our knowledge of van Eyck's donor portraits it is very regrettable that the little altar-piece, which Bartholomeus Facius describes in 1456 as belonging to King Alfonso of Naples, has been lost. It consisted of a centre panel of the Annunciation, and two wings showing St. Jerome in his study and St. John the Baptist. The donors, Battista Lomellino and his wife, were depicted on the outside of the wings, which usually only occurs in the case of large altar-pieces (Ghent, Beaune, Danzig) and in company with figures of saints executed in grisaille. Moreover, they were depicted in an interior, for Facius expressly mentions that a ray of sunlight from a crack fell between them. The text runs: 'In eiusdem tabulae exteriori parte pictus est Baptista Lomellinus, cuius fuit ipsa tabula, cui solam vocem deesse iudices, et mulier, quam amabat praestanti forma, et ipsa, qualis erat, ad unguem expressa, inter quos solis radius veluti per rimam illabebatur, quem verum solem putes.'

In Jan van Eyck's works we find the motive of a direct inflow of sunlight only in the early Virgin in the Church, on the outside of the Ghent altar-piece, and in the Madonna in her chamber in Melbourne, dated 1433.

[2]Panofsky was the first to call attention to the stylistic similarity between this epitaph and Jan van Eyck's portraits of donors (*The Art Bulletin*, XVII, 1935, p. 445, note 21).

[3]The inventories of the Archduchess Margaret, Regent of the Netherlands, dated 1516 and 1524, mention as being 'de la main de Johannes' a portrait not painted in oils ('sans huelle et sur toile') of a Portuguese lady (of a lady dressed in the Portuguese manner). Friedländer (I) thought of Isabella of Portugal and suggested that the St. Nicholas, patron of seafarers, who appeared on the scroll in the hand of the Portuguese lady, probably painted as being a miniature, was a reference to Isabella's imminent journey.

the prototypes are among the pictures preserved. From 1433 on, uniaxial alternate with biaxial portraits and, similarly, as regards format, an occasional return to the older type can be noted.

The earliest independent portrait by Jan van Eyck that has come down to us is that of Niccolò Albergati, Cardinal of Santa Croce, now in the Vienna gallery (*Pl.* 134).[1] The sitting must have taken place either on the 3rd or 4th November 1431 in Ghent, or, more probably, between the 8th and 11th December of the same year in Bruges. On one of these days Jan made a silverpoint drawing now preserved in the cabinet of engravings at Dresden (*Pl.* 133). This is the only known draft sketch made by Jan for a painting. It is drawn with the utmost care and the artist himself inserted numerous notes regarding the colouring, obviously because the Cardinal, during his brief stay in the Netherlands, could grant him only one sitting. The drawing not only gives us the sitter's features in great detail, but also already contains the whole construction of the picture. In executing the painting, the artist had only to make a proportional enlargement. The one alteration he made was a negligible reduction of the width of the picture on the right edge.

The simple construction, with head and body three-quarters turned, the glance following the same direction and the picture terminating beneath the shoulders so that no room is left for the hands, while the body merely stands out as a mass against the neutral ground, is still completely traditional. Moreover, the Cardinal's is the only self-contained portrait by Jan van Eyck in which the sitter is shown bare-headed, like King John the Good seventy years before (*Fig.* 60). It is one of the last Netherlandish examples of the type evolved during the fourteenth century, which we find for the first time in the portrait of 'Archduke' Rudolph (*Fig.* 61). The same tightness within the frame as in this prototype of Jan's self-existent portraiture can be seen in Campin's portrait of Robert de Masmines,[2] in the Berlin gallery (*Fig.* 68). The format, too, of the Albergati portrait (*Fig.* 69), which shows more of the body, is likewise to be noted in the œuvre of the Master of Flémalle, in the portrait of a man wearing a chaperon in the National Gallery, London (*Fig.* 66). It is also to be found in a contemporary work of a completely different school, in the portrait of the Emperor Sigismund painted on parchment by the Veronese painter Pisanello, now in the Vienna gallery (*Fig.* 67).[3]

If we compare these portraits—the Albergati portrait of 1431, Robert Campin's contemporary panels and Pisanello's effigy of the Emperor Sigismund painted in 1432 or 1433—as regards their final execution, we see that the Italian artist's method of executing his painting in the manner of a draughtsman is the most traditional. Like the portrayer of Jean sans Peur (*Fig.* 62), Pisanello reproduces only the outstanding features of the face. The beard and the locks on the temples are put together out of so many single hairs. The general effect still reminds us of the abbreviated methods of the 'international' style and evokes the impression of a recording from memory rather than of a real reproduction from nature. It is easy to see why Pisanello's drawings appear to be truer portraits than his painted effigy of the Emperor. They give us only the skeleton of the construction and leave it to the imagination to supply what is lacking. In the painting, however, the artist, in order to achieve real portraiture, has to give more than a skeleton. Robert Campin (*Fig.* 66) goes considerably further. He grasps all the details as well as the general scheme, taking great pains to achieve real characterization. And lastly, Jan van Eyck (*Fig.* 69) goes still further into detail, but at the same time clearly subordinates the details to the general scheme. The self-contained portraits of the Master of Flémalle—all created during his third period—with their sharp emphasis on the forms and above all on their contours, sometimes (*Fig.* 68) evoke the impression of being made after painted wood-carvings rather

[1] It is noteworthy that the full title of the sitter was still known in 1659. It may be that it was written on the then existing frame. The inventory merely says: 'in a half green and half gilded ('halb zier verguldten') frame.'

[2] In his catalogue Tolnay calls it a copy.

[3] The portrait of this last Emperor of the Luxembourg dynasty was first published by J. Wilde (*Jahrbuch d. kunsth. Sammlungen*, New Series, IV, Vienna 1930) and, for understandable reasons, was attributed to a German painter. W. Degenhart (*ibid.*, XIII, 1944) proved convincingly that it was painted by Pisanello during the Emperor's visit to Italy (1432–33). A work painted by this celebrated Northern Italian master a little later—between 1433 and 1438—the fresco in Sant' Anastasia at Verona, narrating the legend of St. George, shows exactly the same brushwork, despite the difference of the technique.

Unfortunately, Pisanello's preliminary drawing for this picture is not known, but at this time he also drew the Emperor twice in profile (Paris, Louvre). The first of these drawings possesses all the charm of a quick improvisation. In the second, more finished drawing, we notice that the artist has not yet rid himself of a schematic method of presentation. Further crayon drawings by Pisanello in the Louvre prove that he also portrayed other personages, believed to have been dignitaries of the Emperor's suite, in two views (reproduced in Degenhart, *Pisanello*, Vienna 1940). It thus appears that Pisanello used both types of fourteenth-century potraits, namely the profile, well known from Italian donor portraits, and the three-quarters turned, which we find for the first time in Austria, but which may have been of French origin. Only the former of these found followers in Italy at that time; the second do not occur before Mantegna and Paolo Uccello (in his latest style).

66. Robert Campin: *Portrait of a Man.*
London, National Gallery

67. Pisanello: *The Emperor Sigismund.*
Vienna, Gemälde-Galerie

than after living sitters. In Jan van Eyck's works we see a painter's treatment of form, rich in nuances. Once again his prime achievement lies in the execution.

The novel element is already manifest in the Dresden drawing (*Pl.* 133). The artist is no longer content with stressing the essential characteristics of the head, as did Pisanello at that time,[1] but follows every single form with his silverpoint and then models them by means of careful modulations of light and shade. This carefulness was, of course, necessary if a living, thoroughly individual portrait was to be made from a drawing. We see clearly to how great an extent the drawing, for Jan van Eyck, was the design for the picture. The aim was not, as it was for Pisanello, to give the painter the choice between the various possibilities of pose, bearing, turning of the head, etc. All these things, as well as the whole construction, are already contained in the drawing, which was his most valuable medium of approach to the execution. It thus follows that here the artist's draughtsmanship is given no independent function of its own. The concise lines are made to follow every detail of the full plastic form of the Cardinal's face, aged beyond his years, they have to reproduce every fold and dimple, and even some short, refractory hairs. In the same way, in the draperies, they emphasize the contours, they work out the folds, and here and in the background they render the contrast between light and dark. In the treatment of light we notice one peculiarity. Since it falls from the left, there ought to be a noticeable, light patch in the background near the cheek, but it is precisely this spot which Jan makes darker, thus producing a contrast between the ground and the lighted portions of the face; in other words, the background is not a wall, as it is in the case of the donor portraits of the Ghent altar-piece, but a neutral foil, subject to no natural laws, the light and dark portions of which can be freely disposed by the artist in the interests of effect.

It may be assumed that soon after the sitting at the end of 1431 Jan began work on the painting (*Pl.* 134), while everything was still fresh in his mind and he did not have to rely on his very extensive

[1]Pisanello and Jan van Eyck made their portrait drawings about the same time, but they do not, as Degenhart (*Europäische Zeichnungen,* Zürich 1943) maintains, form a complete parallel. The Italian artist's work is still bound up with the 'international' style. He is content to emphasize a few, especially typical features, but does not yet attempt to follow his model in every detail of form and to do justice to him in every respect.

68. Robert Campin: *Robert de Masmines.*
Berlin, Deutches Museum

69. Jan van Eyck: *Cardinal Albergati.* Cat. No. 19.
Vienna, Gemälde-Galerie

notes concerning the colouring. That, during the execution, he went still further into detail, is shown by the eyes, which are not merely yellowish-brown in colour, as Jan jotted down in his notes, but also show an outer blue ring round the iris. The chromatic effect of the picture is surprising and is based mainly on the marked contrast between the glowing red of the Cardinal's white-edged robe and the vigorous intermediate blue of the background.[1] The tones of the face, from the whitish lips to the sanguine patches on the nose and round the eyebrows, are set down in Jan's notes, but it is nevertheless astonishing that the painter achieved such a lifelike rendering of the flesh without further sittings.

The stylistic affinity between the Albergati portrait in Vienna (*Pl.* 134) and the contemporary portrait of the donor Jodocus Vyd (*Pl.* 98) on the Ghent altar-piece is very great. In the self-contained portrait Jan did not have to endow the sitter with a definite expression (that of devoutness), but was able to depict this prince of the Church in a moment of complete, untroubled tranquillity.

In the same year 1432[2] in which in all probability the Albergati portrait was completed, Jan painted another portrait (*Pl.* 135) of a young man whose name was probably Tymotheos and who may have been of foreign[3] origin, in which we see a similar vivid contrast of colours, based on raspberry red and on green, and a great display of skill in the reproduction of materials (note the fur and the wool). In this painting, now in the National Gallery, London, the artist remained faithful to the type of portrait he had chosen in 1431, but he reduced the dimensions, changed the format, included

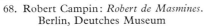

[1]Until the dark, eighteenth-century overpaintings of the background have been removed, it is impossible to say whether the original glowing blue, still visible immediately behind the head, was spread regularly over the whole of the ground, or whether, as in the drawing, the surface was modulated in varying degrees of light tones.

[2]Whereas, with the exception of the Ghent altar-piece, Jan's religious works bear only the year of their completion, on the portraits, with one exception, the exact date of completion is given.

[3]For Panofsky (*Journal of the Warburg and Courtauld Institute* XII, 1949, p. 80) the only possible interpretation seems to be that Tymotheos was a complimentary nickname, comparing him to the famous Timotheos of Miletus, the revolutionary of Greek music. He thus ventures the hypothesis that the Tymotheos portrayed was a musician renowned for his bold, innovatory spirit. And he makes the further assumption—supported by the fact that the 'Tymotheos' portrait bears an inscription in French while all the other paintings by Jan van Eyck are inscribed in Latin or Flemish—that this young genius, like Jan himself, belonged to the entourage of Philip the Good. He further assumes that 'the new Tymotheos' was Gilles Binchois, who was well established at court in 1430 and in 1438 and 1440 was even made 'secretaire aux honneurs du duc'.

forearm and hands[1] in the picture[2] and added a stone sill at the foot, which reveals some very picturesque marks of decay. The chief inscription is planned to be seen from a distance and thus forms part of the pictorial idea, or was perhaps included in the commission, for which reason it is given in the form of block letters incised upon the stone.[3] The wording is in French: ' *Leal souvenir*', an expression certainly chosen by the patron, which better than any other describes the essence of Jan's art.[4] The sill, extending right across the picture, creates an effect of depth, since the sitter is shown behind it. A deep black background emphasizes, even more strongly than the blue of the Albergati portrait, the fact that it is not to be considered as real. In the composition the hand fulfils the function of introducing a second patch of light colour, somewhat smaller than that provided by the face. The left hand is barely visible, while the right holds, as attribute, a letter and is thus devoid of action. Once again we see a purely factual unemotional likeness, which has something timeless about it.

A change is seen in another male portrait, the original frame of which (*Fig.* 70) bears the date 1433, in the National Gallery, London (*Pl.* 136). Here the artist retains the much reduced size of the head, but omits the hands and abandons the uniaxial view. The sitter's glance is no longer in line with the turning of the head and trunk, but, for the first time in the history of painting, is directed straight towards the spectator.[5] In its colours the painting is based on the contrast between the dark red of the chaperon, wound round the head like a turban, and the black of the robe and background. On the original frame of this picture and on that of the Melbourne Madonna, painted in the same year, we see the artist's well-known, modest, but at the same time proud motto: 'als ich kan', 'as (well as) I can'.

70. Jan van Eyck: *The Man with the Chaperon*. 1433. Frame with inscription. Cat. No. 21. London, National Gallery

From the following year, 1434, dates one of Jan van Eyck's greatest masterpieces, the wedding portrait of Giovanni Arnolfini and his wife in the National Gallery, London (*Pls.* 137–140). This creation can only be described as unique. It contains three outstanding features, at that time extremely or completely isolated, namely the use of the full length, the placing of a portrait in an interior and the creation of a double portrait combined with an action.

The first of these features is, comparatively speaking, the least surprising. It is true that the full-length portrait did not become popular until after 1500, and then at first for lifesize effigies.[6] But at times when a new branch of pictorial art is beginning to develop on a large scale (as was the case with portraiture at the beginning of the fifteenth century), a departure from the normal practice

---

[1]The female counterpart to Robert Campin's male portrait in London (*Fig.* 66) also shows one of the hands.

[2]'Jan van Eyck adopted a scheme of composition derived from those Gallo-Roman and Germano-Roman tombstones in which France and the Rhineland still abound ' (Panofsky, l.c.).

[3]The name Tymotheos—which can only refer to the sitter—written above it in small Greek characters, the calligraphically written date and the signature in Latin beneath are items which in later works the artist wrote on the frame.

[4]It is hardly necessary to contradict the attribution, made by E. Renders in the Brussels paper 'Le Soir' of 10th July 1947, of the celebrated 'Fool' in the Vienna gallery to Jan van Eyck. Neither the colouring itself nor the manner in which it is applied, nor the composition, nor least of all the modelling of the hands, has any resemblance to his work. Nevertheless, M. W. Brockwell (*The Connoisseur*, December 1949, p. 79) tries to fit it into the sequence of Jan's portraits, placing it between 1432 and 1433. His identification of this work with a picture mentioned in the Archduchess Margaret's inventory of 1524 is likewise unjustified.

    The picture seems to me to be a very early genre painting rather than a portrait. It stands in a loose school relationship to Jan van Eyck and it is strange that no other work by the same hand has been discovered. The question which should be investigated is whether it was not created towards the middle of the century in (Southern) France by a painter who had learned his art in Flanders, as the 'Maître de l'Annonciation d'Aix' did.

[5]We find the same motive, not very much later, obviously inspired by the same desire for more animated effect and perhaps not unconnected with Jan's art, in a work by one of the immediate followers of Robert Campin, that is to say a painter from his milieu (in 1947 it was in the possession of P. Cassirer, Amsterdam). This is a female portrait of very personal conception. Rogier van der Weyden (Portrait of a lady in Berlin) must have taken the same motive from Campin.

[6]It is found for the first time in Southern Germany in the first decade of the sixteenth century; in the third decade it appears in Venetian art circles, and was adopted some time later by Flemish artists. In the Netherlands, and in France, we first find isolated instances in small format, until, in the seventeenth century, it becomes more frequent.

seems all the more natural since figures of donors, confined to religious pictures, were represented in full length.[1] As examples of this departure from the norm I will not cite the effigies of Emperor Charles IV in Karlstein, since in their case we are dealing with depicted religious ceremonies, *i.e.* the reception and installation of relics, but will mention that remarkable little portrait, painted on parchment, of Lysbet van Duvenvoorde (*Fig.* 71), which was acquired a few years ago for the Mauritshuis in The Hague. This is a charming, though provincial, work, still containing in its whole pose many reminiscences of the 'international' style. The direction of the glance coincides with the angle of head and body. The lady holds in front of her a scroll bearing a jocular[2] line of poetry, a motive found again—though at a later period—in German portraits. In the background behind her we see the combined coats of arms of her family and that of her husband Simon van Adrichen, whom she married on 19th March, 1430, their presence dispelling all doubts as to the identity of the sitter. The composition, which seeks merely to fill the plane and thus produces no effect of depth, sets off the face as the point where the colour is lightest. The features are thoroughly individualistic and thus constitute a portrait. Despite the decorative composition, reminiscent of a tapestry, we could call this portrait of Lysbet van Duvenvoorde a contemporary parallel to Jan van Eyck's creation of a full-length portrait,

71. Dutch School, 1430: *Lysbet van Duvenvoorde.*
The Hague, Mauritshuis

were it not for the fact that other outstanding features of the Arnolfini portrait make it clear that its origin cannot be explained as due to a casual or experimental departure from the norm.

In the Arnolfini wedding portrait there are two things—the fact that it is set in an interior and that it is a double portrait depicting an action—which are found in this work alone in Western European painting during the fifteenth century.[3] A solitary imitation of it will be discussed later. Even double portraits devoid of action and with half-length figures are not usual before the second half of the century, when they occur in Germany.

The only possible explanation[4] is that the primary idea of the picture was to represent an action and this automatically involved the portrayal of full-length figures in an interior. The depicting of two human beings performing an action in the milieu appropriate to that action was not, therefore, just an idea which occurred to the artist after he had been commissioned to paint a double portrait; on the contrary, these characteristics were there from the beginning and were the factors which determined the form of the picture. It is idle to speculate whether this completely novel idea occurred to Arnolfini, or whether the artist suggested it to his friend, at whose marriage he had acted as witness, since it could only be undertaken because the art of Jan van Eyck, not only in portraiture

---

[1] Standing full-length portraits are found in miniature-painting from the beginning of the fifteenth century, *e.g.* that of the Duchess Maria of Gelderland and Jülich in her breviary, written in 1415 (Berlin, Staatsbibliothek; reproduced in Hoogewerff, *De Noord-Nederlandsche Schilderkunst*, I, The Hague 1936, p. 167).

[2] Hoogewerff, II, 1937, p. 53, for this reason suggested that it is a betrothal portrait. On the other hand the combined coats of arms would seem to indicate that the wedding had already taken place.

[3] To the north of the Alps I know only one example of a similar picture, the genre-like representation of two lovers by a painter from South-Western Germany in the style of 1475, now in the Cleveland Museum of Art (publ. *Burlington Magazine*, Oct. 1932). The couple is placed in a garden among trees and flowers, which are rendered in an abbreviated way. Similarly the faces reveal a typical rather than an individual conception.

More like a real portrait is an Italian half-length in the Metropolitan Museum of Art, New York (reproduced in the 1941 Catalogue). Painted in the style of Fra Filippo Lippi, it shows a young lady in profile conversing with a young man who is looking in through a window. M. Davies (London, *National Gallery Catalogues, Early Netherlandish School*, 1945, p. 34) holds it to be a less certain example of a marriage portrait. In any case there is no stress laid on the action.

[4] See Panofsky's exhaustive iconographical analysis of the picture (*Burlington Magazine*, 1934, p. 117 f.).

and in the rendering of an interior, but also in the power of expressing inner feeling, had reached heights which made the realization of this idea possible.

Giovanni Arnolfini,[1] a merchant from Lucca resident in Bruges from 1421, married Giovanna Cenani, daughter of Guillaume Cenane, of Lucca, who lived in Paris. It is noteworthy that both Arnolfini and his wife are shown wearing Netherlandish costume, like Tommaso Portinari and his wife thirty years later (whereas Jacopo Tani and his wife Caterina, who also lived in Bruges, were portrayed in Italian dress[2]). Since the features of the Arnolfini couple are devoid of southern characteristics—Huizinga speaks of 'the most un-Italian face that ever looked out upon the world'— (as were later those of the Portinari couple), we should probably, but for the information given in the inventories of the Archduchess Margaret, have taken them for compatriots of the painter.

Giovanni Arnolfini stands before us in an almost frontal position, grasping in his left hand the back of the hand of his bride, who stands close by, turning towards him. He is on the point of placing his own right hand in hers, as a symbol of his binding vow of fidelity. The two personages are thus about to enter into matrimony and in accordance with the Catholic faith they themselves are administering the holy sacrament to each other. As, in order to complete the validity of the marriage after the binding vow of fidelity, its consummation is necessary, the scene is laid in the bridal chamber. Jan van Eyck's signature is on the rear wall above the round mirror, in clearly visible calligraphic letters (*Pl.* 138), the wording being most unusual; instead of the normal Latin formula found in other works, *me fecit (fieri fecit per)*, or *complevit (completum per)*, or the Flemish form, *gheconterfeit heeft mi*, we here read: *Jan van Eyck fuit hic*, *i.e.* 'was here', was present, which can only mean that he was present at the ceremony as

72. Jan van Eyck: *Apples, from the Arnolfini Wedding Portrait*. Cat. No. 22. London, National Gallery

a witness to the marriage. In the round mirror hanging on the wall beneath the inscription the backs of the young couple are reflected, as well as the remaining half of the room in front of them. Through the door, which must be imagined as being in the place of the spectator, two men are entering, and they, too, are clearly visible in the convex mirror. They are obviously Jan van Eyck and the other witness to the marriage.

Both bride and bridegroom are in ceremonial dress, with their heads covered, and they have removed their footwear—to him belong the light clogs,[3] to her the red leather slippers—as is still

---

[1] The detailed description in the Archduchess Margaret's second inventory (1524) dispels all doubts as to the identification. Here, too, the question is, whether at the time the original frame bearing the sitter's name—in the inventories (1516 and 1524) it is gallicized as 'Hernoul le fin' or 'Arnould fin'—was not still in existence.

[2] *Cf.* the Portinari altar-piece by Hugo van der Goes in the Uffizi, Memling's Portinari portraits in New York and his altar-piece of the Last Judgement in Danzig.

[3] In the Liverpool copy of a lost Deposition by Robert Campin one of the men helping to take down the body of Christ is seen slipping off a similar pair of clogs, because he cannot climb the steps of the ladder while wearing them. Panofsky thinks that the removal of the footwear denotes that the bridal chamber is a sacred place.

the custom among Dutch peasants when entering a room. The bride's little dog (*Fig.* 73), which is present at the ceremony, has been interpreted by Panofsky as a symbol of fidelity.[1] It is broad daylight, but above the bridegroom one candle is burning in the chandelier, as a wedding candle and a symbol of the all-seeing wisdom of God. The aspergillum hanging over the back of the armchair by the bed has presumably been used to besprinkle the room with holy water. The top of the chair is embellished with a carving of St. Margaret, to whom women in childbirth were wont to appeal. More surprising is the fact that the arms of the chair and the prie-dieu are adorned with the lions of the throne of Solomon. The orange-like apples, which, as in the pictures of the Virgin in her chamber (*Pls.* 104, 126), lie near the window (*Fig.* 72), may likewise be presumed not to be there by chance. Probably they are intended to remind the spectator of the Fall and to stress the fact that all men are burdened with the Original Sin. Tolnay, however, interprets them as symbols of eternal bliss ('*gaudia paradisi*'). The frame of the round mirror contains ten concise scenes from the Passion, resembling coloured woodcuts. They range from the Agony in the Garden to the Resurrection and are intended to emphasize that the Original Sin is atoned for by the Passion of Christ.[2]

We have thus before us a unique picture of its kind, a double portrait of a bridal couple at the decisive moment when they are joined together for ever. To stress the solemnity of the moment, various symbols, as in pictures of the Virgin, are included in the representation. It is here part of

---

[1] For another reason for introducing a lapdog into a wedding picture see Chapter VI, p. 85, note 1.

[2] Among the pictures of the Passion the scene of the Resurrection is in no way stressed and is not even in a central position, so that there is nothing to prove that Jan was here combining a representation of the marriage sacrament with the idea of the Resurrection. The convex, diminishing mirror is there in order that the whole of the room may be seen (the reflected image of the room includes even the ceiling) and to make the representation of the witnesses possible without distracting attention from the bridal couple or from the room itself. Convex mirrors are always round, for which reason the roundness in this case is not to be interpreted as a symbol of the world.

73. Jan van Eyck: *Dog, from the Arnolfini Wedding Portrait.* Cat. No. 22. London, National Gallery

F

the theme that the room should be depicted in the greatest detail, for it has an importance almost equal to that of the personages. The bride reminds us of the St. Catherine in the Dresden triptych (*Pl.* 106), or even of the Holy Maiden (*Pl.* 25) standing between St. Barbara and St. Dorothy in the Ghent altar-piece. This coincidence, however, proves nothing except that Jan, like all his contemporaries, was in the habit of depicting Saints in the fashionable attire of noble or well-to-do ladies. The reserved, rather shy expression of this healthy young woman,[1] forming a contrast with the solemn earnestness of the bridegroom, has been most successfully rendered by the artist. Once again we have to admire the way in which everything in the picture is observed down to the last detail, while at the same time nothing is allowed to become too prominent or to claim more of our interest than is due to its significance in the representation. This is also true of the little griffon (*Fig.* 73), sparkling with life, who is nevertheless fitted into the ensemble in a most masterly way. This is the oldest portrait of a dog that we possess.[2]

For a work of Jan van Eyck's the colouring is unusually light, though in this connection it must be noted that the general harmony has been slightly impaired by the last cleaning. In particular, we see now that Arnolfini's countenance and his raised right hand have faded, since some of the glazes here have been lost. This fact makes it doubly evident that the Bordeaux red of his robe is now too dark, this being due to the absorption of the old varnish (now cleaned away in all the lighter parts of the picture), since the dark portions appear to have been less cleaned than the light. Owing to this over-cleaning of large portions, the figure of Giovanna, clad in pale green, blue, cream and white, now seems too bright and thus appears to advance too far towards the spectator, so that the original perfect equilibrium of all values as regards effect of depth has now been somewhat impaired. Jan created a strong contrast by opposing the dominant green of her dress (see *Pl.* 140)—the colour of affection, as blue is that of fidelity, both being the genuine colours of love[3]—directly with the cherry-red of the coverings of the bed, canopy and prie-dieu, which occurs again in the slippers and, together with blue, in the carpet and also on the inner edge of the mirror. The symmetry of the pictorial construction is heightened still more by the treatment of light. The pronounced brightness of the open window on the left is counterbalanced by the gleam of the ray of light falling upon the coverlet of the bed.

Chronologically close to the Arnolfini wedding portrait is the painting of the Virgin with Chancellor Rolin, with its magnificent portrait of the donor (*Pl.* 118). In the interests of the general construction Jan chose for his head an unusual pose, almost a profile, showing, except for the eye, only a small part of that side of the head which is turned away, so that the tip of the nose intersects the contour of the cheek.[4] The countenance is not, like those of Jodocus Vyd and Isabella Borluut, endowed with an expression of pious devotion, but looks as impenetrable as most of the faces in Jan's single portraits. This Chancellor,[5] even in the midst of his devotions, cannot forget his worldly position. In the donor portrait of the Virgin with Canon van der Paele (*Pl.* 122), completed in 1436, his impenetrability, as we have already mentioned, becomes spiritual absorption. Despite the exact reproduction of every feature and the under-lifesize format, an effect of monumentality is produced by these faces. The portraits of the Chancellor and the Canon belong to Jan's greatest achievements in portraiture.

Jan's next two portraits are that of the Bruges goldsmith Jan de Leeuw in the Vienna gallery, bearing the date 1436 on the original frame, and the probably somewhat earlier likeness formerly in

---

[1]*Cf.* p. 79, note 1. F. Winkler (*Pantheon*, 1931, p. 255 f.) points out that the little picture in Berlin, which according to the inscription should be a portrait of Bone d'Artois, second wife of Philip the Good, repeats, with only a few alterations (to the costume), the figure of Giovanna Arnolfini in the wedding picture.

[2]Jan does not confine himself to representing the zoological peculiarities of the species, such as we see in Lombard sketch-books about 1400 (*cf.* O. Pächt, *Early Italian Nature Studies*, in *Journal of the Warburg and Courtauld Institute*, XIII, 1950), but manages to grasp and portray the characteristics of the breed, going far beyond Pisanello, who often took his animals from models and generally retained the traditional profile position. The chief thing is, however, that Jan was the first artist to give us pulsating life in a portrait of a dog.

[3]Huizinga, *loc. cit.*, p. 407. In any case this colour symbolism is not invariably used by painters. In Jacquemart de Hesdin's miniature of the Marriage at Cana in the 'Grandes Heures du Duc de Berry' in Paris (Ring, No. 43), the bride, whose figure, seen completely *en face*, dominates the whole composition, is wearing a brilliant red dress.

[4]A similar overlapping is found in the portrait head with very striking contours now in the Johnson collection, Philadelphia, which on account of the whole conception of form seems to me to be the work of another painter, who was merely influenced by Jan van Eyck (*Pl.* 154).

[5]It appears to me to be a very arbitrary interpretation, quite contrary to the spirit of the fifteenth century, when A. Rudolph (*Das Werk des Künstlers*, I, 1939–40, p. 45) asserts that all the duplicity of Rolin's character is evident in his portrait and that Jan shows us the inner contradiction (existing according to Rudolph) between Rolin's principles and the nature of this commission.

the Baron Bruckenthal gallery at Her-
mannstadt (Sibiu, Roumania), now re-
ported to be in Bucharest. In the latter the
sitter, like Jan de Leeuw, is holding up a
ring in his hand (*Pl.* 141), which makes
it probable that he, too, was a goldsmith.
In this portrait in the Bruckenthal gallery,
later enlarged on all sides (a sill being
added at the foot), the upper part of the
body is fitted into the narrow frame in
the same way, showing the same simplicity as the Tymotheos of 1432 (*Pl.*
135), but including both hands. The light
blue of the chaperon, the ultramarine of
which has in part dissolved to a dull grey,
gives in contrast with the black of the
robe and background a strong accentuation to the picture. A peculiar, brooding,
and at the same time melancholy expres-
ion is seen in the still youthful features
and the deeply furrowed brow. In contrast, the face of the 35-year-old Jan de
Leeuw (*Pl.* 142), who lets his observant
glance rest upon the spectator, seems all
the more animated. The artist has kept
his work as simple as possible. No vivid
colour is to be seen in the picture. The
contours of the black cap and of the robe
enlivened with strips of brown fur stand
out against a dark blue background. The
yellowish colour of the flesh, hardly
broken by the rather pale lips, is the only
patch of brightness in the picture and

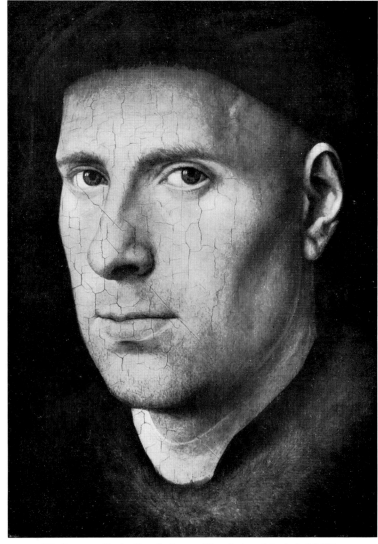

74. Jan van Eyck: *Jan de Leeuw (Detail, in original size)* 1436.
Cat. No. 24. Vienna, Gemälde Galerie

the spectator's eye is thus drawn at once to the unusually animated countenance of the Bruges
goldsmith (*Fig.* 74).

Probably a little later than this picture are two more portraits, both of them now in the Berlin
gallery. In these Jan returns to the uniaxial form, but uses a higher format, which enables him in
each case to show more of the upper part of the body, so that one of these pictures, probably the
later of the two, is already a half-length. The presumably earlier portrait represents Baulduyn de
Lannoy, Sieur de Molembais and one of the first knights of the Order of the Golden Fleece, who had
been given the sobriquet 'Le Besgue' (*Pl.* 143). In 1428–29 this nobleman, a scion of a distinguished
Hainault family, was a member of the same mission that Jan van Eyck accompanied to Portugal. At
the time he was portrayed he was between fifty and sixty years old. From his proud, but at the same
time sour expression, we can easily believe that he suffered from the physical defect which earned
for him the nickname of the stutterer. The face is strangely deformed. The right eye is higher in
the head, but closer to the nose, than the left. The sitter is wearing a dark-brown fur hat, similar
to Arnolfini's in the wedding portrait, and the golden chain of the Order of the Fleece over his
crimson brocaded robe, threaded with gold and edged with fur. In his right hand he holds a light-
coloured chamberlain's staff. The general colour effect is once again dark, so that the animated face
stands out strongly against the black ground.

Much more vigorous in its colouring is the single portrait of Giovanni Arnolfini (*Pl.* 144) in Berlin,
based on the contrast between the glowing red of the chaperon and the sap-green of the robe faced
with reddish-brown fur. The striking colours completely surround the face and thus make the
light-brown flesh, which they separate from the black ground, seem paler than it really is. When

compared with the 1434 wedding portrait, the face of the sitter, who is holding a folded letter in his right hand, seems more worn and reserved. This is not the friend in all the exaltation of his wedding day, but the official Arnolfini, the great merchant whom Duke Philip made his chamberlain and ennobled. In its accentuation of the enigmatic features this portrait is a psychological masterpiece.

The last work of Jan's portraiture that has come down to us is the portrait of his wife Margaret, now in the museum at Bruges, which he completed on 17th June 1439, when she was thirty-three years old (*Pls.* 145, 146). She sits erect for her husband, arrayed in her best scarlet robe trimmed with mouse-grey fur and fastened with a girdle of grey silk. The then fashionable cornets of gold brocade hide the hair on her temples. The white, crisply folded hood rests on top of it. A light-brown, marbled frame shows off the colours to particular advantage. As Jan does not give his wife an attribute, her hands rest folded in her lap and only part of the right is shown. She turns her intelligent eyes attentively towards the beholder.

All the single portraits by Jan van Eyck that have come down to us are of the same type, with only slight variations—in format, inclusion or exclusion of the hands, direction of glance. All of them are devoid of action, in all of them the mouth is firmly closed, all have uniform, neutral backgrounds, in other words no setting is shown behind the sitter. The only drawing known to us that seems to be a true copy after a lost original portrait by Jan[1] (*Pl.* 152) does not differ in any respect from the type we have just briefly outlined.

There can be no doubt that, if we possessed nothing by Jan except his single portraits, we should still be able to affirm that with him there begins a new era in the history of painting. They contain none of the summary qualities of mediaeval portraits, but are the expression of a pronounced objectivity. Here we have before us an art, the creator of which studied nature with the keenest penetration, but reproduced his models without any attempt at interpretation, that is to say without giving expression to his personal opinion as to the character of the sitter, a point in which he will be followed by the younger Hans Holbein. The chief stress is laid upon the face, the hands being given prominence only when they hold an attribute.[2] Even in cases when the uniaxiality is abandoned and the eye of the sitter is directed towards the beholder, the gaze is so quietly observant that the portrait does not strike with a note of instantaneity. This makes it unlikely that Jan ever painted likenesses with mouths opened in speech.[3] The opening of the mouth and the showing of the teeth are, for that matter, archaic traits, going back to a more primitive stage in the representation of reality. We find it in the 1430's in Pisanello's portrait of the Emperor Sigismund (*Fig.* 67),[4] but it hardly ever occurs in the latter part of the fifteenth century. On the other hand, the introduction of settings into portraiture is found for the first time in works of the master's followers. Every elaboration of the background distracts the spectator's eye from the face of the sitter. The unusual concentration prevalent in all Jan van Eyck's works, compels us to assume that the artist, if he had wanted to include a second feature, in this case the setting (even if it had been stipulated in the commission), would have made this dualism serve some inner purpose.[5] In the works of this creator of a new style in portraiture the utmost simplicity is

---

[1]Only the silverpoint drawing in the Louvre of a man wearing a chaperon (*Pl.* 152) seems to me, on account of the similarity of the draughtsmanship (which, however, is a little less precise) to that of the Albergati portrait in Dresden, to be a composition by Jan van Eyck, reproducing a lost drawing by the master probably made at the beginning of the 1430's, as a model for a painted portrait. As for the portrait drawing of Jacqueline of Bavaria, as long ago as 1905 (*Mitteilungen der Gesellschaft für vervielfält. Kunst*, 1905, p. 1) G. Glück rightly maintained that it is by an unknown contemporary artist. Apparently it is a drawing made after a painting. The sketched female heads in Turin and Rotterdam and the two male portraits in Berlin are by followers of the master. The beautiful portrait of a man wearing a chaperon in London (*Cat. No.* 88) has nothing to do with Jan van Eyck. For the falconer in Frankfurt (*Pl.* 151), *cf.* note 5.

[2]It is invariably a very simple attribute (a letter, ring or staff). The Archduchess Margaret's inventory of 1524 mentions a picture of a beautiful Portuguese lady holding in her right hand a little roll of paper. *Cf.* p. 68, note 3.

[3]We find this speaking mouth again in two portraits painted by artists from the master's immediate entourage. Of these, the portrait of a cleric in the Musée Ingres at Montauban (*Pl.* 153) is very difficult to judge from the photograph, which appears to reproduce an original somewhat obscured by layers of varnish. As regards format and uniaxiality, it is, like the drawing in Paris (*Pl.* 152), very close to the Albergati portrait, but seems to have, besides the very marked *craquelée*, a less plastic modelling and less sharply defined details. The grouping is also less successful.

The other portrait is the celebrated Man with the Pinks in Berlin (*Pl.* 156), which recent scholars have almost unanimously deleted from Jan's œuvre. This painting, which on purely external grounds is often given an early dating, produces an archaic effect on account of various stylistic elements such as the additive putting together of the features and the badly drawn thumb. Nevertheless, it cannot be of an early date, since it contains three stylistic elements not found in Jan's works until the 1430's, namely the sharp drawing of the folds in the skin (not yet noticeable in the Jodocus Vyd on the Ghent altar-piece), the inclusion in the picture of both hands and the fact that the sitter's glance is directed towards the spectator. The chronological problems are easily solved if we attribute this work to a follower.

[4]And also in the St. George of the fresco in Sant'Anastasia at Verona.

[5]The charming drawing of a falconer at the Städelsches Institut in Frankfurt am Main (*Pl.* 151) is more likely to be derived from a painting than from a drawing. There is no other instance of a preliminary drawing for a portrait giving the complete setting, including even the still-life details, and it would be difficult to adduce a reason for a painter's doing this. The far too graphic technique, *e.g.* the purely linear

everywhere predominant.[1] Huizinga has rightly spoken of the miracle of this fathoming of the innermost secrets of a personality and stressed that it is something that must be painted and cannot be expressed in words, so that it is impossible to find literary parallels to this art.

rendering of the fur edging and the hat and the hesitant, hatching-like modelling of the robe, is too remote from the Dresden drawing (*Pl.* 133) and becomes comprehensible only if we suppose a transposition of a painting into a drawing. The modelling of the head and the handling of the contours certainly belong to Jan's style in the middle of the 1430's, but the excessively slender, curiously boneless hands (similar to those of Jacqueline of Bavaria, *cf.* p. 78, note 1) are foreign to his art. It is possible—though this would be a very complicated hypothesis—that the painted model for the dawing was an enlarged copy of a portrait without hands by Jan. In this case the whole composition would be parallel to the effigy of Jean sans Peur in Antwerp (*Fig.* 62).

F. Winkler (*The Art Quarterly*, Detroit 1950, p. 216, *cf.* O. Kurz, *Burlington Magazine*, 1951, p. 238) also points out that the drawing is a copy—though a particularly good one—of a painting, but he ascribes the lost original to Rogier van der Weyden. In Rogier's pictures we find no example of an interior like that of the Frankfurt drawing. Only the hands are similar to his style. The face is much richer in details and far more individualized—one need only compare the ears, which Rogier always rendered in a typical manner.

The earliest preserved portrait in which the setting is included in the picture is the likeness of Edward Grymeston by Petrus Christus, dated 1446. It is no longer possible to ascertain why Carel van Mander maintained that Jan van Eyck repeatedly—van Mander himself appears to have seen only one, and that an unfinished work (*cf.* Catalogue, Nr. 14)—painted portraits with landscape backgrounds. The first portrait of a sitter in a room with an open window is also by Petrus Christus, but the first known examples of portrait heads being depicted against sky and landscape are by Memling and by Antonello da Messina (dated 1474, Berlin).

It seems conceivable that Jan van Eyck might have represented a portrait model in the attitude of prayer, as Rogier van der Weyden did later in his diptychs. (It is curious that half-length Virgins, found in Franco-Flemish and German pictures of the 'international' style, disappear completely from Netherlandish art about 1425 and do not reappear until 1449 in the works of Petrus Christus and until 1450 in those of Rogier, that is to say after his journey to Italy.) The miniature of King René praying, in the 'Heures du Duc d'Anjou' (Paris Bibliothèque Nationale, MS. lat. 1156a; Ring, No. 87), illuminated during the 1430's, proves that half-length portraits of donors were customary during Jan's lifetime.

In the fragment (cut off at the foot) of a donor portrait in Leipzig (*Pl.* 155) the clumsy composition, together with the ostentatious gesture of prayer, the dull, uninspired face and the weakness of the hands, makes it impossible not only that it can have been executed by Jan, but even that it was conceived by him. This work, too, must be ascribed to a follower, but not to the painter of the 'Man with the Pinks (*Pl.*156).

[1]The observation occasionally made to the effect that Jan van Eyck painted men better than he did women is incorrect and is contradicted by those two masterpieces alone, the portraits of Isabella Borluut and of the painter's wife. We must remember that Facius praised both the Lomellini portraits, saying that the man lacked only voice and that the representation of the woman was perfect, even down to the nails of her fingers. Probably the notion of the inferiority of Jan's female portraits is due to the pretty, but not very expressive face of Giovanna Arnolfini. We must, however, consider that it never entered Jan's mind to give a face more expression than he could read in it.

Chapter VI: OTHER PROFANE WORKS BY JAN VAN EYCK

CONTEMPORARY documents and almost contemporary literary references tell us that Jan van Eyck was commissioned to paint not only portraits, but also other works of a secular nature. Some of these were works which show the master in the service of the art of sculpture. Others, and these appear to have been far more important, were paintings of profane narrative art.

At that time the work a painter did in connection with sculpture might be of two kinds—the painting over and gilding of sculptures,[1] or the designing of them. I have already mentioned that the series of twelve Apostles, known to us only through drawings made after them (*Pls.* 108–111), may have been designed for plastic execution in comparatively small dimensions by a woodcarver, a bronze-founder or a silversmith. To the same category belong four drawings for portraits of princes, which were only discovered in 1936 and have been attributed to Jan van Eyck.

These are four silverpoint drawings (*Pls.* 147–150), of which two are now in the van Beuningen collection at Vierhouten, while the other two were destroyed together with the Mannheimer collection during the 1939–45 war. According to the inscriptions they represent Dukes John and Philip of Brabant, the Duke of Savoy and Count Philip of Nevers. The sculptures made after these drawings exercised a clearly visible influence on the slightly later bronze statues known as the 'Gravenbeeldjes' in the Rijksmuseum at Amsterdam (*Figs.* 75, 76).[2] The very first mention of these drawings[3] relates them, quite correctly, to the twenty-four figures cast in bronze on the base of the black marble tomb erected by Duke Philip the Good in the church of St. Pierre at Lille for Louis de Mâle, Count of Flanders, who died in 1385, though the tomb was not completed until 1455. Rough drawings made after them in 1602 and clumsy engravings of 1731 do, in fact, show clearly that these drawings were used as models for four of the figures of princes on this monument, which was destroyed during the French Revolution.

Although the van Eyck character of these figures is clearly manifest, it is impossible to establish their authenticity solely on the basis of stylistic comparisons with Jan's known works. The draughtsmanship is

75–76. *Duke John of Brabant and Count Philip of Nevers.* Bronze figures from the Gravenbeeldjes. Amsterdam, Rijksmuseum

[1] Jan van Eyck received payment in 1435 for the painting and gilding of six statues destined for the façade of the town hall.

[2] *Cf.* C. M. A. A. Lindeman, *De dateering, herkomst en identificatie der 'Gravenbeeldjes' van Jacques de Gérines,* in *Oud Holland,* 1941.

[3] In the catalogue, edited by D. Hannéma, of the Jeroen Bosch exhibition at the Boymans Museum in Rotterdam in 1936. A historical justification of the attribution was attempted by J. C. Ebbinge Wubben, *De Tentoonstelling 'Tekeningen van Jan van Eyck tot Rubens' in het Museum Boymans, Maandblad v. beeldende Kunsten,* 1949.

obviously more hesitant than in Jan's drawing at Dresden (*Pl.* 133), but despite the less careful execution the handling of the line is similar, both in the accentuation of the main folds on the breasts and in the hatching. Weaknesses can be discerned, above all in the incorporeal, in part barely more than sketchy reproduction of the hands, and sometimes also in the standing pose, which achieves an artistically perfect solution only in the figure of the Duke of Savoy (*Pl.* 147). A remark of Tolnay's carries us still further. He rightly draws attention to the fact that style and draperies appear to be more archaic than in the paintings of Jan van Eyck known to us, from which we must conclude that they are youthful works of the master. In the four standing figures there is, in fact, still a relic of the slenderness and delicacy of the 'international' style. The long, sweeping train, with only one break where it touches the floor, of Duke John of Brabant (*Pl.* 148) reminds us of that of the Berlin Virgin in the Church (*Pl.* 10). If, however, these figures were designed about the middle of the 1420's for the Duke of Burgundy, then it is highly probable that their original author was Jan van Eyck.[1]

If we wish to realize the scope of Jan van Eyck's art, these drawings are important. They give us an idea of his activity in the service of the most sumptuous court in Europe. What we here see are dignified figures, posing with tranquil and natural charm. The excessively elongated proportions of Paul de Limbourg's courtiers (*Figs.* 13, 36) have given way to normal stature, rendered in simple but effective poses. Three of the princes are wearing ceremonial dress and have their heads covered. The fourth is bare-headed,[2] in hunting attire with a falcon on his wrist. For a figure on the base of a tomb which, with the others, takes the place of the 'Pleureurs', this attribute seems so unusual that the almost insoluble problem arises, whether the drawings were not originally intended for a purely profane purpose, *e.g.* as models for sculptures in the hall of a palace, and were only at a later date used as models for figures on the base of a tomb which was not completed until several decades later.[3]

It is remarkable at how late a date self-contained panel-paintings of secular subjects make their appearance. In the natural course of things secular books of the most varied kinds were illustrated throughout the Middle Ages. In Avignon (some now in the Louvre), in Italy, in Tyrol, etc., fourteenth-century frescoes have been preserved, proving that towards the close of the Middle Ages it was customary to decorate the halls of castles with mural paintings of secular themes. In miniature-painting—at first in Northern Italy from the end of the fourteenth century and then, from the beginning of the fifteenth, in France and Flanders—we find scenes of everyday life with figures in modern costumes placed in contemporary interiors. These stand at the beginning of genre-painting. But, so far as we know, the very beginnings of secular cabinet-painting, that is to say of self-contained, portable pictures painted on wood, parchment or canvas, which are neither religious nor portraits, date from the time of the brothers van Eyck. This is all the more surprising since secular miniatures, such as the illustrations, painted about 1400, to the 'Livre de la chasse' (*Fig.* 8), the miniature from the 'Conversations' of Pierre Salmon (*Fig.* 12) and the calendar miniatures in books of hours (*Figs.* 11, 13, 36), show that painters in their compositions did not differentiate between religious and secular subjects. We see this throughout the fifteenth century in the secular historical scenes[4] to be found far more frequently in tapestries and miniatures than in cabinet-paintings. But in his third period, with its plastic rendering of reality, we already find Robert Campin painting—it would be instructive to know for what location and at whose orders—the scene of Queen Tomyris with the head of

[1] One can hardly assume that, in addition to Jan himself, an artist who had already been influenced by him was working for the Duke between 1425 and 1430. Evidence of Jan's influence is not found elsewhere before the 1430's. Probably the drawings were one of the first tasks assigned by Philip the Good to Jan when he appointed him his court painter on 19th May 1425.

The lack of comparative material, for we possess only one drawing certainly made by Jan, and, moreover, of later date, makes it impossible to give more than a personal opinion as to the authenticity of these sketches.

[2] The drawing made from it in 1602 unfortunately does not tell us exactly whether the bronze figure of Duke Philip of Brabant showed him out hawking. We see him without the falcon, but in the same pose, so that it is possible that the falcon, which would have been cast separately, may have already been lost by that time. It is hardly possible to assume that the artist was merely given the task of producing a series of drawings portraying princes, without any more indication of the purposes for which they were intended.

[3] Stylistically very close to these works is a drawing in Berlin of another bare-headed gentleman, which P. Wescher (*Berliner Museen*, 1938, p. 31) believes to be the remnant of a full-length sheet. Friedländer calls it an original by Rogier van der Weyden. I do not see any difference of style between this work and the four drawings of princes (*Pls.* 147–50). That it formed part of the series cannot be proved, but seems probable. The portrayed person appears neither in the drawings of 1602 nor in the engravings of 1731. As an explanation, Wescher supposes the figures, which stood on the two narrow sides of the tomb, to be lacking in both series.

[4] Historical scenes were represented at a very early date, *cf.* the important Bayeux Tapestries, executed at the end of the eleventh century.

77. After a Franco-Flemish Painter, about 1425.
Hunting Festival of Duke Philip the Good. Cat. No. 68.
Versailles, Chateau

Cyrus with precisely the same rigid solemnity as he would have used for a scene of Christian martyrdom.[1]

One representation of a contemporary event has at least come down to us in copies, of which that in the Palace of Versailles (*Fig.* 77), however, to judge by the manner of painting, cannot have been made before the middle of the sixteenth century, though in its general appearance and costumes it seems to be a faithful reproduction of the lost original. Only the landscape background must have been somewhat enriched. It represents a hunting festival, which takes place in the vicinity of a castle surrounded by water after a hawking expedition. The appearance in three places of the Burgundian coat of arms[2] and the presence of Duke Philip the Good's fool show that a festival given by the Duke is represented, although there is no apparent effort to achieve direct portraiture. Judging from the costumes, which are invariably white, Roblot-Delondre[3] deduced that the original must have been executed in the middle 1420's or while Jan was in Portugal. It was painted by a minor artist still entirely in the style of the second decade of the century, who knew nothing of the innovations of Robert Campin and Hubert van Eyck in the representation of the setting, who anxiously avoids overlappings and forms his crudely drawn figures into awkward groups which he distributes more or less symmetrically about the completely unorganized inclined plane. The historical significance of the composition lies in the fact that the commission must have been given to the artist before Jan van Eyck entered the Duke's service or during his absence. The commission testifies to the general interest in secular pictures and to the entry of genre pictures, or to put it more exactly, of subjects drawn from daily life, into the sphere of cabinet-painting.

Of a considerably higher artistic quality was the model for the engraving of the large Garden of Love (*Fig.* 78). Although some abbreviated elements in the rendering of the landscape must surely be attributed to the engraver, it is nevertheless clear that the original author also used schematic stock-pieces for his landscape. In contrast to the painter of the hunting scene, however, he knew how to give rhythmic movement to his single figures and his groups. The composition seems to be too spacious to allow us to assume that a tapestry could have served as a model for it. The model must, therefore, have been a mural or a cabinet-painting. I shall return later to the hypothesis[4] that the model was a fresco painted by Jan van Eyck at The Hague. In any case the ladies and cavaliers

---

[1] Copies in the Museum, Berlin, and (with variations) in the Academy at Vienna. F. Winkler (*Der Meister von Flémalle und Rogier van der Weyden*, Strasbourg 1930) accepts Hulin's reference to the *Speculum humanae salvationis* and thinks that, as in the case of the representations of Judith and of Jael, we have to do with an 'assimilation' to the Virgin Mary. Nevertheless this unusually large picture can hardly have been hung in a church, *e.g.* as a component part of an altar-piece, but was probably intended for the embellishment of a secular, probably official room.

[2] F. Post (*Jahrbuch d. preussischen Kunstsammlungen*, LII, Berlin 1931, p. 120 f.), judging from the form of the coat of arms on the one hand and the absence of the chains of the Golden Fleece on the other, concluded that the original had been created between 4th October 1430 (date of the form of the coat of arms) and 3rd December 1431 (date on which the Statutes of the Order were promulgated). It is true that the obligation for the knights to wear the Fleece constantly was not written down until 1431, but we may assume that the rule existed from the foundation of the Order. It seems extremely unlikely that Duke Philip, after the institution of the Order, would have commissioned a painting in which he himself and the whole of his court were depicted in white ceremonial dress, but without the Order. This being a copy painted a century later, it is quite conceivable that the copyist might have corrected the original painter's heraldry, introducing, instead of the coat of arms he found on the original, a version of it which he considered to be the only correct one.

[3] *Revue archéologique*, 1911, p. 420 f.

[4] Irmgard Schüler, *Der Meister der Liebesgärten*, 1943, p. 38 f.

78. *The Large Garden of Love*. Engraving. Cat. No. 89

of this composition belong to the same courtly world as Jan van Eyck's figures of princes. Whereas in the hunting scene the intention would appear to have been to reproduce some specific episode, namely a festival held on a certain day in which certain persons took part, the large Garden of Love is obviously an allegory. In a similar court milieu the company is split up even more emphatically into pairs and this creates an amorous note. This is entirely in accord with the courtly spirit prevailing in the remnants of fourteenth-century frescoes brought from Avignon to the Louvre, a spirit which exercised its influence upon the artists of Burgundy and Flanders as well as on those of Lombardy and Tyrol. In the hunting festival scene the erotic element is confined to dancing and flirting. In the large Garden of Love the couples have detached themselves from the company. It needed only one step more in order to attain an even greater unequivocalness and this step was quite in harmony with the spirit of the time.[1]

   This marked accentuation of the erotic element now makes its appearance in the new category of cabinet-pictures. In 1456 the Italian humanist Bartholomeus Facius wrote a little book entitled *De viris illustribus*, in which, among other famous men, he included Joannes Gallicus (Jan van Eyck) and Rogerius Gallicus (Rogier van der Weyden). He describes Jan as the first among painters, well versed in all branches of knowledge, especially in geometry (this can only refer to the perspective foreshortenings in his pictures), and finally as the founder of a new method of painting ('*multa de colorum proprietatibus invenisse*'), after which he gives us remarkably lucid descriptions of the few pictures by Jan that he had seen. Among these he mentions a particularly fine one in the possession

---

[1]*Cf.* Julius von Schlosser, *Die Wandgemälde aus Schloss Lichtenberg in Tirol*, Vienna 1916.

of Cardinal Octavianus. In it[1] were to be seen women emerging from the water after bathing, covering the secret parts of their reddened bodies with fine linen, the reverse of their bodies being visible in a mirror, so that their backs as well as their breasts could be seen. Together with other details, such as a perspiring old woman, a burning lamp and a little dog drinking water, Facius also describes various features in the landscape. From the wording it is clear that mountains, woods and castles could be seen, shown in such a way that they seemed to be fifty thousand paces apart. Facius was obviously impressed by the fact that the landscape details were brought into a correct relationship of dimensions. After enumerating all the things to be seen in the picture, he returns once more to the mirror, which reflected everything he described and seemed to the Italian to be the most admirable part of the whole painting. His description is so vivid that he might have dispensed with mentioning the artist's name. Only Jan van Eyck could have painted such a picture. Facius also knew a similar picture by Rogier van der Weyden in Genoa—a woman perspiring in a bath. Close to her was a little dog and two smiling youths were peeping through a crack without her knowledge.[2]

These two pictures, which the humanist describes only fifteen years after the premature death of Jan van Eyck and at a time when Rogier van der Weyden was still alive, are among the oldest real genre-paintings of which we have cognizance. They are works which neither reproduce a specific episode, such as a hunting festival that actually took place, nor express an allegorical idea, such as a Garden of Love or the occupations of a certain month, but depict a daily occurrence, in which the name of the person depicted is of no interest and which does not symbolize anything. It is noteworthy that in each case the artist chose an erotic theme. That this choice was deliberate is proved in the one case by the fact that the women cover the secret portions of their bodies with fine linen and in the other by the introduction of the youths peeping through a crack.[3] The representation of such subjects was possible only as a result of the new realism. Only a method of painting capable of giving material characterization to the surface of things could endow such a theme with significance. It is probably no mere chance that Facius gives us a detailed description only of the picture by Jan and not of Rogier's bathing scene.

Fortunately, the composition of a similar picture has been preserved in the form of a small copy dating from the beginning of the seventeenth century. In 1628 the well-known Antwerp collector Cornelis van der Geest commissioned the painter Willem van Haecht to record on a panel for posterity the room in which he kept his treasures, by means of one of the so-called 'gallery pictures' which at that time were popular, choosing the culminating moment in his career as a collector, when he was honoured by the visit of his sovereigns, the Archduke Albert and the Infanta Isabella Clara Eugenia. This picture was formerly in the collection of Lord Huntingfield, whence it passed to the van Berg collection in New York.[4] In it we can recognize a number of well-known pictures by Rubens, Wildens, Quentin Metsys, Pieter Aertszen, etc. On the wall opposite the window hangs a picture which can only have been painted by Jan van Eyck. If the proportions of the pictures shown are correct, which can never be assumed *a priori* in 'gallery pictures', the painting must have been a little larger than the Arnolfini wedding portrait.[5] Van Haecht reproduces this picture (*Figs.* 79,

---

[1]The text runs: Sunt item picturae eius nobiles apud Octavianum Cardinalem virum illustrem eximia forma feminae e balneo exeuntes occultiores corporis partes tenui linteo velatae, notabili rubore, e quibus unius os tantummodo pectusque demonstrans posteriores corporis partes per speculum pictum lateri oppositum ita expressit, ut et terga quemadmodum pectus videas. In eadem tabula est in balneo lucerna ardenti simillima et anus, quae sudare videatur, catulus aquam lambens et item equi hominesque perbrevi statura, montes, nemora, pagi, castella tanto artificio elaborata, ut alia ab aliis quinquaginta millibus passuum distare credas. Sed nihil prope admirabilius in eodem opere, quam speculum in eadem tabula depictum, in quo quaecumque inibi descripta sunt, tanquam in vero speculo prospicias.

[2]The text runs: Eius est tabula praeinsignis Jenuae, in qua mulier in balneo sudans, juxtaque eam catulus, ex adverso duo adolescentes illam clanculum per rimam prospectantes ipso risu notabiles.

[3]Huizinga (*loc. cit.*, p. 458 f.), discussing Facius' descriptions of these pictures, mentions that at the Burgundian court, on the occasion of solemn entries, stages were erected at certain points, on which naked women posed as 'personnages', representing scenes such as the Judgement of Paris or bathing sirens. An exposure of the body producing a particularly obscene effect can be seen in the Limbourg brothers' February miniature at Chantilly, in which a man and a woman are warming themselves in front of a fire, in attitudes which clearly expose their genital organs.

[4]There are numerous reproductions in *The van Berg Collection of Paintings*, Catalogue issued by Mrs. Mary van Berg, New York 1947.

[5]It is represented as being somewhat higher than the male portrait (69 cm. high) by Quentin Metsys, now in the Städel Institute at Frankfurt-on-Main, or than the so-called portrait of Paracelsus (70 cm. high) in the style of Metsys, now in the Louvre (there attributed to van Scorel) or than the copy of the latter (77 cm. high) by Rubens in the Brussels gallery. In any case, Rubens' Battle of Amazons (Munich), Aertszen's Woman making pancakes (Rotterdam) and the Adoration of the Shepherds by a follower of F. Floris and J. Bueckelaer (Vienna) are all shown in the correct relationship of size to these two portraits. All the above pictures, like van Eyck's, are hanging on the walls. That the Winter Landscape with a Hunter by Wildens, now in the Dresden gallery, is shown as being considerably smaller is probably due to reasons of composition. This picture is shown standing on the floor in the foreground and care was taken that no portion of the pictures behind it should be concealed.

79. Willem van Haecht, after Jan van Eyck. *The Toilet*. Cat. No. 36. New York, Van Berg Collection

80. The same picture.
(with the distortion corrected)

80)—as he does the other known works—with the utmost fidelity; in fact he even includes a gaping transverse crack caused by the glued-on strip of the frame, which has prevented the panel from expanding.

This picture likewise represents a toilet scene. A young woman, wearing only a pair of sandals and with her hair hanging loose, is washing herself in front of a round mirror similar to that seen in the Arnolfini wedding picture, assisted by a pretty, smartly dressed girl. The careful attire of the companion is obviously intended to form a contrast to the nude body, thus fulfilling a similar function to that of the old woman among the young ones in Facius' description of the bathing scene and in Dürer's drawing of a women's bath-house. The girl holds a glass bottle, presumably containing some sweet-smelling perfume. The picture has exactly the same box-like room with a ceiling of wooden beams, as the Arnolfini wedding picture. Moreover, the window and bed are in the same position and even the cast-off slippers and the little dog are not lacking. From Facius' description it would appear as if lapdogs were an indispensable element in such pictures.[1] The mirror is proportionately larger than that in the Arnolfini wedding picture and is hung on a nail in the window-frame, presumably for the express purpose of the toilet.

---

[1] A little dog is also to be seen in the 'Love-spell' in the museum at Leipzig, painted by a Cologne master in the third quarter of the century and representing a popular old legend which also forms the subject of Friedrich Hebbel's poem 'Liebeszauber'.

This presence of a lapdog in all the four erotic paintings showing female nudes which are known to us in this category, makes it legitimate to doubt whether Panofsky is right in interpreting Giovanna Arnolfini's dog as a symbol of fidelity, as found on late mediaeval tombstones. The juxtaposition of symbols of Salvation and erotic allusions would not be in conflict with the spirit of the late Middle Ages. The cheerful behaviour of the exuberant little animal (*Fig.* 73), of a breed which at that time was evidently popular both with women of rank such as Giovanna Cenani and with other more frivolous ladies, seems to support this theory. From van Eyck's lost toilet scene (*Figs.* 79–80) obviously derives a large panel-painting by Hans Memling, showing Bathsheba emerging from her bath. In this picture, now at Stuttgart, we also find the hairy grey lapdog. In mature pictures by Rogier van der Weyden a little dog of the same breed appears near the representation of the Sacrament of Matrimony (Antwerp) as well as in scenes from the Gospel (Munich).

This little copy (measuring 11.5 by 6.5 cm.) reveals not only in its composition, but also in the types, the hands and the treatment of the folds, the mature style of Jan van Eyck, who must have painted the original during the 1430's. We may assume that he was the creator of this type of picture. Such an intimate scene is hardly conceivable in mural paintings. It was probably painted for some princely patron and was obviously intended for a private cabinet. Jan's masterly rendering of a female nude in the Ghent altar-piece may have evoked in some connoisseur the wish to possess a similar picture of a profane subject. It is characteristic of the Netherlandish mentality that a mythological subject was not chosen.[1] Despite the general admiration for antique heroic legends, the patron evidently wanted not only a realistic representation of a female nude, but also an equally realistic representation of the milieu. It is noteworthy that so soon afterwards two of the pictures of this kind, which cannot have been very numerous, had already found their way to Italy. Obviously Italians, as Facius' eulogy proves, were peculiarly susceptible to this kind of representation.

Facius also mentions another picture by Jan van Eyck, a *Mappa mundi*, that is to say a painted map of the world, said to have been made by Jan for Duke Philip. In this picture,[2] which, according to the Italian humanist, was at that time perfect beyond all imagination, were to be seen not only the places and the locations of the countries, but also the correct distances between the various points. We can see in the Chantilly book of hours (*Fig.* 81) what was the artistic conception of a map at that time. It is true that Facius says nothing about the technique, but we may assume that it was a cabinet-painting, perhaps a water-colour on canvas. As he also mentions its circular form, it is probable that the general effect was similar to that of the Limbourg brothers' miniature, though this does not show the whole world, but only Rome. Jan probably enriched the scheme with numerous naturalistic details, to bring out the character of the various views of towns and landscapes.

It is probable that Jan van Eyck also painted other secular pictures. In the first half of the sixteenth century Marcantonio Michiel mentions seeing in the house of the philosopher Leonico Tomeo at Padua a small landscape,[3] by the hand of 'Gianes da Brugia', showing some fishermen capturing an otter. Of the fact that on another occasion this Venetian connoisseur confuses Jan van Eyck with Memling, or rather makes one person out of the two, we shall speak later.

A hunting picture might very well have been by Jan's hand, for such representations were by no means confined at that time to calendar miniatures, but were also popular in the art of tapestry. Among the four tapestries of hunting scenes in the Duke of Devonshire's collection, executed in Tournai during the second quarter of the fifteenth century, that is to say about the same time,[4] there is one showing the hunting of otters and wild swans. The subject was therefore familiar in Jan's time. As no real genre pictures from Memling's period of activity, *i.e.* the second half of the fifteenth century, have come down to us or are known to have existed in the Netherlands, we

81. Paul de Limbourg. *Plan of Rome.* Chantilly, Musée Condé

[1] In Italy mythological nudes are not found in panel-paintings until the second half of the century.

[2] The text runs: Eius est Mundi comprehensio orbiculari forma quam Philippo Belgarum Principi pinxit, quo nullum consummatius opus nostra aetate factum putatur, in quo non solum loca, situsque regionum, sed etiam locorum distantiam metiendo dignoscas. It is most remarkable that Facius praised Jan's map of the world so highly, since it seems rather unlikely that he would not have known Ambrogio Lorenzetti's 'Mappamondo' in the Palazzo Pubblico at Siena, mentioned as 'Cosmografia' by Ghiberti (the fresco, since destroyed, was commissioned in 1344). As to the relationship between the maps of Rome in the 'Très riches heures' and the vault fresco by Taddeo di Bartolo in the Palazzo Pubblico at Siena, *cf.* Pächt in *Journal of the Warburg and Courtauld Institute*, XIII, 1950, p. 40.

[3] The text runs: Lo quadretto in tela d'un piede, ove è dipinto un paese con alcuni pescatori, che hanno preso una londra, con due figurette, che stanno a vedere, fu de mano de Gianes da Brugia. The use of the word 'tela' (canvas) led Friedländer to suppose that it was a water-colour ('Tüchlein') like the portrait of the beautiful Portuguese lady, but Michiel is occasionally mistaken in his indications of materials.

[4] B. Kurth, *Gotische Bildteppiche aus Frankreich und Flandern*, Munich 1923.

must assume that Michiel was referring either to a picture by some contemporary artist of Patinir's school,[1] or else to a lost work by Jan van Eyck.

In another passage Michiel says that in the Casa Lampognano at Milan[2] there was a small half-length showing a master settling accounts with his steward: 'fu de man de Juan Heic, credo memelino, Ponentino, fatto nel 1440.' The figure 1440, which, since Michiel rarely mentions dates, must have been in a prominent position, probably on the lower edge of the frame, proves that he is referring to a work of Jan's painted during the last year of his life. We shall see in the next chapter that the first instance of a half-length genre picture is one of a religious nature painted in 1449 by Petrus Christus (*Fig. 86*), who could hardly have invented the idea, so that it becomes highly probable that the half-length genre picture was first introduced into art by Jan van Eyck. The only question remaining unsolved is whether the prototype was a real genre picture, such as we find later among the works of Quentin Metsys, though without the latter's moralizing tendency, which did not appear until about 1500. It is also possible that it was a portrait combined with action such as the Arnolfini wedding picture.

Facius' descriptions, the copy in van Haecht's 'gallery picture', Marcantonio Michiel's notes and the elaboration of a pictorial idea by Petrus Christus in the spirit of Jan, give us so clear an idea of Jan's activity as a painter of profane subjects, even if an error may have crept in, that we are compelled to see in him a very many-sided artist. All Jan's profane works, in so far as they are known to us from literary or artistic sources, are narrative pictures showing an action which is simple, but typical of a certain class or occupation. (In these respects they are quite different from the picture of Duke Philip's hunting festival or the large Garden of Love,[3] for Jan never depicted numerous scenes of equal value side by side, but invariably produced a highly concentrated representation.) Thus Jan would seem to have been, not a precursor, but the initiator of the new art of genre-painting. His ideas were at first followed by Rogier van der Weyden and Petrus Christus, two artists who in other respects also occasionally followed in his footsteps. In the second half of the century these ideas were not pursued any further.[4] About 1500, however, when great artists turned once more to this field of painting, masters who ensured the continuity of genre-painting down to the eighteenth century, they drew their inspiration from works of the founder of the school. It is characteristic that the first two to return to genre-painting were artists of retrospective tendencies. Whether the manner in which Hieronymus Bosch represents the follies of the world in the setting of his time and with landscapes of his native country as background was inspired by Jan van Eyck we cannot say, since Marcantonio Michiel's description of the otter-hunt does not go into detail. But Bosch's rendering of the interior in his wing-panel of the Death of the Miser is entirely in accord with Jan's style. And lastly, Quentin Metsys' half-length genre-pictures follow in every way the manner which we find in Petrus Christus' painting of 1449, and this manner originated with Jan van Eyck.

---

[1] Take, for instance, the hunting scene, including, it is true, several scenes and not just one episode, painted by the Master of the Female Half-lengths (erroneously attributed to Patinir), in the former Wesendonck collection in Berlin (reproduced in *Jahrbuch d. kunsthist. Sammlungen*, XXXIV, Vienna 1918, pp. 124, 125).

[2] The text runs: El quadretto a mezze figure, del patron che fa conto con el fattor, fu de man de Juan Heic, credo Memelino, Ponentino fatto nel 1440.

[3] As is always the case when an attempt is made to reconstruct early works, there is plenty of scope for fancy. For us the important point is that Jan van Eyck's mature genre pictures seem to have been of a different stamp from the 'large Garden of Love'.

[4] The fact that there is a picture of this kind by an artist from the Lower Rhine does not disprove this assertion, since it was a characteristic feature of fifteenth-century German art that the achievements of Netherlandish art began to exercise influence at the very time when they were being supplanted by new ideas in their country of origin.

Chapter VII: THE FOLLOWERS OF JAN VAN EYCK

WE do not know of any painter whose art derives so completely from Jan van Eyck's as the style of Rogier van der Weyden or Jacques Daret does from that of the Master of Flémalle. As we have already seen, this is due, not so much to the 'courtly' character of Jan's works and the 'burgher' character of Campin's pictures, as to the exclusive nature of Jan's art which always made the highest demands upon the painter. His method of providing a new solution for every problem according to the nature of each separate task did not leave younger artists any scheme which they could easily take over. Hulin has already pointed out that the Ghent altar-piece must have had a discouraging effect on imitators. Jan's pictures of the Virgin, too, were so carefully planned, painted in such a finished way and withal so natural in appearance that his contemporaries could seldom discover an element in this system which allowed of further development.

As is well known, we possess a whole series of documentary notices referring to Jan, but in none of these is there any mention of his having trained a pupil. For Jan's immediate successors there were thus three possibilities. The first was the occasional appropriation of various features. More important than this is the only known instance of the exploitation of the second possibility, when a painter, obviously not trained by either of the brothers van Eyck, comes under the influence of their art, makes a thorough study of their works and, without actually copying them, endeavours to achieve effects which prepare the way for further developments. The third possibility, instances of which are found mainly in portraiture, consisted in an imitation of Jan's artistic principles, which led to important results in individual cases.

1. *Influence on Robert Campin and Rogier van der Weyden*

ESSENTIALLY, the two chief masters of the Tournai school were independent of the art of Jan van Eyck. The points of contact which can be established, however, give us a deeper insight into the general development of old Flemish painting.

Robert Campin's most important works were those of his second period. At a moment that we cannot exactly determine, probably at the end of the third decade, he entered upon his third period,[1] during which his realism inclined to heavy forms. He strives to achieve the effect of utmost plasticity. While the other stylistic elements remain as they were, we notice a change in the use of colour which was beginning towards the end of the second period. The excellently preserved Ingelbrecht altar-piece shows bright colours, without the differentiation achieved by heightening a colour with a lighter one. The light colours of the Nativity at Dijon, still reminiscent of the 'international' style, have become saturated. The light effects of the background, such as the rose-coloured sky over the gay view of the town, are less striking than the material rendering of wood (painted or waxed in the main room, raw in the workshop), of leather and metal. Only the clothes do not yet reveal what they are made of. At the beginning of the third period, however, in the fragment of the Thief, now at Frankfurt-on-Main, the material characterization was still achieved by a linear pattern. Only steel and precious stones are rendered by superimposed lights. The elaborately modelled nude owes its plasticity above all to the marked alternations of light and dark, *i.e.* by genuine means of painting. As an exception, the landscape remains schematic. In the more advanced wing-panels with the standing figures of the Virgin and St. Veronica, in the same museum, many details (treatment of the flesh, clothing materials, such as veil, cloth, fur, leather, brocade backgrounds and grassy terrain with minutely rendered flowers) reveal a material characterization of their texture. We must here assume an influence exercised by Jan van Eyck's art, probably derived from the panels of the Ghent altar-piece, which at that time had just been completed. The grisaille group of the Trinity, too, with its marked plasticity, is closely akin to the grisailles in the Ghent altar-piece.

---

[1]The following authentic pictures, in addition to the portraits already mentioned, date from this period: the Fragment with the Wicked Thief in Frankfurt-on-Main (Städel Institute); the fragment of the Virgin in her chamber in London, and above all, the wing-panels in the Städel Institute at Frankfurt, which are said to have come from an abbey of Flémalle near Liége, *cf.* Winkler in *Thieme's Künsterlexikon*, XXXVII. A few compositions preserved only in the form of copies (*e.g.* p. 82, note 1) serve to round off the œuvre.

The works of Robert Campin's third period, together with Jan van Eyck's pictures of the Virgin in Frankfurt and Bruges, represent the culminating points of the stylistic phase of plastic realism in the Netherlands. This phase, which everywhere prevailed only for a relatively short time, soon gives way to Campin's fourth period, characterized by an exaggeratedly delicate modelling of the human figure—cf. e.g. the Werle wing-panels in the Prado, dated 1438,[1] or the Virgin in Aix.

Rogier van der Weyden (or, to give him his French name, de la Pasture) was the most important pupil of the Master of Flémalle. Born in Tournai, he entered Campin's atelier as an apprentice in 1427 and in 1432 was admitted as a master to the Guild of St. Luke. He must have been a mere boy when he began his apprenticeship, for he appears in the rolls under the diminutive appellation of Rogelet de la Pasture.[2]

Two elements of style are of outstanding importance in the work of Rogier van der Weyden— first, the formative influence of Robert Campin, which remained with him all his life, and secondly, a deliberate tendency towards archaism. The first of these elements is revealed in his continuance of Campin's technique, in his adoption not only of various compositional ideas, but also of Campin's facial types, gestures and folds, and in the similar reproduction of inanimate objects and landscape details. The relationship is sometimes so close that the attribution of certain works to one or the other of the two artists has given rise to controversy.[3] The second element is manifest, as was pointed out by Hulin, in a return to the linear art of the fourteenth century—cf. the Parement de Narbonne executed for King Charles V (1364–1380). This retrospective trait must be ascribed to a deviation from the naturalistic tendencies of the 1420's and 1430's. Among the leading Netherlandish painters of the fifteenth century Rogier is perhaps the only one who did not depict nature for her own sake, i.e. on account of her beauty. Content takes the foremost place in his pictures. To heighten the accentuation of the religious significance he returns to the predominance of line, the chief vehicle of expression in fourteenth-century art. His clearly and expressively outlined figures are welded together by a significant interplay of lines, continued in the architecture surrounding them. There thus enters into all his works a factor which is not only idealistic, but also non-individualistic. The very essence of Rogier's art has rarely been grasped; his influence goes into breadth. There are two cogent reasons why he became the most influential painter of the fifteenth century outside Italy. In the first place his retrospective, completely non-revolutionary art was in harmony with the many traditional tendencies still existing everywhere, at all events in a latent form, and secondly, the essential character of his style proclaimed itself, not, as in the works of Jan van Eyck, in the execution, but in the design, for which reason it was easier to learn and led to a more or less satisfactory result, even if the pupil was incapable of rising to the height of mastership.

Even a retrospective artist is, up to a certain point, bound to the artistic tendencies of his own time. Rogier van der Weyden was thus in many respects subservient to the stylistic demands of the new naturalism. In the reproduction of the human form, of interiors and landscapes and in his

---

[1]As is well known, there is a close relationship between the figures of St. John the Baptist, represented as patron of Canon Werle on Robert Campin's left wing in the Prado, and of Christ appearing to the Virgin in the painting by Rogier van der Weyden in the Metropolitan Museum, New York. The fact that in this case it was Rogier who imitated a figure by Campin, and not the other way round as supposed by some scholars, becomes evident as soon as we consider the way in which the bodies rest on the legs and feet. St. John's left leg bears the main weight of his body, whereas his right leg takes no weight at all. With Rogier's Christ the centre of gravity has shifted: he stretches out his right knee, while bending the left. Nevertheless the way in which the feet contact the ground has remained the same as on the Werle wing, i.e. only the toes of the right leg, which now bears the main weight of the body, touch the ground, whereas the sole of the left foot, now carrying no weight, rests flat on the ground. It is clear that Rogier here used a model, as he so often did. The artist, whose interest in the lifelike rendering of figures had always been of a secondary nature, obviously chose the position of legs and feet for linear reasons, in order to give more determination and verve to the outline of the figure. He was highly successful, however, in transforming the protecting gesture of St. John's right hand, perfectly suited to a picture of situation, into the expressive movement of Christ in his picture of action.

[2]This was a custom in Tournai; similarly, Jaques Daret was entered as Jaquelotte, Mahieu Vangermez as Mahieuvet, Pierart Laingniel as Pierotin, Bauduin de Almekerke as Baudechon, etc. The assumption that Campin's pupil Rogelet is identical with the 'Maistre Rogier de la Pasture', to whom on 17th November 1426 the town council of Tournai offered eight lots of wine, i.e. that the artist was then a grown man, already a master when he entered Campin's atelier for the purpose of becoming a master in yet another craft, is not at all convincing. The master of 1426 must have been another member of the family with the same Christian name, of whom, moreover, we know nothing, not even his craft. The painter and pupil of Campin, Rogier de la Pasture, was not, therefore, as is generally assumed, born about 1400, but about, and perhaps even shortly after 1410; he thus belonged to a younger generation of artists than the brothers van Eyck. Rogier spent most of the remainder of his life in Brussels, where is he mentioned in 1436 as official painter to the city.

[3]One of these works is the little picture of St. George and the Dragon in Lady Mason's collection. I am convinced that in this case the youthful Rogier (Hulin de Loo, Rogier van der Weyden, Bibliographie nationale publieé par l'Académie des Sciences, des Lettres et des Beaux Arts de Belgique, Vol. XXVII, 1938, rightly places the painting at the head of the list of his works) here made a faithful copy of a lost painting of Campin's second period, with, however, a few minor alterations, e.g. in the type of the Princess and the style of the folds or in the modernized armour. The authorship of the younger master is recognizable in small peculiarities of style and in the very characteristic brushwork.

characterization of the surfaces of things, he, too, had to strive to achieve a certain lifelikeness of effect, which, however, is only a concomitant feature in his paintings and not, as it is in the works of Robert Campin and, above all, of Jan van Eyck, an essential factor. This is the explanation of the curious fact that fifteenth-century painters outside the Netherlands, especially the Germans and Spaniards, as well as a number of French artists, became acquainted with the new Flemish realism through the works of the most unnaturalistic of all old Netherlandish masters.

Even though the art of Rogier was derived entirely from that of Robert Campin, he occasionally made a thorough study of works by Jan van Eyck and borrowed motives from them.[1] We find the first parallels to Jan's art in two small early works by Rogier, the standing Madonna in the Vienna gallery and the Virgin Enthroned which has passed from the Earl of Northbrook's collection to the Thyssen collection at Lugano. Architectonic settings similar to those behind the two Madonnas were to be seen in the burned portion of the 'Heures de Turin', in miniatures probably painted by the illuminator schooled to the art of Jan van Eyck who also copied lost works of his such as the Agony in the Garden and the Crucifixion (*Figs.* 31, 33). The representations[2] of Christ enthroned as King of Kings and of the standing Christ as Salvator Mundi both show clear traces of Jan's influence and it seems highly probable that they are versions of lost paintings by Jan. In these miniatures we see the figure surrounded by elaborate architecture cut off by the top edge of the picture, similar to what we find in pictures by Rogier. It is thus quite possible that we have here an after-effect of some compositional idea of Jan's.

In Rogier's Madonna with St. Luke we find a sure instance of his appropriation of one of Jan's pictorial ideas. Here Rogier was obviously drawing his inspiration from the Rolin Madonna. Nevertheless he took over only the external elements of the setting, the hall with the three apertures opening on a garden terminated by a crenellated wall, the two figures of loiterers with their backs to the spectator, and the view of both banks of a river. More interesting than this is the use made of the spatial image of Jan's early Virgin in the Church in the centre panel of a mature work by Rogier, the altar-piece of the Seven Sacraments in the Museum at Antwerp.[3] Here Rogier borrowed the setting and gave a reflected image of it. He followed it quite accurately and even included the rood-screen and gave the same heights to the pillars, arcades and windows of the nave and to the various parts of the choir. In the two wing-panels, as in Jan's Dresden triptych, we look into the side-aisles of the church in which the scene is laid.

From such borrowings we can see what aspects of Jan van Eyck's art made the greatest appeal to Rogier. To the younger master the architectural solutions of the older artist seemed, above all other things, to be worth imitating.

2. *The Chief Master of the 'Heures de Turin'*

A. *The 'Heures de Turin'*

ONE of the most grievous losses suffered by art history in the twentieth century was the destruction by fire of a book of hours in the royal library at Turin. These miniatures can now be studied only in the indistinct and sometimes blotchy collotype illustrations of a volume edited in 1902 by Paul Durrieu.

---

[1] While Rogier van der Weyden was still alive, Bartholomeus Facius described him as a pupil of Jan van Eyck, an error which persisted for a long time. The mistake is understandable, since to the Italian humanist, who knew only the few pictures by Jan and Rogier that had crossed the Alps, the difference between their art and contemporary Italian painting must have seemed so great as to obliterate the differences of aims and artistic temperament which distinguished the two great Flemings from each other.

[2] Durrieu, *Les Heures de Turin*, Paris 1902, Plates XLI, XXV.

[3] It is noteworthy that we possess four compositions, all dating from the second quarter of the fifteenth century, by four different artists, who all made use of the spatial image of Jan's Virgin in the Church, though they avoided Jan's mistake in perspective at the point where the transept intersects the nave. At least three of these works must have been created independently of the others. The oldest of them is probably the drawing in Wolfenbüttel (reproduced by H. Zimmermann in *Jahrbuch der preussischen Kunstsammlungen*, 1915, p. 215 f.). The draughtsman is at pains to give the setting a uniform foreshortening; he omits the rood-screen and enlivens the scene with the rather crude figures of an Annunciation in the van Eyck manner, but on the left edge—an archaic feature—he adds, like Hubert van Eyck and Robert Campin, a system of buttresses as an indication of the exterior of the building. We shall return shortly to the use made of Jan's composition in the 'Heures de Turin'. Thirdly, a Presentation in the Temple, a panel-painting probably by the hand of a Tournai painter, about 1440, acquired by the French government in 1930 from the Pelletier sale in Paris and now in the museum at Dijon, shows a spatial image which reveals a striking similarity with the latest of the four from the stylistic point of view, Rogier van der Weyden's altar-piece of the Sacraments. The possibility cannot be excluded that a lost painting derived from Jan's Virgin in the Church served as model for the two pictures at Dijon and Antwerp.

The illumination of this book of hours was begun about the year 1400 in the style of Jacquemart de Hesdin, by order of the Duke of Berry, and was not finished until long after the latter's death.

Fortunately, soon after the fire Georges Hulin de Loo discovered a second large fragment of the same manuscript in the Trivulziana at Milan. In addition to this, there were a few isolated folios in the Louvre and in the collection of Baron M. de Rothschild in Paris. Shortly before the 1939–45 war the rather considerable fragment in the Trivulziana was acquired by the Museo Civico in Turin. The term 'Heures de Turin' is now used as a comprehensive designation for all parts of this manuscript, whether extant or destroyed.

In the 'Heures de Turin' we find a series of miniatures which are stylistically very closely related to the art of the brothers van Eyck.

In Chapter II we have already had occasion to speak of one of the illuminators, who made faithful copies of at least two lost compositions by Jan, the Agony in the Garden and the Crucifixion (*Figs.* 31, 33). He also painted a number of other miniatures in the van Eyck style and in one case imitated a painting of the Descent from the Cross[1] by Robert Campin. His best achievements are marginal miniatures of his own invention depicting narrative scenes from the Bible (*Fig.* 32), some of them set in spacious landscapes. In these he inclines towards the style of the other miniaturist of van Eyck

tendencies. This artist made no almost literal copies, or at all events only variants of works by the van Eycks, but for the most part painted miniatures of his own invention. Despite the small number of his works we can justly describe him as the chief master of the 'Heures de Turin'.

One of the miniatures, destroyed in the fire, of this chief master represented a cavalcade by the seashore (*Fig.* 82), the meaning of the scene being not yet quite certain.[2] One of the armour-clad knights holds a standard, on which some scholars have claimed to recognize the Dutch-Bavarian coat of arms[3]—in the reproduction it

[1]Durrieu, Plate XXI. A copy of the whole work, with the Descent from the Cross as centre panel, is in the Walker Art Gallery, Liverpool.
[2]It is usually called the Thanksgiving for Delivery from the Peril of the Sea, but this interpretation is by no means convincing. The mounted prince in fashionable attire at the head of his armoured knights and accompanied by several dogs would appear to be setting out on some expedition rather than returning from some perilous undertaking. As to the old man at the prince's feet and the kneeling women, it is more likely that they are trying to present a petition to the leader of the cavalcade, who is touched by a ray from the 'gloria' of God the Father, rather than that they are returning thanks to heaven. The sea dotted with little ships is only slightly ruffled. Nothing indicates that a violent storm has just jeopardized the life of the prince.
[3]In a second (extant) miniature showing a Requiem (*Pl.* 158), tiny coats of arms are depicted on the coffin, among which scholars have claimed to recognize those of Holland and of Hainault-Flanders. A third miniature, perhaps by the hand of the other miniaturist with van Eyck tendencies, showed a French King praying in his tent before a battle.

82. Chief Master of the 'Heures de Turin'. *Cavalcade by the seashore*. Cat. No. 60.
A page destroyed by fire

G

can no longer be seen distinctly. From this coat of arms it was assumed with absolute certainty that the chief master's miniatures were painted for Count William IV of Bavaria and Holland and must therefore have been executed before his death on 31st May 1417. This hypothesis gave rise to others of equally complete assurance. It was affirmed that before 1417 only one of the van Eyck brothers—according to Hulin, Hubert; according to Friedländer, Jan—could have painted miniatures in such an advanced style.[1] One solitary critic, Max Dvořák,[2] protested vehemently against the attribution of these miniatures to either of the brothers.[3] As the originals of three pages illuminated by the chief master have been preserved, a precise critical investigation of the style of these is the only method by which we can arrive at a satisfactory conclusion.

Most scholars attribute to the chief master of the 'Heures de Turin' two main miniatures with large figures, five with small figures, five of the initials beneath them and six of the miniatures in the bottom margins. I intend here to confine myself to those works which have been preserved, discussing those that have been destroyed only as regards their composition.[4]

The marginal miniature of the Baptism of Christ (*Pl.* 159) is one of the most significant productions of the chief master. Tiny little figures, with the main group in the centre (God the Father giving his benediction is in the initial above) and a number of curious spectators approaching from the right, stand in a correctly foreshortened, delightful, exuberant landscape. This landscape has not only no affinity whatsoever to Hubert's landscapes, but also surpasses by far those of Jan's early works, such as the Stigmatization of St. Francis (*Pl.* 13). It stands, as Tolnay has pointed out, on the same stylistic level of development as the landscape of the Rolin Madonna (*Pl.* 119), with which it has in common the organizing motive of the river flowing towards the spectator out of the distance. The miniaturist must surely have seen this or some similar work, since lost.

Of the same relatively late origin was the destroyed miniature of the Voyage of St. Julian (*Fig.* 83). The sea in the foreground is shown as if seen slightly from above. The termination of the landscape by a skilfully interlaced range of mountains has no affinity with the art of the second decade, *i.e.* with the miniatures of the master of the 'Heures du Maréchal de Boucicaut' (*Figs.* 9, 10) or of the Limbourg

---

[1] The confidence was such that nobody thought it necessary to make stylistic comparisons between the miniatures and authenticated paintings by the brothers van Eyck. It did not occur to any of the champions of this hypothesis that in the settings and in the structure of the landscapes the miniatures are more advanced than the wing-panels of the Ghent altar-piece and cannot, therefore, have been executed before 1432. Moreover, nobody was willing to admit that the style of the figures in the miniatures is as remote from that of Hubert as it is from that of Jan, so that they cannot have been executed by either of the two brothers.

[2] *Jahrbuch der preussischen Kunstsammlungen*, XXXIX, p. 51 f.

[3] Dvořák stressed the fact that the coats of arms do not exclude the possibility that the miniatures were commissioned by Wilhelm's daughter, Jacqueline of Bavaria. In the blotchy photogravure reproduction the coat of arms is no longer clearly visible and it is therefore improbable that a definite identification will ever be possible. In any case one cannot, merely on account of this coat of arms, upset an extremely logical course of development. Dvořák's explanation has either been completely ignored or else attempts have been made to counter it with vague arguments derived from the history of costume. These, too, were accepted without critical examination, despite the fact that they were untenable.

Dr. Ortwin Gamber, of the Vienna Armoury, has been kind enough to send me the following remarks on the armour in the 'Cavalcade by the Seashore' in the book of hours (*Fig.* 82): 'The two horsemen behind the standard-bearer are wearing breastplates horizontal-edged in the lower tierce, which were unknown before the third decade of the fifteenth century (*cf.* the altar-piece of St. Thomas by Meister Franke commissioned in 1424) and did not become frequent until about 1430 (*cf.* Speculum humanae salvationis, 1427, Library of the Benedictine Monastery, Gries; Jan van Eyck, Ghent altar-piece, completed 1432; Thomas von Rieneck, died 1431, parish church of Lohr, Unterfranken; Hans Multscher, Wurzach altar-piece, 1437, Berlin, etc.).

'In the second decade of the fifteenth century the wide deep iron skirts (*cf.* the standard-bearer) did not yet exist, but only jupons of mail or short skirts of lames. The first skirts extended to just below the waist (*cf.* Bedford Hours, about 1425, British Museum, Add. MSS. 18850, fol. 288; the armour in this case coincides exactly with that of Gentile da Fabriano's Quaratesi altar-piece, 1425, Florence, Uffizi). Subsequently the skirts of lames remained equally short (*cf.* Ghent altar-piece, second horseman; Philipp von Ingelheim, died 1431, Oberingelheim am Rhein—coinciding almost exactly with the medal of Philip the Good, 1434, Paris, Bibliothèque Nationale, MS. français 4923; both skirts correspond to that of the horseman on the left behind the standard-bearer). Only in the course of the 1430's did the skirts of lames reach the length and width of those shown in the 'Heures de Turin' (*cf.* Multscher, Wurzach altar-piece, 1437; MS. of the Trojan War, 1441, Nürnberg, Germanisches Museum; K. Witz, altar-piece of St. Peter in Geneva, 1444).

'The standard-bearer's helmet is already different from the early form as seen in the Bedford Hours (see above) and resembles those on the medal of Philip the Good and on Witz' altar-piece of St. Peter in Geneva.

'On the basis of the general development of armour in Europe, therefore, the armours shown in the "Heures de Turin" cannot be dated before the period after 1430. The forms of the armour in the New York picture of the Crucifixion (*Pls.* 163, 164) belong to the same period'.

[4] One of the destroyed marginal miniatures (*Fig.* 84) showed a group of Holy Maidens with prayer-books in their hands approaching the symbol of Christ, the Lamb, which is standing on a grassy hill, emitting rays. Although not a single figure is identical, this group was just as compactly arranged as the host of Maidens in the Adoration of the Lamb in Ghent. For this reason it has been assumed that it was the first form of a pictorial idea which was subsequently used for the centre panel of the Ghent altar-piece. Curiously enough, the fact has been overlooked that these worshippers do not approach the object of worship from the front, as is normally the rule, but come upon the Lamb from behind. That the figures in the marginal miniature approach from the right can be explained as due to the presence of the initial above on the left, but it is impossible to find an explanation for the fact that the Lamb, too, turns its head towards the left. Even the most mediocre artist would not have naively invented such a contradiction. The only explanation is that the various portions of the composition have been taken from a larger work, the Adoration of the Lamb in Ghent.

brothers (*Fig.* 11), or with that of the third decade, *i.e.* Robert Campin's second period and the art of Hubert van Eyck, but presupposes a knowledge of Jans' mature landscapes, such as we find for the first time in the Ghent altar-piece (*Pls.* 44, 45). We can perceive completely new motives on the destroyed page containing the Cavalcade (*Fig.* 82), *i.e.* in the main miniature the terminating of the landscape in a slightly ruffled sea, and the rendering, in the margin, of a simple flat Netherlandish landscape. These motives, which the other miniaturist with van Eyck tendencies used as models for his marginal miniature of Jonah (*Fig.* 32), were possible only after the creation of Jan's landscapes, *e.g.* the hilly country on the right wing of the Dresden triptych or the environs of the town in the Rolin Madonna, and therefore are of the same order as those in the miniature of the Baptism of Christ. We notice here that the illuminator, not in the narrow marginal miniatures, but in the larger ones, invariably shows his landscapes as if seen slightly from above. This is the only traditional element in these works. Apart from that, the construction is quite uniform and in certain cases the landscapes are foreshortened without the aid of coulisses. Such

83. Chief Master of the 'Heures de Turin'. *The Voyage of St. Julian.* Cat. No. 60. Destroyed by fire

a construction was determined by Jan's method of perspective rendering of space, a method which he did not elaborate until the early 1430's. The difference lies merely in the fact that the miniaturist achieves the impression of distance without using perspective foreshortening.

Let us now consider how the chief master renders interiors. In the extant miniature of the Requiem (*Pl.* 158) we find two motives identical with Jan's early painting of the Virgin in the Church (*Pl.* 10). The miniature-painter shows us only the choir of the cathedral, its side-wall being constructed in exactly the same way as in the panel-painting, though the vaulting is that of Jan's nave. The miniaturist also uses a wider spatial image, showing portions of the transept, intersected on the right and left by the edges of the picture. Instead of the enclosed interior of the Virgin in the Church we thus have the interior, open on three sides, of the Rolin Madonna (*Pl.* 116). Uniform though the setting of the Requiem may appear at a first glance, it is nevertheless compounded of two elements from different stages of stylistic development. The essential novelty of the Berlin picture, the treatment of light, is not taken over, because miniature-painting has not the means with which to express it.

Lastly, when we consider the miniature, very rich in its colouring, of the Nativity of St. John (*Pl.* 157), it becomes quite evident that here an artist is endeavouring to transplant into the art of miniature the mature achievements of Jan van Eyck's panel-paintings. The scene is laid in a sumptuously furnished, lofty and spacious room, closed at the top, but open on the right side, and otherwise conceived in exactly the same way as the settings of the Arnolfini wedding picture (*Pl.* 137) and the toilet scene (*Figs.* 79, 80). We thus have once again a setting of the 1430's, merely foreshortened with less skill. Jan must have made a thorough study of the perspective, but his follower seems to have thought he could dispense with that and was concerned only with the visual effect. The effort the miniaturist made to compete with the achievements of panel-painting is shown in one detail, in the reflex lights on the metal vessels, to which Paul de Limbourg (*Fig.* 13) still gave a uniform colouring by means of painter's gold. The miniaturist also tries to achieve a certain lighting effect by alternating light and dark strips of wall, but is finally compelled to suggest the glass in the windows by the application of silver foil.

84. Chief Master of the 'Heures de Turin'. *The Adoration of the Lamb.* Cat. No. 60. Destroyed

85. Chief Master of the 'Heures de Turin': *The Betrayal of Christ; the Agony in the Garden; Peter denying Christ.* Cat No. 60. Destroyed by fire

Of all the stylistic features in these miniatures[1] it is the style of the figures that shows the greatest divergence from the art of the brothers van Eyck. Nevertheless the free arrangement in space of the group in the miniature of the Discovery of the Cross by St. Helena and the natural rendering of the movement of the diggers (*Pl.* 161) are far in advance of the style of the Limbourg brothers and presuppose a knowledge of the Ghent altar-piece. Artistically by far the most important are those miniatures in which the illuminator, to a greater extent than Jan van Eyck, subordinates his figures to the interior or the landscape. Of the figures, the most successful are those in the initials. God the Father above the Baptism of Christ (*Pl.* 159) and the figure of the Saviour on the slope of the Mount of Olives (*Fig.* 85) are conceptions with a very personal charm. In the draperies of both these figures the folds are sharply angular, with no trace of the 'international' style of the second decade. These idealistically conceived figures contrast strangely with the narrative realism that distinguishes the smaller figures in the margins beneath them (*Figs.* 82, 85; *Pl.* 160). In the groups of small figures such as we see in the scene of the Nativity or the Requiem, a preference for figures seen from behind is noticeable. The curiously abrupt movements do not always seem to be justified by the subject.

B. *The Other Works by the Chief Master of the 'Heures de Turin'*

OTHER works by the painter of the most important miniatures in the 'Heures de Turin' are also known, so that a tangible artistic personality stands before us, whose development we can follow fairly closely. Of the compositions attributed by scholars to this artist, the beautiful silverpoint drawing in the British Museum is undoubtedly the earliest. It represents the Betrayal of Christ (*Pl.* 169) and is still almost at the same stage of development as the works of Paul de Limbourg.[2] It differs from the Passion scenes in Chantilly in its freer rendering of movement; certain of its stylistic features anticipate those of the burnt miniature of the same subject in the 'Heures de

[1] In the monochrome photographic reproduction this miniature looks far more like a panel-painting than it does in the original, where we can clearly recognize its character as an illustration.
[2] The drawing has occasionally been ascribed to the Limbourg brothers. For the literature on this subject, see Ring, No. 69.

Turin' (*Fig.* 85). The drawing shows only the group of figures, without any setting.[1] To me it seems almost impossible to establish with certainty whether this composition is a work of our miniaturist's first teacher or an early work of his own invention. The style of the chief master is clearly discernible in a silverpoint drawing on a green ground in the Rijksmuseum at Amsterdam (*Pl.* 167), though this is not on the same high artistic level as the Betrayal in London. The Amsterdam drawing shows only the chief personages in a representation of the Epiphany, but in the treatment of the folds and the types (note especially the figure of St. Joseph) it is already completely in the manner of the miniaturist. Richer, though of earlier origin, is the composition of a pen-drawing in Berlin showing the Adoration of the Magi (*Pl.* 168), which may be assumed to be an approximately contemporary reproduction of a lost painting by the master. Some of the slender figures, *e.g.* the St. Joseph or the standing King seen in profile, are already quite in the style of the 'Heures de Turin'. The spatial image still shows the coulisses of the 1420's. As the landscape fills the whole middle ground, there was little room left for the retinue, for which reason these figures had to emerge from a cleft in the rocks. Obviously the artist wanted to utilize the depth, too, for his figure composition. In the structure of the landscape realistic details are not yet to be seen.

It is in his earliest surviving panel-painting that we find the first obvious traces of van Eyck influence in the œuvre of the chief master of the 'Heures de Turin'. It represents Christ on the Cross between the Virgin and St. John (*Pl.* 162) and is now in the Berlin gallery.[2] The way in which the body of Christ hangs on the Cross is reminiscent of Jan's lost version of the subject, known to us only through copies (*Pl.* 11, *Fig.* 31). The heavy figure of St. John with its wiglike hair is akin to the Disciples in the Agony in the Garden (*Fig.* 33). The structure of the landscape and the rendering of the city of Jerusalem, on the other hand, derive from the art of Hubert rather than from that of Jan. The inspiration may have come from the Three Maries at the Sepulchre (*Pl.* 1), from which the pine tree may also have been borrowed. The range of snow-covered mountains which terminates the composition is, however, set further back into depth than in the presumed model. Here we have an artist who endeavours to combine inspirations drawn from Hubert's works with elements from Jan's early style.[3] At the same time he is obviously striving to do justice to the significance of the theme, an aim which he tries to achieve, in contrast to his two models, by means of an exaggeration of the gestures and contortion of the faces.

The chief master of the 'Heures de Turin' creates an independent composition of his own in his next work, two narrow wing-panels formerly in the Hermitage at Leningrad and now in the Metropolitan Museum, New York. Whether tradition is right in affirming that the lost centre panel interrupted the historical sequence of the theme by showing an Adoration of the Magi—in this case the representation, the combination of which with the Last Judgement is unusual, must have contained considerably more figures than was customary in the Netherlands—is a question which must remain unanswered. The two surviving wing-panels are at the same stage of development as the miniatures in Turin. Like many a picture of Jan's, the right wing contains explanatory inscriptions.

On the left wing (*Pls.* 163, 164) we see the Crucifixion with numerous figures. The artist, who in his miniatures also showed a preference for depicting the terrain as if seen from above, constructs his foreground in accordance with the old principle of the inclined plane, obviously in order to fill up the whole of the unusually high and narrow panel. Here, however, a realistic touch is given to the inclined plane by making it represent the steep slope of Golgotha.[4] Some persons in the foreground,

---

[1] As regards fifteenth-century drawings, it is only in the case of very few masters, who have left us a considerable number of drawings, that we are able to distinguish with any probable degree of exactitude between designs and drawings copied from paintings for use in the workshop. The high quality of a drawing is not an absolute criterium of design, for obviously even the best artists occasionally made sketches of other artists' compositions. Drawings which look like completed pictures (*Pl.* 168) can hardly be considered as designs. If we try to arrange them according to the purpose for which they were made, our task is rendered more difficult by the fact that the drawing of St. Jerome in the Paris manuscript (MS. fr. 166; *Fig.* 24) shows that even at the beginning of the fifteenth century drawings were occasionally made for their own sake, though it is true that such drawings are always very minutely executed.

[2] A little drawing of the same subject in the possession of Count Moltke, Copenhagen, published by F. Winkler (*Festschrift für M. J. Friedländer*) as a copy after Jan van Eyck, shows so few of the characteristics of the lost model, that one can only speak in general terms of the master's entourage. The same may be said of a drawing-copy, dated 1521 (reproduced in *Jahrbuch der preussischen Kunstsammlungen*, LVIII, Berlin, 1937, p. 158), now in the Goethehaus at Weimar, which represents a cavalcade of horsemen (the Three Magi?).

[3] Besides the stylistic elements mentioned above, it is especially the clustering of the clouds and the system of folds that are taken from pictures painted by Jan about 1430. This Crucifixion, of all the works of the Chief Master's of the 'Heures de Turin', shows most clearly the realistic style of the 1430's with its plasticity of forms.

[4] After the achievement of Jan van Eyck—and until the days of Bruegel—we invariably find the inclined plane shown as if seen from above when the theme involves a very large number of figures or motives.

like single figures in the miniatures, are seen from behind; the sentiment of the Holy Women is conveyed more by their general bearing than by their facial expression. On the middle of the hill rise the three Crosses, so high that even the feet of Christ and the Thieves are above the heads of the horsemen. The faces of some of the wicked riders grimace in a way never found in the works of either of the brothers van Eyck. The contorted figure, outlined by a sweeping curve, of the Wicked Thief on Christ's left hand reminds us that in the initial of the Agony in the Garden (*Fig.* 85) the illuminator was most successful in conveying emotion by means of flowing movements. The extensive landscape would alone suffice to prove that the picture was painted in the 1430's.

The counterpart to the Crucifixion, the Last Judgement (*Pls.* 163, 165), is dominated still more emphatically by a *horror vacui*. The top half, in which Heaven is depicted, is composed with strict symmetry in a very hieratical manner. The figures are modelled with a slight awkwardness which can also be observed in certain miniatures of the 'Heures de Turin'. This ungainliness must not be confused with the severity found in works dating from the beginning of the century.[1] Beneath them is a narrow strip of this world, divided into land and sea, the only portion of the picture which is carried into depth. On closer examination we see that land and sea are nothing but the upper sides of the widespread wings of Death, represented by a gigantic, hovering skeleton. On his shoulders stands the exaggeratedly large figure of St. Michael, moulded entirely in the style of Jan van Eyck. Beneath the outstretched limbs of Death Hell extends, a wild confusion of tumbling bodies, twisted with pain, and of fearsome infernal monsters, the whole being constructed with a curious lack of space. It is easy to see that the artist was unable to cope with the formidable task of representing Heaven, Earth and Hell in one narrow panel.

The most important composition of the chief master of the 'Heures de Turin' is a work unfortunately known to us only through a copy painted during the second quarter of the sixteenth century and now in the Budapest gallery.[2] This is a multi-figure Bearing of the Cross (*Pl.* 166), set in an extensive landscape, which anticipates not only the figure composition of Martin Schongauer's large engraving of the subject,[3] but also a number of landscape effects to be found in the paintings of Joachim Patinir. A detailed copy in silverpoint of part of the group of horsemen (*Pl.* 170), executed just after the middle of the fifteenth century and now in the Ducal Museum at Brunswick, proves that the painter of the Budapest picture made a true copy of the essentials of his model, making only slight modifications to certain archaic features in the treatment of form. As in the miniatures, the artist's starting-point was the spatial image, which in its structure is closer to Hubert van Eyck's Three Maries than it is to the Ghent altar-piece, since it is dominated in the foreground by the traditional coulisses. The city of Jerusalem, here shown in the middle distance, is executed with great minuteness of detail. The landscape terminates in a spacious distant prospect, similar to that of the marginal miniature of the Baptism of Christ (*Pl.* 159). The prime factor in the picture is not the figure of Christ bearing the Cross, but the whole procession as it streams out from the gates of Jerusalem, describing a curve in the foreground, and proceeds towards Golgotha. A complete novelty in panel-paintings are the bystanders, who continue the genre-like figures of the Berlin drawing (*Pl.* 167) and, to an even greater extent, the scenes of everyday-life in some of the marginal miniatures in the 'Heures de Turin' (*Pl.* 160).

C. *The Localization of the Chief Master of the 'Heures de Turin'*

THE chief master of the 'Heures de Turin', a painter of panels who occasionally made miniatures, was still bound by a few threads to the art of the second decade. He can thus have been only slightly younger than Jan van Eyck and must have learned his craft from some painter of the older generation, that is to say from a contemporary of Paul de Limbourg. For the earliest composition connected with

---

[1]A similarly hieratic arrangement is found in the Last Judgement in Brussels (published by Tolnay, *Münchner Jahrbuch*, 1932) whither it was brought from the town hall at Diest. In view of its system of folds, this picture, too, must have been created as late as around 1430.
[2]A drawing in the Albertina in Vienna reproduces the chief types of a similar, but richer composition by a follower (*cf.* O. Benesch, *Jahrbuch der preussischen Kunstsammlungen*, 46, p. 81, and the Albertina Catalogue, II, No. 22). In addition, there was another, probably earlier version in high format, which was imitated in the burned portion of the 'Heures de Turin'. Two more variants in high format are a panel-painting in the Suermondt Museum at Aachen (*cf.* G. J. Kern, *Die verschollene Kreuztragung des Hubert oder Jan van Eyck*, Berlin 1927) and the fine picture in the Metropolitan Museum in New York (*cf.* H. B. Wehle and M. Salinger, *A Catalogue of early Flemish . . . Paintings*, 1947, p. 23, Nr. 4395).
[3]Hans Memling, too, must have known the composition of the Bearing of the Cross, since he borrowed some figures from it for his panel with Passion scenes, painted shortly after 1470 (Turin, Galleria Sabauda, *cf.* L. Baldass, *Hans Memling*, Vienna, 1942, p. 15).

his art (*Pl.* 169) show a relationship to Paul's style and is on the same level of development. Afterwards he studied with close attention the achievements of the brothers van Eyck and endeavoured to transplant Jan's mature style into miniature-painting. There is always a remnant of conventionalism in his rendering of figures, which are rarely borrowed from van Eyck's. He never frees himself entirely from the training he received from his first teacher, whom we do not know. Our master's talent is most apparent in his renderings of interiors and landscapes. In landscape painting, especially, he explores new paths. Through his association with miniature-painting an effort to achieve genre-like representation makes itself felt in his panel-paintings, which include scenes of popular life. In his largest work, preserved only in the form of a copy, he deviates from Jan's art, from which he takes only a few figures of horsemen, and endeavours to achieve a new solution by making the landscape the chief focus of interest in a panel-painting, as he had already done in some of his miniatures.

We do not know the name of the chief master of the 'Heures de Turin', or where he worked. Max Dvořák, to whom the credit is due for discovering the period when these miniatures were painted, suspected that he was of Dutch origin,[1] a view which gained a certain amount of support. Nevertheless caution is necessary. The hypothesis that the creator of the most important miniatures was a Dutchman, can ultimately be ascribed to the desire to prove that the basic elements of the Dutch art of the seventeenth century already existed in the fifteenth. A conclusion *a posteriori* of this kind involves numerous dangers. The chief difficulty lies in our choice of the starting-point. We reach widely differing results according to whether we start from the great realists, the painters of landscapes and interiors (Tolnay was reminded by these miniatures of Emanuel de Witte, Vermeer and Pieter de Hoogh), or take as a basis Rembrandt's biblical scenes with their spiritualized narrative and their introspective human beings.[2] The only point that appears certain is that the chief master of the 'Heures de Turin' had his roots in Flemish art. Whether he was born in Holland is a question which for the time being must remain unanswered.

At first sight it seems strange that the art of the chief master of the 'Heures de Turin' found no followers among his younger contemporaries. The reason for this seems to me to be the overwhelming influence exercised about 1440 by the art of Rogier van der Weyden on the whole artistic production of the Netherlands, both in Flanders and, as we shall see below, in Holland. At that time interest was centred primarily upon the representation of the human figure. The strength of the chief master of the 'Heures de Turin', however, lay in those elements of style that did not until later become the primary object of interest.

3. *Petrus Christus*

THE works of Petrus Christus reveal an artist who did not become acquainted with the art of Jan van Eyck until he had already formed a style with a distinctive stamp of its own and who only in his maturity conceived it to be his task to take over the art of the dead painter, which led him to produce many imitations, but also, on occasion, some really remarkable inventions.

---

[1]E. H. Zimmermann (*Amtliche Berichte aus den königl. Museen*, XXXIX, Berlin, p. 15 f.) has supported the theory that these are early works of Albert van Ouwater, a hypothesis which at the time (*Jahrbuch der kunsth. Sammlungen*, XXXV, Vienna 1919, p. 4 f.) I accepted, as Tolnay (1938) also did. As regards this Haarlem painter, Carel van Mander assumes that he lived at the same time as Jan van Eyck. He praises his gift for the rendering of landscape and maintains that, in fact, the earliest and best system of constructing landscapes was evolved in Haarlem. This hypothesis would seem to find further confirmation in the diary of Marcantonio Michiel. It has long been suspected that Albert van Ouwater must be identical with the 'Alberto da Olanda' of whom Michiel says that he saw 'molte tavolette de paesi' by his hand in the Casa Grimani. A close study of van Mander's vita shows, however, that he had only a vague idea of van Ouwater's art and relied on the oral tradition of the ateliers, since he had no opportunity of forming an opinion of his own.

The fact remains that *before* the works of Geertgen van Haarlem, *i.e.* before the last thirty years of the century, we know only works by provincial Dutch artists, which, of course, as we shall see below, does not exclude the possibility of the existence in Haarlem of an independent school of panel-painting as early as about 1440.

[2]That various stylistic characteristics of the chief master of the 'Heures de Turin' can be detected in the works of Hieronymus Bosch, proves little, for this artist, though he had his roots in provincial Dutch artistic practice, soon became acquainted with the works of the Flemish school and in some of his relatively early works returns deliberately to already long-forgotten stages of development.

The fact that the genre-like rendering of the spectators in the Budapest Bearing of the Cross finds its continuation in Dutch panels, for example, in the picture of the Healing of the Sick in the Kleiweg collection at Amsterdam (reproduced in Hoogewerff, *De Noord-Nederlandsche Schilderkunst*, I, 1936, p. 557) or in the Bearing of the Cross in the Brussels museum, painted by a master from Hertogenbosch (reproduced by F. Winkler, *Jahrbuch der preussischen Kunstsammlungen*, 1923, p. 145) does not necessarily mean that the chief master of the 'Heures de Turin' was of Dutch origin. It may do no more than make probable that works in the style of the Bearing of the Cross were in Holland during the 1470's. This seems to find support in the observation that one of the illuminators of the volumes of the Dutch Bible in the Vienna National Library, the so-called 'Master Zeno', in his background landscapes and in popularly conceived figures (*cf.* Hoogewerff, l.c. I. *Figs.* 309, 311), apparently follows the style of the chief master of the 'Heures de Turin'.

86. Petrus Christus: *St. Eligius.*
New York, Robert Lehman Collection

Petrus Christus—this is the name under which he appears in documents; he himself signed several of his works PETRUS XPI—became a master in the Guild of St. Luke at Bruges on 6th July 1444 and from that time until his death in 1472 or 1473 he appears to have worked in that city. He came from Baerle, a small town in the province of Limbourg, now in Dutch territory, distant about thirty miles north-east of Antwerp. For a long time it was assumed that Petrus Christus learned his craft from Jan van Eyck during the last years of Jan's life, until in 1926 Otto Pächt proved in a convincing manner that the hitherto accepted chronological arrangement of his works was wrong.[1]

Two early works by Petrus Christus reveal his knowledge of the art of Rogier van der Weyden.[2] This influence, however, is confined to a few motives; the pictorial construction and formal language of these early works are as remote from the art of Rogier as they are from that of the brothers van Eyck. Characteristic of his style at this time is a block-like awkwardness of the figures, which are placed in the picture with a curious lack of mutual relationship. A certain affinity with Robert Campin's second period can be detected.[3] Campin's pupil, Jacques Daret, is the artist most likely to have been the source of inspiration for Petrus Christus, but the work showing the greatest affinity of style is of somewhat later date. This is the altar-piece in the Prado showing four scenes from the Life of the Virgin, the earliest extant work of the Haarlem painter Dirk Bouts, which likewise shows Rogier's method of enframing the figures, but also has the same tendency for clumsy block-like figures and lack of relationship between them as the early works of Petrus Christus. It seems possible that we ought to regard the early works of Petrus Christus and this first work of Dirk Bouts as the beginning of a specifically Dutch style in panel-painting.[4] We are bound, however, to agree with Pächt that the question must still remain unanswered, whether the relationship between the early works of Petrus Christus and that of Dirk Bouts is to be explained as the result of development from the common basis of the style of the Master of Flemalle or as being due to a direct connection.[5]

It may be assumed that the early works of Petrus Christus were painted before he became a master at Bruges.[6] We find traces of van Eyck influence for the first time about the middle of the 1440's in his

[1] *Belvedere*, 1926, p. 155 f. Chronologically, the first would be the large painting of the Lamentation for Christ (Brussels), which shows no trace of the van Eyck influence. We would therefore have to assume that Petrus came to Bruges from elsewhere and did not become acquainted with the art of van Eyck until after he had become a master at Bruges. This supposition of Pächt's is confirmed by two paintings of Petrus Christus, which in 1926 were still unknown and must likewise be considered as early works, a Dormition of the Virgin in the Knoedler Gallery at New York (reproduced by van der Elst, *The Last Flowering of the Middle Ages*, New York 1945, Plate 47) and a Nativity in the National Gallery, Washington (reproduced by Friedländer, XIV, Supplement, Plate III).

[2] In the Brussels Lamentation, the central figure of the fainting Virgin is taken from the celebrated early Deposition by Rogier van der Weyden (now in the Prado) and the figure of the weeping St. Mary Magdalen also shows Rogieresque pathos. The Nativity in Washington is enframed by a sculptured arch similar to those which the city painter of Brussels placed round several of his compositions.

[3] The Nativity in Washington reminds us most of all of Jacques Daret's painting of the same subject in New York, whereas the Dormition is reminiscent of a composition by the Master of Flémalle preserved only in the form of copies (*e.g.* London, National Gallery; *cf.* Chapter I, p. 21, Note 2).

[4] Very similar characteristics of style are found again in the Berlin Raising of Lazarus, the only picture, if Carel van Mander was right, by Ouwater that we possess; then in the panels of the Master of the Tiburtine Sibyl, a Dutch pupil of Dirk Bouts; and finally in the early paintings of Geertgen van Haarlem.

[5] The works of the Master of the Gathering of the Manna, a Dutch painter, active after the middle of the century (*cf.* K. G. Boon in *Oud Holland*, LXV, 1950, p. 207), still show the influence of Robert Campin's second period.

[6] P. Richardson (*Flemish Paintings of the 15th and 16th Century*, The Detroit Institute of Arts, 1936, p. 7) mentions that on the picture of St. Jerome in the Detroit museum (*Pl.* 9) he found the tiny date 1442. As, in my opinion, we have here to do with an early composition by Jan van Eyck, I can only think of two possible solutions, that is either that Petrus Christus may have made with exceptional care a faithful copy of a work by Jan or that he may have completed an unfinished picture in the manner of the original designer. In either case we cannot draw any conclusions from this concerning the development of Petrus Christus.

portraits, for which Petrus Christus had a special talent. The substitution of the neutral ground by an interior would appear to be due to him. His most original work is the painting of St. Eligius, dated 1449, in New York (*Fig.* 86). The Saint, in contemporary dress and characterized only by the halo, is weighing on a small pair of scales the wedding rings of a bridal couple in fashionable attire who stand behind him. There is no doubt here that Petrus Christus has combined two pictorial ideas of Jan van Eyck, that of the Arnolfini wedding picture and that of the half-length picture of the master settling accounts with his steward, known to us only through Michiel's mention. Like the Arnolfini wedding picture, the St. Eligius panel is primarily a picture of action. The chief stress is laid, not on the Saint, but on the bridal couple, rendered in the manner of portraiture. Even Jan van Eyck's convex mirror, here reflecting the street in front of the shop and two witnesses, is not lacking.

About 1450 the artistic power of Petrus Christus begins to fail. From then on he was content to produce variants of Jan van Eyck's pictorial ideas and occasionally of a composition by the chief master of the 'Heures de Turin', without ever achieving the vivacious fidelity to nature of his models. Only in cases where a new subject prevents him from using an existing scheme, *e.g.* in the little devotional picture of the Virgin by the barren tree, does he contrive to manifest originality.

CHAPTER VIII: THE PLACE OF JAN VAN EYCK'S ART IN THE HISTORY OF FIFTEENTH CENTURY EUROPEAN PAINTING

THE art of Jan van Eyck represents the absolute zenith of old Netherlandish painting. This is evident in the marked artistic individuality of this painter, who added so many new achievements to the art of panel-painting, as well as in the high standard of craftsmanship in all his pictures. There is no painter besides him who ever reached the intensity and harmony of his glowing and yet deep colours. The large centre compartment of the Ghent altar-piece shows most clearly the skill of his hand. The Adoration of the Lamb, designed and in important parts executed by his brother, he brought to completion, and did so in combining it harmoniously with the wing pictures and with the big figures of the lower row, thus creating a homogeneous colouristic system of the whole. Through assimilating glazes he brought the main parts, painted by Hubert, up to the higher standard of his own rich and differentiated additions. This feat is not inferior to the creation of his masterpieces, Adam and Eve, the Madonna with the Chancellor Rolin and the Arnolfini wedding picture. We see that Jan's skill in execution and completion equals his power of invention and composition.

The artist's influence on his contemporaries in the Netherlands and the neighbouring countries was, as we remarked at the beginning of the preceding chapter, slighter than that of Robert Campin's works. About 1440 Campin's style gave way to that of the youthful Rogier van der Weyden. The artists of the next generation—Dirk Bouts, Hugo van der Goes, Hans Memling—were at first influenced by Rogier's style, from which they freed themselves comparatively slowly.

The example offered by Jan van Eyck's works may have helped them to achieve this freedom. That this example was still a living force, is proved by the later activity of Petrus Christus, who painted pictures in the style of Jan van Eyck for lovers of that artist. From the 1460's artists paid more attention to the purely colouristic qualities of paintings than they had done about the middle of the century. Everywhere we see a striving to make the lifelike rendering of nature one of the chief aims of art. In his maturity Dirk Bouts carried the conquest of space a step further and paid an increasing attention to the arrangement of his figures in depth. Hugo van der Goes, although he was strongly influenced in the compositions of his early works by Rogier van der Weyden and endeavoured merely to give a more varied and greater profundity to their power of psychological expression, nevertheless strove to surpass Rogier's stereotyped rendering of nature and to equal Jan's versatility in the choice of motives, his mastery in the characterization of materials, in the handling of light and in the treatment of landscape. True, it was only in details that Bouts and van der Goes (despite their high artistic standards) enriched Jan's representation of the world. The cosmic character of this representation, as has been stressed particularly by Tolnay, was never equalled, probably because nobody ever attempted to show the whole of Creation in one picture. Even the greatest work of the second half of the century, Hugo van der Goes' Portinari altar-piece, confines itself to bringing before our eyes, in as clear and lively form as possible, a scene from the story of Salvation. Not until Hieronymus Bosch did an artist once more undertake, obviously quite independently of Jan's achievement, to give us in his paintings an image of the world, though in his case it was seen from a more subjective angle and with a moralizing tendency (an aim which was far from Jan's mind). The art of Hieronymus Bosch formed the basis of that of Peter Bruegel, who built a new image of the world out of various sources. Most significant for the future was his new treatment of landscape, which, however, would have been impossible but for Jan's achievement. In the sixteenth century Bruegel was the only artist to realize that for the creation of a world-wide landscape a loving and faithful absorption in the details of the foreground is just as important as the consistent treatment of space and the pictorial construction of the far distance.

The significance of Jan's art can, however, be correctly gauged only if we remind ourselves that the technique he evolved was adopted by French and German painters during the second half of the fifteenth century. All the masterpieces of German sixteenth-century painting were executed in his technique, or in one derived from it, and ultimately German art produced a painter who strove to achieve, and did achieve, the same perfection in rendering the visible world with the same fidelity in the observation of nature and, in portraiture, a similar, passionless objectivity. That artist was Hans Holbein the Younger.

Jan's greatness becomes evident if we consider it from the general European standpoint. In the fifteenth century there were only two completely independent schools of painting—the Netherlandish and the Italian, which only very exceptionally were in communication with each other. Since Giotto the Italian school had won for itself a particular position. Vis-à-vis all the schools to the north of the Alps, the Western European as well as the German, which followed ever more closely the Flemish, it appears, despite its numerous local trends, as a compact entity. But, if we compare contemporary productions on either side of the Alps, a striving towards similar goals becomes apparent.

A comparison between the achievements of Jan's art and the abundance of Italian Quattrocento painting would thus lead to a very interesting result. Such a comparison is made easier by the fact that at the beginning of the century the predominance of the 'international' style in Florence, Siena, Verona, etc., was just as undisputed as it was in Paris, Burgundy and Flanders or on the banks of the Rhine and in Bohemia. The reactions to this style—though independent in themselves—were almost identical in Flanders and Italy. Simultaneously with the evolution which in the Netherlands began with the works of Robert Campin, and was continued by the brothers van Eyck, we see in Tuscany during the second decade a striving towards completely new aims. Here, too, thanks to the towering genius of Donatello, sculpture was a step in advance of painting, just as in Burgundy the art of Claus Sluter anticipated essential features of the realistic style, but in Florence the art of painting did not lag very far behind. Two tendencies are now perceptible in Italy, each independent of the other. The one remains in a certain sense faithful to the fundamental principles of the 'international' style, but at the same time seeks (think, for example, of Gentile da Fabriano and Pisanello) to permeate its purely idealistic tendencies with others of a naturalistic kind. The *horror vacui* and the idealistic composition are connected with a realistic rendering of the human figures, especially of the subsidiary figures, and with an accurate study of animals and vegetation. The other tendency is manifest above all in the work of a single revolutionary artist, the Florentine Masaccio. Returning to the art of Giotto, and at the same time deeply impressed by the animation, grandeur and simplicity of Donatello's plastic forms, Masaccio places himself in strict opposition to the principles of the 'international' style. He starts from a naturalistic conception, but endeavours to monumentalize it, and arrives at 'the discovery of material conformity to rule and of objective causality as the most important problem in the observation of bodies, their functions and their spatial inter-relationship'.[1] The last works of Masaccio were followed, probably only a short time after his premature death, by those of Paolo Uccello, showing equally revolutionary achievements. This artist was a few years older than Masaccio, but seems to have matured somewhat later. He, too, was still under the overwhelming impression of Donatello's sculptures, but he was concerned less with monumentality of effect than striving after animation of action and fidelity to nature, and thought that he could best achieve this end by devoting himself to an intensive study of anatomy and above all of perspective.

In the Netherlands about the year 1430 the 'international' style had been completely superseded. Even Rogier's stylized counter-tendency to Jan van Eyck's world-embracing representations could not help making use, in details, of the naturalistic language of forms elaborated by Robert Campin and the brothers van Eyck. In Italy the influence, on the one hand, of Masaccio's objective monumental art based on realism and of Uccello's naturalism founded on mathematics and, on the other hand, of the last phase of the 'international' style, still idealistic despite all the naturalistic details, persisted side by side for several decades; in fact, the two opposing tendencies can be observed until the end of the century. The factor common to both these tendencies in Italian painting was summarized ninety years ago in a masterly manner by Jacob Burckhardt, who spoke of the new spirit which came over Occidental European painting at that time. 'While still remaining in the service of the Church, from now on it evolved principles which no longer had any relationship to the purely ecclesiastical task'.[2]

---

[1] Max Dvořák—'Entdeckung der materiellen Gesetzmässigkeit und der objectiven Kausalität als der wichtigsten Aufgabe in der Beobachtung der Körper, ihrer Funktionen und ihres räumlichen Zusammenhanges.'

[2] 'Im Dienste der Kirche verharrend, entwickelt sie fortan Prinzipien, die zu der rein kirchlichen Aufgabe in keiner Beziehung mehr standen.'

This schism between the detailed reproduction of earthly things and the justifiable demand for an ideal representation of heavenly things had been perceived by Hubert van Eyck, who endeavoured to achieve a reconciliation. His brother Jan achieved it by giving to his image of the real world a clear stamp of being the reproduction of God's Creation, so that in his religious works all his rendering of the beauties of this world is made to serve the glory of the Almighty.

From the earliest times the two pictures of the Ghent altar-piece which excited the greatest admiration were those of Adam and Eve. These first naturalistic nudes of the new Flemish painting have very close parallels in the first lifelike portrayals of nude figures by the masters of the revolutionary tendency in Florentine Quattrocento painting, namely in Masaccio's frescoes, painted only a few years earlier, of the Expulsion from Paradise and the Baptism of the Converts in the Brancacci Chapel and in Paolo Uccello's mural painting of the Deluge in the cloister of Santa Maria Novella. The affinity is all the more surprising since the task is different. In the one case we have an altar-piece intended to be viewed from close at hand, painted in the new technique which gives characterization to the surfaces; in the other, frescoes designed to be seen from a certain distance. The contrast between Jan's representative picture of situation and the Italian artists' pictures of action also renders comparison difficult. The common factor lies in the abandonment of the idealization and of the mediaeval conformity of type still found in the 'international' style, *e.g.* in Paul de Limbourg's nudes (*Fig.* 43) and in the figures of the fresco of the Fall in the Brancacci Chapel, attributed by most scholars to Masolino. Between Masaccio and Jan van Eyck there is above all the following contrast, attributable to the difference of nationality. The great Fleming is intensely absorbed in the rendering of every detail of the human body, whereas the Florentine is more particularly concerned with the representation of the movements, which he endeavours to make as expressive as possible. His figures show a new conception of the human body, based on realism and anticipating the canon of classical art. Paolo Uccello, on the other hand, shares with Jan the passionate striving after truth in the rendering of the nude. Uccello made a thorough study of plastic anatomy, but the nude interests him more from the point of form than from that of naturalistic rendering of surfaces. Despite all the differences, the aims of painting in Ghent and Florence about 1430 were akin.

If we now turn to Jan's other contributions to the artistic conquest of the visible world, we notice that his achievements in the observation of nature do not occur in Italy until later, sometimes even several decades later, and that it is not possible to detect any direct influence exercised by his artistic principles on any of the great Italian artists, with the exception of Antonello da Messina.

A number of stylistic peculiarities in Jan van Eyck's works defy comparison since they are at first exclusively typical of Flemish art and later of fifteenth-century art to the north of the Alps. One of these stylistic peculiarities, which was a prime factor in the development of the new oil technique, is the effort made by the artist to immerse himself completely in the reproduction of every detail of the human form, the landscape and the interior, and to depict every detail with the utmost fidelity to nature, including the characterization of the surfaces, a thing which the Italians never attempted.[1] Another characteristic is the imperative urge to individualize human beings. Jan's art of portraiture was at that time an isolated phenomenon in Europe. Even this urge, however, is to be found in Italy. We have already seen how in the heads of the singing angels on the Ghent altar-piece the pitch of their voices is revealed by the shape given to their mouths. A parallel to this differentiating realism can be found in contemporary Florentine sculpture, for there is something similar in the lifelike reliefs of singing girls and boys in the tribune which Luca della Robbia began for the cathedral of Florence in 1431 and finished in 1438.

A decisive alteration made by Jan to Hubert's original project for both the inside and the outside of the Ghent altar-piece was the attention paid to the position of the spectator, this being particularly noticeable in those panels of the upper rows which were designed entirely by Jan. Figures and settings are here clearly shown as if seen from below. In the middle of the century a Northern Italian artist, Andrea Mantegna, who was certainly unacquainted with Jan's achievement, made a very similar experiment. In one of the frescoes in the Eremitani Chapel at Padua, apparently

---

[1] I cannot see any close stylistic parallel—not to mention Flemish influence—in the fact that Piero della Francesca in his Flagellation at Urbino wrapped one of the onlookers in a brocaded garment. Like many of the painters of the Tre- and Quattrocento Piero merely wanted to show a rich contemporary costume (Mantegna did the same in some of his cabinet-paintings), without attempting to elaborate the material character of the surface in the manner of Jan van Eyck (*cf.* R. Longhi, *Piero della Francesca*, Rome 1928, pp. 43 and 118).

the most advanced of the four dedicated to the story of St. James the Great, he chose a point of vision lower than the bottom edge of the picture, so that, unlike his scenes from the legend of St. James above it, the spectator views the figures and buildings from below and can see how the vanishing lines of the latter seem, consequentially, to drop steeply. Mantegna never repeated this experiment, which found no followers in Italian fresco-painting, any more than did Jan's foreshortening executed with regard to the position of the spectator in panel-paintings—a circumstance which, it is true, coincides with the decline in popularity of tiered altar-pieces in the Netherlands. Nevertheless, the foreshortening of this fresco in Padua with regard to the spectator was the harbinger of Mantegna's ceiling painting in the Camera degli Sposi at Mantua, with its illusionistic aim of tearing open the room in order to give the effect of a view of the sky. Here the great Paduan was the first to tread the path followed by so many artists from Correggio to Pozzo and Tiepolo.

Mantegna's frescoes in the Eremitani Chapel have yet another feature in common with the art of Jan van Eyck. They are the first works in Italian painting (note, in particular, the scene of the Martyrdom of St. James) to be terminated by an extensive landscape prospect, which we can follow exactly from the foreground to the point where the sky meets the range of mountains.

For Masaccio, landscape was still nothing more than a setting for the action. It is true that he monumentalizes the landscape by confining himself to a few large motives of mountains, but he does not assign to it any independent existence. Paolo Uccello, the promoter of perspective, introduced into the landscape the unified, deep-set horizon. Moreover, it represents a novelty for Italy when we find that in his hunting scene at Oxford the proportion between the size of the figures and the height of the picture is similar to that found in the wing-panels of the Adoration of the Lamb, that is to say that the figures are in approximate proportion to the lofty trees. Subsequently we occasionally find in the works of Florentine painters a subsidiary motive observed from nature, such as the rose-bower in Domenico Veneziano's little predella of the Annunciation in Cambridge. In his sketch-books Jacopo Bellini, returning to Altochiero's spatial image with its preponderance of architecture, also expanded the landscape setting and sometimes individual motives gave a certain similarity to nature.

Mantegna was the first to achieve a detailed rendering of an extensive landscape panorama, which, in order to avoid coming into conflict with the rules of perspective, he showed as a rising mountainous region. It is astonishing what a wealth of the visible world he manages to include in the two narrow sections of landscape in his cabinet-painting of St. Sebastian in Vienna. The few small figures, depicted in a thoroughly naturalistic manner, which he inserts into this landscape, may very well be compared with the workmen in Jan's little picture of St. Barbara at Antwerp. Only exceptionally do certain of Mantegna's landscape details reveal a study of nature, though this can be discerned in the birds and animals which fill his pictures (e.g. the Agony in the Garden in London).

Independently of Mantegna (and likewise quite independently of Flemish art) we find in Tuscan painting shortly after 1450, in the works of Piero della Francesca, Benozzo Gozzoli, Alessio Baldovinetti and Antonio Pollaiuolo, extensive landscape backgrounds. In the 1460's and 1470's the feeling for clearness, unity and natural effect in landscapes became stronger and stronger, without, however, reaching a solution as convincing as the landscape of the Rolin Madonna. Nevertheless, the ground was prepared for the advent of the youthful Leonardo, who in 1473 was the first artist in Europe (and without having any followers in Europe for the next twenty years) to go further than Jan van Eyck. Leonardo set himself down in front of nature and with his pencil (the superimposed execution with the pen may have been done later at home) recorded a view of the Arno valley as it presented itself to his eyes.

In Jan van Eyck's works the rendering of landscape is closely bound up with his endeavour to achieve correct foreshortening of interiors and, as a consequence, the study of the problem of lighting. In his efforts to achieve correct perspective, the great Fleming followed the same paths as his Florentine contemporaries, above all Paolo Uccello. Only sporadically does the problem of lighting play a role in fifteenth-century art, and then in most cases a subordinate role. When Gentile da Fabriano, in one of the small predella pictures of his 1423 altar-piece of the Epiphany, tries to give a naturalistic stamp to a very summarily rendered landscape by introducing little red sunset clouds, he is doing little more than Paul de Limbourg did when he painted the Betrayal of Christ (*Fig.* 15) as a nocturnal scene. A real study of lighting effects is found for the first time in the works of Jan van Eyck. In the main these studies are confined to scenes set in interiors and only occasionally exercised a slight influence. A quarter of a century later Dirk Bouts terminates his Gathering of the Manna in the Louvain altar-piece with an evening sky, but the protagonists of the action in the foreground are not affected by the lighting. In the last thirty years of the century a few versions of the Nativity with the Child as sole source of light constitute an exception. A lighting effect similar to that used in one single instance by a French miniature-painter, the 'René Master'[1] (probably not uninfluenced by Flemish art), is found in Southern Europe, as an independent element in a painting by Piero della Francesca. In his fresco at Arezzo of the Dream of Constantine the light is no longer an accessory motive, but dominates the scene. This, too, seems to have had no subsequent influence on other artists.

These parallels between Italian art and that of Jan van Eyck do not extend to other stylistic elements, by means of which Italian artists, during Jan's lifetime, would have carried the observation of nature to an even higher pitch of perfection than the painter who completed the Ghent altar-piece. All the great achievements of Jan's art, the lifelike portrayal of men and women, the perspective foreshortening of the interior, the thorough rendering of the landscape, the solving of the problem of lighting, etc., etc., are found in Italy at the very most at the same time, but generally later,[2] and above all each individual Italian artist adopts only one or two of these inventions. Jan van Eyck applied them all at once. In the perfection of his rendering of nature by means of colour he stands alone. We must thus rank Jan van Eyck as by far the greatest painter before Leonardo.

Despite all the admiration professed by Italian art-lovers for Flemish painting, it is only exceptionally that it exercised even a transitory influence on Italian art, which, vice versa, did not divert from their paths those few painters from north of the Alps, such as Rogier van der Weyden and Jean Fouquet, who visited Italy. Only Joos van Wassenhove (Justus van Gent), who settled at the court of Urbino, changed his style in Italy.

When in 1480 Ghirlandaio—in life size and in the technique of fresco—adopted the scheme of composition of Jan's St. Jerome (*Pl. 9*), little remained of the stylistic features of the model. Even when the masterpiece of Hugo van der Goes, the Portinari altar-piece, was installed in a Florentine church, at a time when in the rendering of nature, and above all in the landscapes, the tendencies of Tuscan art were already very close to those of the Flemish school, its effect on the painters of Florence was limited. Only a few naturalistic details, notably the heads of the shepherds, were taken over and freely transformed by Ghirlandaio. It was perhaps impossible to gain an understanding of the essence of this art from a single work.[3] Another instance, however, has an unusual importance.

The Flemish, and that, in reality, is equivalent to saying Jan van Eyck's, manner of painting, of characterizing the material surfaces of things and of making colour the most important factor in the picture, was appropriated by the Sicilian painter Antonello da Messina, who was the first artist in Italy to break with the convention of considering colour as an accessory element. This is the fact although it has not yet been explained how Antonello arrived at this new technique. He transmitted it to the great Venetian painters, above all to Giovanni Bellini. This was the impetus that paved the way for the efflorescence of Venetian painting in the sixteenth century.

---

[1] *Cf.* E. Trenkler, *Das 'Livre du cuer d'amours espris' des Herzogs René von Anjou*, Wien 1946.

[2] The prime achievement of Jan's art is one of form and of theme. Leaving aside the genre pictures, let us not forget that the typical concentric construction of the 'sacra conversazione' is not found in Italy until after Jan's death (Antonio Vivarini, Venice, 1446, and Domenico Veneziano, Florence, about the same time).

[3] The influence exercised about 1490 on Pietro Perugino (*cf.* L. Baldass, *Hans Memling*, p. 32) and occasionally on Lorenzo di Credi or on his school (*cf.* B. Degenhart, *Münchener Jahrbuch* IX, 1932) of Memling's works, brought to Italy, is also no more than sporadic.

THE PLATES

1 (Cat. No. 2). HUBERT VAN EYCK: THE THREE MARIES AT THE SEPULCHRE. Vierhouten, van Beuningen Collection.

2. THE THREE MARIES. Detail from Plate 1.

3. THE ANGEL. Detail from Plate I.

4. THE THIRD WATCHER. Detail from Plate I.

5. THE WATCHER IN ARMOUR. Detail from Plate 1.

6. THE TOWERS OF JERUSALEM. Detail from Plate I.

7. The Closed Garden. Detail from Plate 8.

8. (Cat. No. 3). HUBERT VAN EYCK (original?): THE ANNUNCIATION. New York, Metropolitan Museum.

9. (Cat. No. 5). JAN VAN EYCK (original?): ST. JEROME IN HIS STUDY.
Detroit, Institute of Arts.

10 (Cat. No. 4). Jan van Eyck: The Virgin in the Church.
Berlin, Deutsches Museum.

11 (Cat. No. 34). After Jan van Eyck: The Crucifixion. Venice, Ca d'Oro.

12. (Cat. No. 33). After JAN VAN EYCK: THE AGONY IN THE GARDEN.
Miniature from the Turin Book of Hours. Turin, Musco Civico.

13. (Cat. No. 6). Jan van Eyck: St. Francis receiving the Stigmata.
Philadelphia, John G. Johnson Collection.

14 (Cat. No. 1). HUBERT and JAN VAN EYCK: INSIDE OF THE GHENT ALTAR-PIECE. Ghent, St. Bavon.

15 (Cat. No. 1). Hubert and Jan van Eyck: The Adoration of the Holy Lamb. Ghent, St. Bavon.

16. The Altar of the Holy Lamb. Detail from Plate 15.

17. Landscape with the Holy Bishops and Confessors. Detail from Plate 15.

18. HUBERT VAN EYCK: THE HOLY BISHOPS AND CONFESSORS. Detail from Plate 15.

19. THE PATRIARCHS. Detail from Plate 15.

20. THE PROPHETS. Detail from Plate 15.

21. THE APOSTLES. Detail from Plate 15.

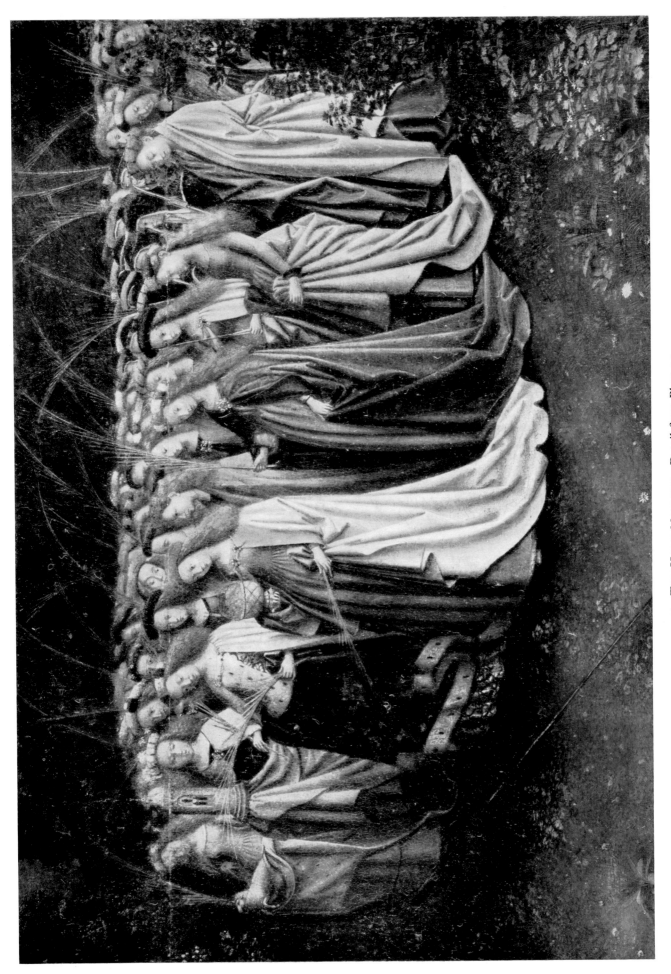

22. THE HOLY MAIDENS. Detail from Plate 15.

23. The Holy Martyrs. Detail from Plate 15.

24. THE ANGEL WITH THE CROSS. Detail from Plate 15.

25. THE FOREMOST HOLY MAIDENS. Detail from Plate 15.

26. CROWN OF THE WELL OF THE WATER OF LIFE. Detail from Plate 15.

27. KNEELING ANGELS. Detail from Plate 15.

28. HEAD OF A PATRIARCH. Detail from Plate 15.

29. HEAD OF AN APOSTLE. Detail from Plate 15.

30. HEAD OF THE SO-CALLED VIRGIL. Detail from Plate 15.

31. HEADS OF APOSTLES. Detail from Plate 15.

32. Heads of Prophets. Detail from Plate 15.

33. HEADS OF TWO POPES. Detail from Plate 15.

34. HEAD OF A PROPHET. Detail from Plate 15.

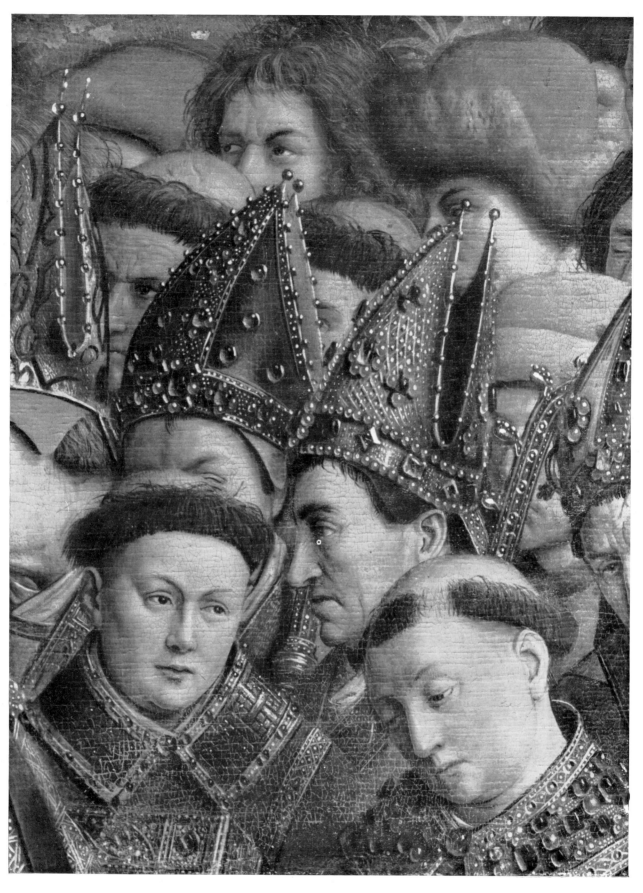

35. HEADS OF THE HOLY DEACONS. Detail from Plate 15.

36. Expanse of Turf. Detail from Plate 15.

37. LILY, IRIS AND PEONY. Detail from Plate 15.

38. TOWN, FROM THE LEFT UPPER CORNER. Detail from Plate 15.

39. WOOD BEHIND THE HOLY CONFESSORS. Detail from Plate 15.

40. Town with Gothic Cathedral. Detail from Plate 15.

41. Town with Romanesque Cathedral. Detail from Plate 15.

42. Hilly Landscape. Detail from Plate 15.

43. Pine Tree, Palm and Cypress. Detail from Plate 45.

44 (Cat. No. 1). Jan van Eyck: The Just Judges and the Warriors of Christ. Ghent, St. Bavon.

45 (Cat. No. 1). JAN VAN EYCK: THE HOLY HERMITS AND THE HOLY PILGRIMS. Ghent, St. Bavon.

46. THE JUST JUDGES. Detail from Plate 44.

47. CHARGERS OF THE WARRIORS OF CHRIST. Detail from Plate 44.

48. ROCKS. Detail from Plate 44.

49. THE WARRIORS OF CHRIST. Detail from Plate 44.

50. Mountain Landscape. Detail from Plate 44.

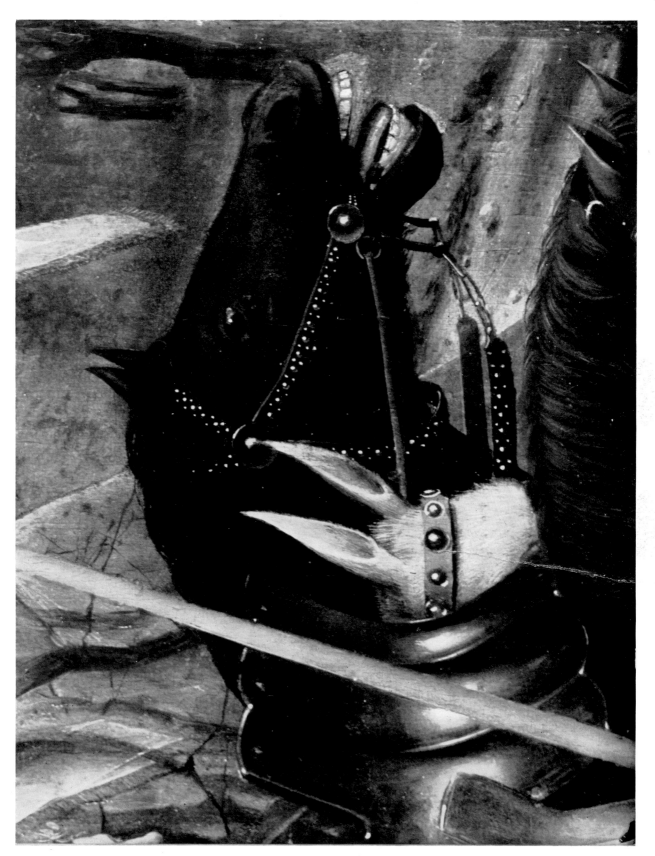

51. HEADS OF HORSES. Detail from Plate 44.

52. THE HOLY HERMITS. Detail from Plate 45.

53. THE HOLY PILGRIMS. Detail from Plate 45.

54. A Holy Hermit. Detail from Plate 45.

55. ST. CHRISTOPHER. Detail from Plate 45.

56. ORANGE TREE. Detail from Plate 45.

57. WOOD. Detail from Plate 45.

58. Palms and Cypresses. Detail from Plate 45.

59. DISTANT LANDSCAPE. Detail from Plate 45.

62 (Cat. No. 1). HUBERT and JAN VAN EYCK: THE VIRGIN MARY. Ghent, St. Bavon.

63 (Cat. No. 1). HUBERT and JAN VAN EYCK: ST. JOHN THE BAPTIST. Ghent, St. Bavon.

64. THE VIRGIN MARY. Detail from Plate 62.

65. THE VIRGIN MARY. Detail from Plate 62.

66. St. John the Baptist's Book. Detail from Plate 63.

67. ST. JOHN THE BAPTIST. Detail from Plate 63.

68. Right Hand of God the Father. Detail from Plate 60.

69. TOP OF THE SCEPTRE. Detail from Plate 60.

70. THE VIRGIN MARY'S CROWN. Detail from Plate 62.

71. Crown at the Feet of God the Father. Detail from Plate 60.

MEUS DEO · LAVS PHĒNIS · ORAR A° 10 ·

72 (Cat. No. 1). Hubert and Jan van Eyck: Singing Angels. Ghent, St. Bavon.

73 (Cat. No. 1). Hubert and Jan van Eyck: Angels making Music. Ghent, St. Bavon.

74. The Singing Angels. Detail from Plate 72.

75. ANGEL PLAYING THE ORGAN. Detail from Plate 73.

76. ANGELS MAKING MUSIC. Detail from Plate 73.

77. STAND OF THE MUSIC-DESK. Detail from Plate 72.

78. The Music-desk. Detail from Plate 72.

79. FLOOR. Detail from Plate 73.

·ADAM·

·EVA·

ADAM NOS I MORTE PCIPITAT·

EVA OCCIDENDO OBFVIT·

80 (Cat. No. 1). Jan van Eyck: Adam and Eve. Ghent, St. Bavon

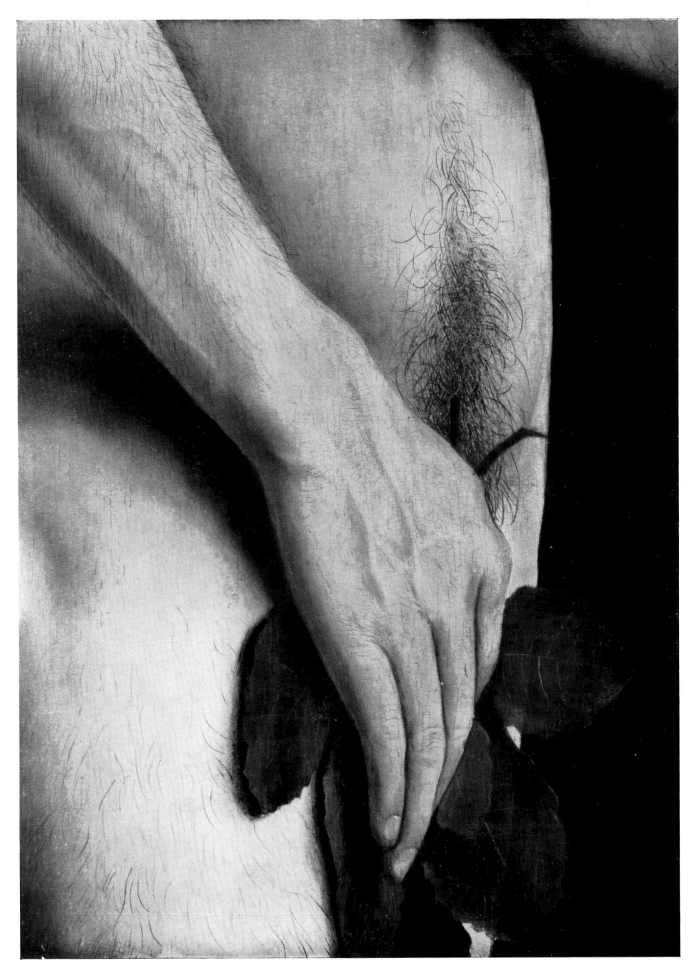

81. HAND OF ADAM. Detail from Plate 80.

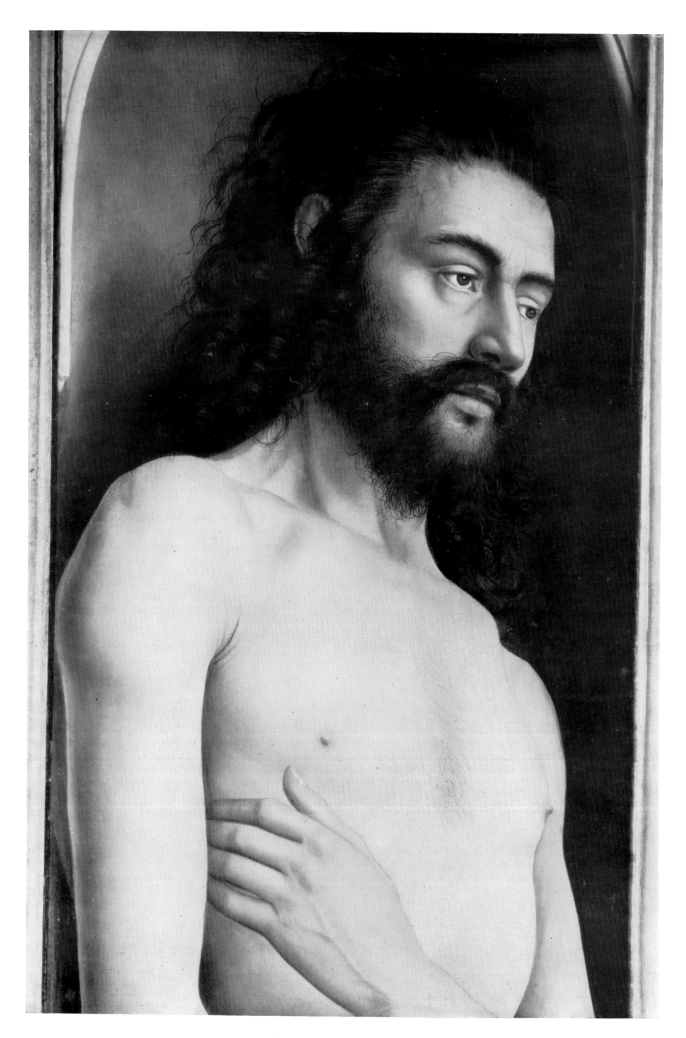

82. ADAM. Detail from Plate 80.

83. Eve. Detail from Plate 80.

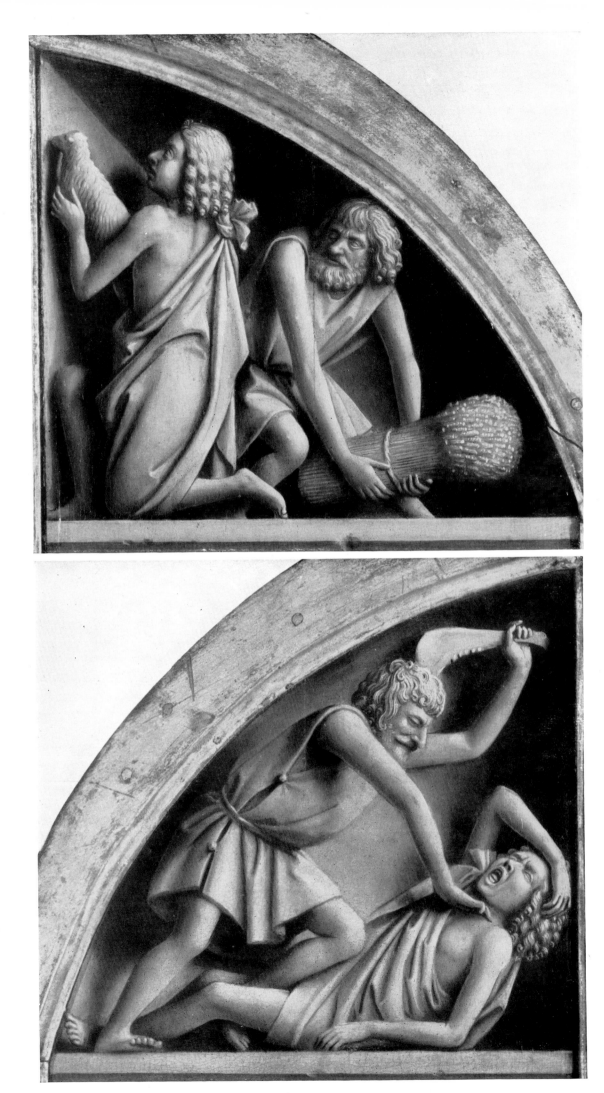

84 (Cat. No. 1). JAN VAN EYCK: THE SACRIFICE OF CAIN AND ABEL; THE MURDER OF ABEL.
Ghent, St. Bavon.

85 (Cat. No. 1). HUBERT and JAN VAN EYCK: OUTSIDE OF THE GHENT ALTAR-PIECE. Ghent, St. Bavon.

86 (Cat. No. 1). HUBERT and JAN VAN EYCK: THE LEFT PART OF THE ANNUNCIATION.

87 (Cat. No. 1). Hubert and Jan van Eyck: The right Part of the Annunciation.

88 (Cat. No. 1). Jan van Eyck: The Erythraean and Cumaean Sibyls.

89 (Cat. No. 1). Jan van Eyck: The Prophets Zechariah and Micah.

90. THE ERYTHRAEAN SIBYL. Detail from Plate 88.

91. THE PROPHET MICAH. Detail from Plate 89.

92. THE ANGEL. Detail from Plate 86.

93. THE ROOM BEHIND THE VIRGIN. Detail from Plate 87.

94. VIEW OF THE STREET ON THE LEFT. Detail from Plate 86.

95. VIEW OF THE STREET ON THE RIGHT. Detail from Plate 86.

96. Washing Recess. Detail from Plate 87.

99. St. John the Evangelist. Detail from Plate 101.

100 (Cat. No. 1). Jan van Eyck: St. John the Baptist and Jodocus Vyd. Ghent, St. Bavon.

101 (Cat. No. 1). JAN VAN EYCK: ST. JOHN THE EVANGELIST AND ISABELLA BORLUUT. Ghent, St. Bavon.

102. JODOCUS VYD. Detail from Plate 100.

103. ISABELLA BORLUUT. Detail from Plate 101.

104 (Cat. No. 7). Jan van Eyck: The Madonna in her Chamber.   Melbourne, National Gallery of Victoria.

105 (Cat. No. 8). JAN VAN EYCK: THE ANNUNCIATION. Outsides of the wings of the Dresden Altarpiece.

106 (Cat. No. 8). JAN VAN EYCK: ST. MICHAEL WITH THE DONOR. ST. CATHERINE.
Insides of the wings of the Dresden Altar-piece.

107 (Cat. No. 8). JAN VAN EYCK: THE VIRGIN AND CHILD. Centre panel of the Dresden Altar-piece.

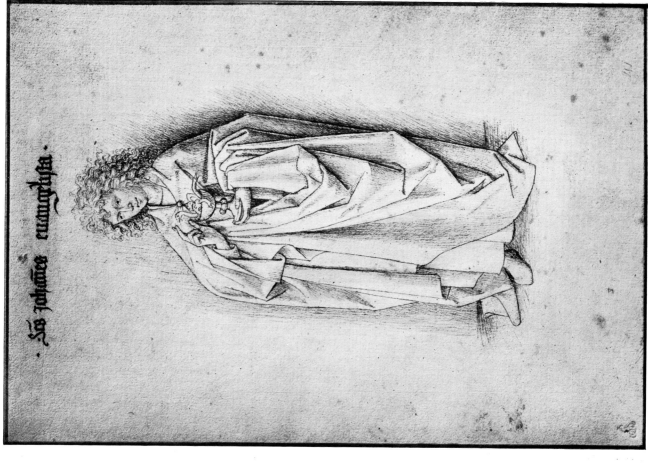

109 (Cat. No. 41). After Jan van Eyck: St. John the Evangelist.
Drawing. Vienna, Albertina.

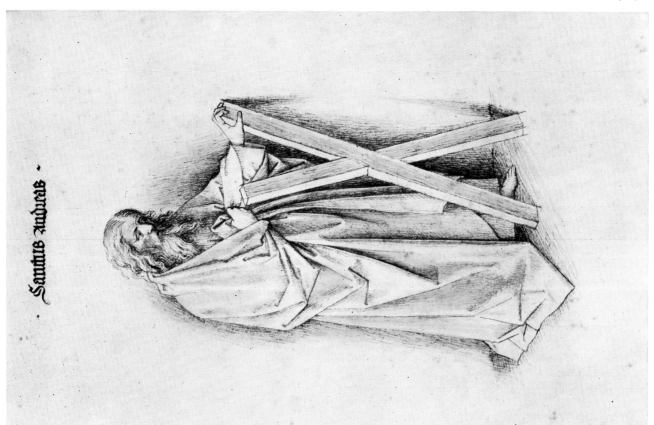

108 (Cat. No. 39). After Jan van Eyck: St. Andrew.
Drawing. Vienna, Albertina.

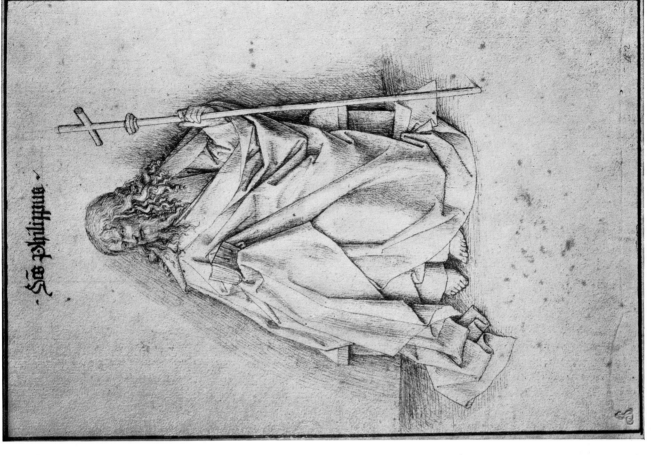

111 (Cat. No. 44). After Jan van Eyck: St. Philip.
Drawing. Vienna, Albertina.

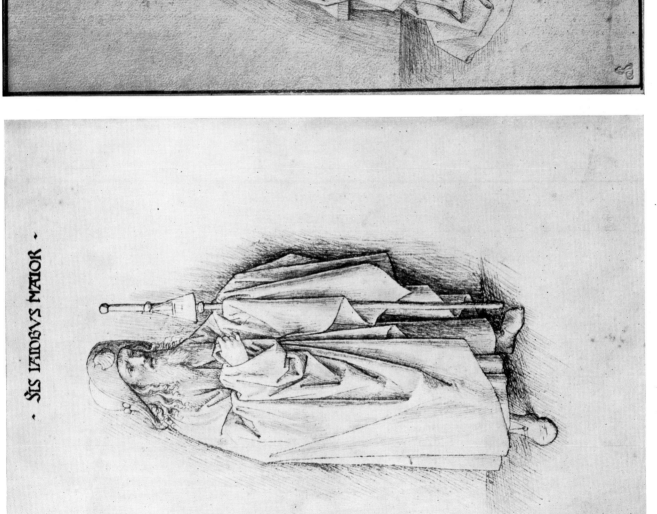

110 (Cat. No. 40). After Jan van Eyck: St. James the Great.
Drawing. Vienna, Albertina.

112 (Cat. No. 11). JAN VAN EYCK: THE ANNUNCIATION. Lugano, Schloss Rohoncz Collection.

113 (Cat. No. 9). JAN VAN EYCK: THE ANNUNCIATION.
Washington, National Gallery of Art.

114. THE ANGEL AND THE VIRGIN. Detail from Plate 113.

115. FLOOR. Detail from Plate 113.

116 (Cat. No. 10). Jan van Eyck: The Madonna with the Chancellor Rolin. Paris, Louvre.

117. THE MADONNA. Detail from Plate 116.

118. THE CHANCELLOR ROLIN. Detail from Plate 116.

119. VIEW OVER THE TOWN. Detail from Plate 116.

120 (Cat. No. 13). JAN VAN EYCK: THE MADONNA WITH CANON VAN DER PAELE. Bruges, Museum.

121. Drapery and Carpet. Detail from Plate 120.

122. CANON VAN DER PAELE. Detail from Plate 120.

123. ST. DONATIAN. Detail from Plate 120.

124. THE MADONNA. Detail from Plate 120.

125. ST. GEORGE. Detail from Plate 120.

126 (Cat. No. 12). JAN VAN EYCK: THE MADONNA IN HER CHAMBER. Frankfurt, Staedel Institute.

127 (Cat. No. 14). JAN VAN EYCK: ST. BARBARA. Antwerp, Museum.

128 (Cat. No. 15). Jan van Eyck: The Madonna by the Fountain. Antwerp, Museum.

129 (Cat. No. 17). JAN VAN EYCK: THE MADONNA WITH ABBOT MAELBEKE. Private Collection.

131 (Cat. No. 16). JAN VAN EYCK: CHRIST AS KING OF KINGS. Private Collection.

130 (Cat. No. 35). After JAN VAN EYCK: CHRIST AS KING OF KINGS. Berlin, Museum.

132 (Cat. No. 18). Jan van Eyck: The Madonna with a Carthusian. Paris, Rothschild Collection.

133 (Cat. No. 28). JAN VAN EYCK: CARDINAL ALBERGATI. Drawing. Dresden, Print Room.

134 (Cat. No. 19). Jan van Eyck: Cardinal Albergati. Vienna, Kunsthistorisches Museum.

135 (Cat. No. 20). JAN VAN EYCK: 'TYMOTHEOS'. 1432. London, National Gallery.

136 (Cat. No. 21). JAN VAN EYCK: MAN WITH CHAPERON. 1433. London, National Gallery.

137 (Cat. No. 22). Jan van Eyck: Wedding Portrait of Giovanni Arnolfini. London, National Gallery.

138. MIRROR AND CHANDELIER. Detail from Plate 137.

139. GIOVANNI ARNOLFINI. Detail from Plate 137.

140. GIOVANNA ARNOLFINI. Detail from Plate 137.

141 (Cat. No. 23). JAN VAN EYCK: A GOLDSMITH. Bucharest, Museum.

144 (Cat. No. 26). JAN VAN EYCK: GIOVANNI ARNOLFINI. Berlin, Deutsches Museum.

145 (Cat. No. 27). Jan van Eyck: Margarethe van Eyck. 1439. Bruges, Museum.

146. Margarethe van Eyck. Detail from Plate 145.

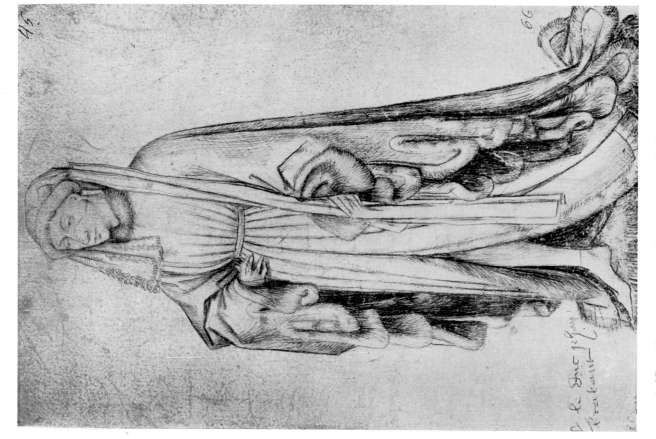

148 (Cat. No. 30). Jan van Eyck: John IV, Duke of Brabant.
Drawing. Vierhouten, van Beuningen Collection.

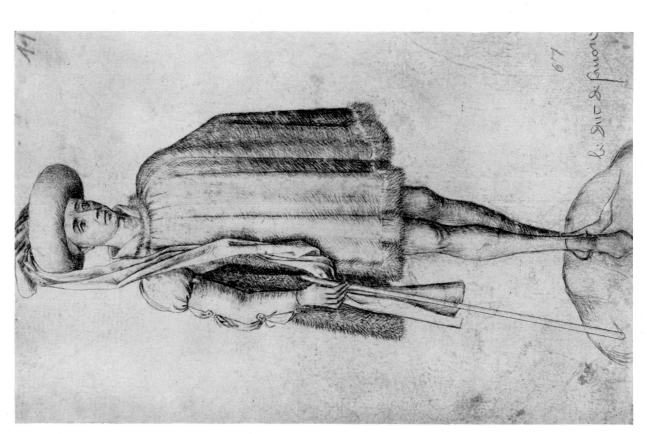

147 (Cat. No. 29). Jan van Eyck: Lodovico, Duke of Savoy.
Drawing. Vierhouten, van Beuningen Collection.

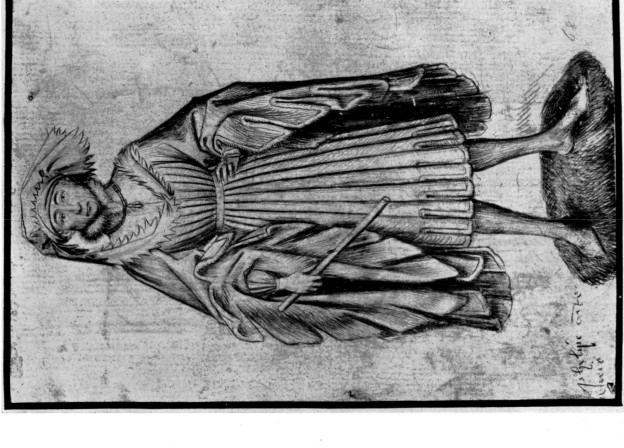

149 (Cat. No. 31). JAN VAN EYCK: PHILIP, DUKE OF BRABANT.
Drawing. Destroyed by fire.

150 (Cat. No. 32). JAN VAN EYCK: PHILIP, DUKE OF NEVERS.
Drawing. Destroyed by fire.

152 (Cat. No. 50). After Jan van Eyck: Man with Chaperon.
Drawing. Paris, Louvre.

151 (Cat. No. 51). Partly after Jan van Eyck (?): The Falconer.
Drawing. Frankfurt, Staedel Institute.

154 (Cat. No. 72). NETHERLANDISH SCHOOL, ABOUT 1440: PORTRAIT OF A MAN.
Philadelphia, John G. Johnson Collection.

153 (Cat. No. 71). FOLLOWER OF JAN VAN EYCK: A CLERIC.
Montauban, Musée Ingres.

155 (Cat. No. 70). FOLLOWER OF JAN VAN EYCK: PORTRAIT OF A DONOR. Leipzig, Museum.

156 (Cat. No. 69). ANOTHER FOLLOWER OF JAN VAN EYCK: THE MAN WITH THE PINKS. Berlin, Deutsches Museum.

157 (Cat. No. 60). CHIEF MASTER OF THE 'HEURES DE TURIN':
THE BIRTH OF ST. JOHN THE BAPTIST. Turin, Museo Civico.

158 (Cat. No. 60). Chief Master of the 'Heures de Turin':
Requiem. Turin, Museo Civico.

159 (Cat. No. 60). Chief Master of the 'Heures de Turin':
The Baptism of Christ. Turin, Museo Civico.

160 (Cat. No. 60). Chief Master of the 'Heures de Turin':
Cemetery Scene. Turin, Museo Civico.

os autem glonan oportet in auce dm
noftri ihelu xpisti in quo est salus uita
et resunrectio nostra per quem saluati *
liberati sumus. ps. deus misereatur

161 (Cat. No. 60). Page from the 'Heures de Turin': St. Helena finding the True Cross.
Turin, Museo Civico.

162 (Cat. No. 61). Chief Master of the 'Heures de Turin': Christ on the Cross. Berlin, Deutsches Museum.

163 (Cat. No. 62). CHIEF MASTER OF THE 'HEURES DE TURIN': THE CRUCIFIXION; THE LAST JUDGEMENT.
New York, Metropolitan Museum.

164. THE THREE CROSSES. Detail from Plate 163.

165. ST. MICHAEL AND HELL. Detail from Plate 163.

166 (Cat. No. 63). After the Chief Master of the 'Heures de Turin': Christ bearing the Cross. Budapest, Gallery.

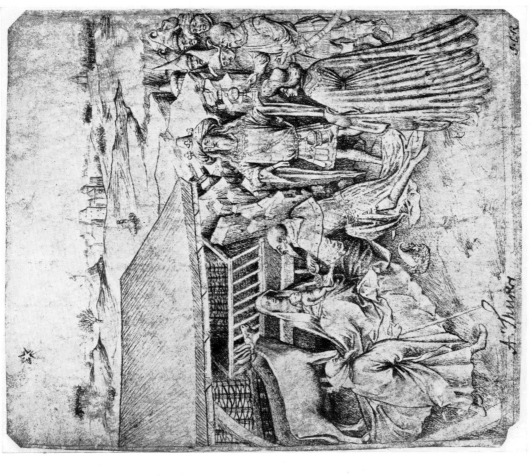

168 (Cat. No. 77). After the Chief Master of the 'Heures de Turin':
The Adoration of the Magi. Drawing. Berlin, Print Room.

167 (Cat. No. 78). After the Chief Master of the 'Heures de Turin':
The Adoration of the Magi. Drawing. Amsterdam, Rijksmuseum.

169 (Cat. No. 76). CHIEF MASTER OF THE 'HEURES DE TURIN' (?): THE BETRAYAL
OF CHRIST. Drawing. London, British Museum.

170 (Cat. No. 80). After the CHIEF MASTER OF THE 'HEURES DE TURIN':
CAVALCADE. Drawing. Brunswick, Museum.

THE CATALOGUE

ARRANGEMENT OF THE CATALOGUE

Nineteenth-century attributions, which since M. J. Friedländer (I) have been generally rejected, have been disregarded here. Of the old copies and drawings after preserved works listed by Weale, I have included only those few which are important for reasons of composition, provenance, dating, etc. The following abbreviations are used for the more frequently quoted works:

> Kämmerer (*Hubert und Jan van Eyck*, Bielefeld and Leipzig, 1898).
> Weale (*Hubert and John van Eyck*, London and New York, 1908).
> Weale-Brockwell (*The Van Eycks*, London, New York and Toronto, 1912).
> Friedländer I (*Die altniederländische Malerei*, I, Berlin, 1924).
> Friedländer XIV (*Die altniederländische Malerei*, XIV, Leyden, 1937).
> Tolnay (*Le maître de Flémalle et les frères van Eyck*, Brussels, 1939).
> Beenken (*Hubert und Jan van Eyck*, Munich, 1941).

An asterisk above a title in the Catalogue denotes that I have not been able to make a personal examination of the work; two asterisks, that I have not seen it for many years.

CATALOGUE OF THE PAINTINGS AND DRAWINGS

I. THE GHENT ALTAR-PIECE

I

THE GHENT ALTAR-PIECE[1]
Ghent, St. Bavon

A. *THE ALTAR-PIECE WHEN OPEN*
(Plate 14)

1. LOWER ROW

Centre Panel: The Adoration of the Lamb (Plates 15-42, Figs. 35, 49). Wood. Height 53 inches (135 cm); width 93 inches (236 cm).
On the altar of the Lamb, whose blood is pouring into the chalice, is the inscription: ECCE AGNVS DEI QVI TOLLIT PEC⟨CA⟩TA MV⟨N⟩DI (St. John, i.29); beneath this on the left: IHES⟨VS⟩ VIA; on the right: VITA V⟨ER⟩ITA⟨S⟩.
On the Well of the Water of Life, the inscription: HIC EST FONS AQV⟨A⟩E VIT⟨A⟩E PROCEDENS DE SEDE DEI ⟨ET⟩ AGNI (*cf.* Rev. xxii.1).
Kneeling round the Well, on the left twelve Prophets, on the right the fourteen Apostles (including Matthias, Paul and Barnabas).
Among the Saints in the foreground on the right, the foremost Holy Deacon has been characterized by stones as St. Stephen; next to him, with his tongue in a pair of tongs, is Bishop Livinus, Patron Saint of Ghent. These personages make it probable that this group clad in red are the Holy Martyrs. The white-robed figure with the crown of laurel in his hair, among the Patriarchs on the left, has been identified as Virgil. Among the Holy Maidens in the second plane can be distinguished Saints Agnes, Barbara, Dorothy and Ursula. The blue-robed clerics opposite them, sometimes, on account of the palm-fronds in their hands, held to be Holy Martyrs, are probably the Holy Bishops and Confessors.
The panel has suffered damage through heat (probably in 1822), especially in the landscape and sky at the back. The dove has been overpainted. The same is the case, as M. Philippot was so kind as to show me, with the head and body of the Lamb, the legs being in the original state.

Inner Left Wing-panel: The Warriors of Christ (Plates 44, 47-51). Wood. Height 57 inches (145 cm); width 20 inches (51 cm). Below on the frame the inscription: CRISTI MILITES.
On the shield of the knight in the centre: D⟨OMINV⟩S FORTIS ADONAY SABAOT V.. EM⟨MANV⟩EL I. H. S. XR. AGLA (Agla—the first four letters of a Hebrew appeal to the Lord).
The three knights are usually held to be Saints Martin (or Victor), George and Sebastian; the emperor has been identified as Charlemagne; the rider of the white mule as Godfrey de Bouillon; the king on the left as St. Louis. King Arthur has also been suggested, and even princes living at the time or recently dead, such as the Emperor Sigismund, Jean sans Peur, Charles VI of France, the Duke of Berry, etc. (*cf.* Durrieu, in *Gazette des Beaux-Arts*, 1910, 1, p. 461; 1920, 1, p. 77, Reinach, *Revue archéologique*, 16, 1910, p. 369, Six, *Revue archéologique*, 18, 1911, p. 401).

Outer Left Wing-panel: The Just Judges (Plates 44, 46). Wood. Height 57 inches (145 cm); width 20 inches (51 cm). Inscription below, on the frame; IVSTI IVDICES.
Lucas de Heere, in 1565, was the first to suggest that the first horseman was a portrait of Hubert van Eyck and the fourth of Jan, a hypothesis which persisted in art literature until well into the twentieth century. Equally unconvincing is the suggestion advanced by P. Post (*Jahrbuch d. preuss. Kunstsammlungen*, 1921, p. 67) that the four horsemen represent Philip the Bold, Louis de Mâle, Jean sans Peur and Philip the Good.

Inner Right Wing-panel: The Holy Hermits (Plates 45, 43, 52, 54, 57). Wood. Height 57 inches (145 cm); width 20 inches (51 cm). Inscription below on the frame: HEREMITE S⟨AN⟩C⟨T⟩I
Two women bring up the rear of the procession, St. Mary Magdalen (with the jar of ointment) and another, probably St. Mary Aegyptiaca.

Outer Right Wing-panel: The Holy Pilgrims, led by St. Christopher (Plates 45, 53, 55, 56, 58, 59). Wood. Height 57 inches (145 cm); width 20½ inches (52 cm). The pilgrim with the shell in his hat has been held to be St. Josse (Jodocus).
Inscription below on the original frame: PE⟨RE⟩GRINI S⟨AN⟩C⟨T⟩I

2. UPPER ROW

Centre Panel, middle: God the Father[2] enthroned and blessing (Plates 60, 61, 68, 69, 71). Wood. Height 82 inches (208 cm); width 31 inches (79 cm). Inscription in pearl-embroidery on the stole: SABAⲰT.
On the seam of his pallium: ⟨A⟩NANXIN PEX PEGV (Rex Regum).
A pelican in its nest occurs repeatedly in the pattern of the brocade, above it a scroll with the words: IHESVS XPS.
Inscriptions in the semi-sircular top of the picture:
+ HIC E⟨ST⟩ DEVS POTE⟨N⟩TISSIM⟨VS⟩ P⟨RO⟩P⟨TER⟩ DIVINA⟨M⟩ MAIESTATE⟨M⟩ + SV⟨MMVS⟩ O⟨MN⟩I⟨V⟩M OPTI⟨MVS⟩ P⟨RO⟩P⟨TER⟩ DVLCEDI⟨NI⟩S BO⟨N⟩ITATE⟨M⟩ //REMVNERATOR LIBERALISSIMVS PROPTER INME//NSAM LARGITATEM.
On the steps of the throne: VITA · SINE · MORTE · IN · CAPITE · IVVE⟨N⟩T⟨VS⟩ · S⟨I⟩N⟨E⟩ · SENECTVTE · I⟨N⟩ · FRONTE · //GAVDIV⟨M⟩ S⟨I⟩N⟨E⟩ MERORE · A · DEXTRIS SECVRITAS · S⟨I⟩N⟨E⟩ · TI⟨M⟩ORE · A · SINIST⟨RI⟩S//.

---

[1]Nearly all the panels have their original edges, the only exceptions being the upper edges of the pictures of God the Father, St. Mary and St. John, which, as M. Philippot told me, have been sawn off. Apart from the exceptions mentioned, the panels have not been cut anywhere, though various writers have assumed this.

[2]In order to prove that the figure is meant to be God the Father and not Christ as King of Kings, Renders (l.c. 1950) stressed the fact that the Holy Figure is wearing shoes, whereas Christ used to be represented barefooted.

Centre Panel, left: The Virgin Mary[1] (Plates 62, 64, 65, 70).
Wood. Height 65 inches (165 cm); width 28 inches (71 cm).
Inscription in semi-circles of the top of the picture: HEC E⟨ST⟩
SPECIOSIOR SOLE + SVP⟨ER⟩ O⟨MN⟩EM STELLARV⟨M⟩ DISPOS-
ICIO⟨N⟩E⟨M⟩ LVCI //C⟨OM⟩PA⟨RA⟩TA I⟨N⟩VE⟨N⟩IT⟨VR⟩ P⟨RI⟩OR
CA⟨N⟩DOR E⟨ST⟩ E⟨N⟩IM LV⟨CIS⟩ ⟨ETER⟩N⟨A⟩E + SPEC⟨V⟩L⟨V⟩M
S⟨I⟩N⟨E⟩// MAC⟨V⟩LA DEI.

Centre Panel, right: St. John the Baptist[2] (Plates 63, 66, 67).
Wood. Height 65 inches (165 cm); width 28 inches (71 cm).
The initial letter 'C' in the opened book of the Baptist has
been interpreted as the beginning of Isaiah XL (in the text of
the Vulgate).
Inscription in semi-circles of the top of the picture: + HIC
E⟨ST⟩ BAPTISTA IOH⟨ANN⟩ES MAIOR HO⟨M⟩I⟨N⟩E PAR ANG-
⟨E⟩LIS LEGIS //SVM⟨M⟩A EWA⟨N⟩GELII SA⟨N⟩C⟨T⟩IO AP⟨OSTO⟩-
LOR⟨VM⟩ VOX SILE⟨N⟩CIV⟨M⟩ P⟨ROP⟩HETAR⟨VM⟩// LVCERNA
MVN⟨DI⟩ D⟨O⟩M⟨I⟩NI TESTIS.

Inner Left Wing-panel: Singing Angels (Plates 72, 74, 77, 78).
Wood. Height 63 inches (160 cm) (with semi-circular top;
Width 27 inches (69 cm).
Inscription below on the frame[3]: MELOS DEO · LAVS P⟨ER⟩-
HEN⟨N⟩IS GRA⟨TIA⟩R⟨VM⟩ AC⟨T⟩IO.
On the music desk are wooden figures of St. Michael and two
Prophets. Some of the tiles of the flooring show the Lamb and
Flag, others the monograms of Jesus and Mary, the inscrip-
tion ΑΓΛΑ, Alpha and Omega, etc.

Inner Right Wing-panel: Angels making Music (Plates 73, 75,
76, 79).
Wood. Height 63 inches (160 cm) (with semi-circular top);
Width 27 inches (69 cm).
Inscription below on the frame: LAVDA⟨N⟩T EV⟨M⟩ IN CORDIS
ET ORGANO.
Tiles of the flooring as in the corresponding panel.

Outer Left Wing-panel:Adam; above, in grisaille: *The Sacrifice
of Cain and Abel* (Plates 80, 81, 82, 84).
Wood. Height 84¾ inches (215 cm) (with quadri-circular top);
Width 15 inches (38 cm).
Inscription below on the original frame: ADAM NOS I⟨N⟩
MORTE⟨M⟩ P⟨RE⟩CIPITA⟨VI⟩T.
On the architecture above Adam's head: · ADAM.

Outer Right Wing-panel: Eve, with a lemon in her hand; above,
in grisaille: *Cain slaying Abel* (Plates 80, 83, 84).
Wood. Height 84¾ inches (215 cm) (with quadri-circular top);
Width 15 inches (38 cm).
Inscription below on the original frame: · EVA OCCIDENDO
OBFVIT · (St. Augustine, *Incarnatio Christi*); on the archi-
tecture above Eve's head: · EVA ·

---

[1]The colour plate shows a detail of the picture before its cleaning in
1951. We see now instead of a mantle overpainted with a dark blue
colour the original one in brightly shining ultramarine.
[2]The triangular spaces beside the semi-circles of the three centre-
pictures are entirely overpainted. The copies of the pictures of
St. Mary and St. John made in 1558 by M. Coxie for King Philip II
of Spain (now in Munich; his copy of God the Father is in Berlin)
lead us to the conclusion that there was underneath the brocades a
gold ground with semicircular lines but without the modelling
shadows, and that the tiles of the floor, painted in two intense
colours, were not separated by gold lines.
[3]The frame of the four middle pictures is modern. The frames of the
wings are described in Posse's 1911 Berlin catalogue as 'old'. On the
other hand Puyvelde (*loc. cit.*) asserts that of the inside panels only
those of Adam and Eve have the original frames, whereas those of the
other wing-panels are copies (in fir-wood) with copies of the original
inscriptions. This information is not correct. All the frames of the
wings are original. The panels that were in Berlin have been lined
with fir-wood only when they were sawn apart about 1900.

B. *THE ALTAR-PIECE WHEN CLOSED*
(Plate 85; Fig. 87)

1. LOWER ROW

*The Two Middle Panels: St. John the Baptist and St. John the
Evangelist.* Grisaille figures (Plates 99, 100, 101).
Wood. Each panel 57 inches (145 cm) high, 20 inches
(51 cm) wide.
Inscription on the socles : IOH⟨ANN⟩ES BAP⟨TIS⟩TA: IOH-
⟨ANN⟩ES EWAN⟨GELIS⟩TA

The Two Outer Panels: The donors, Jocodus Vyd, burgomaster
of Ghent 1433-34, died 1439, and his wife Isabella Borluut,
died 1443 (Plates 100-103).
Wood. Each panel 58 inches (147 cm) high, 20 inches (51 cm)
wide.

2. UPPER ROW

The Two Outer Panels: The Annunciation; above, separated by
strips of the frame[4] bearing the inscriptions: Sacharias
propheta and Micheas p⟨ro⟩pheta, the prophets Zechariah
and Micah. (Plates 86, 87, 89, 91, 92, 93, 96-98).
Wood. Each panel 63½ inches (161 cm) high, 27½ inches (70cm)
wide, the Annunciation pictures being 47¼ inches (120 cm)
high and those of the Prophets 13¾ inches (35 cm).
Inscription near the Angel: Ave gracia plena dns tecv.
Near the Virgin, with letters upside down (*cf.* p. 62):
Ecce ancilla dni.
On the scroll of the Prophet Zechariah: Exvlta satis filia
Syo⟨n⟩ jubila ecce rex tvvs ve⟨n⟩it (Zechariah, ix. 9).
On the scroll of the Prophet Micah: Ex te egredietur qui sit
dominator in isr⟨ae⟩l (Micah, v.2).
The varnish on the wings is too yellow.

The Two Inner Panels: The Room of the Annunciation; above,
separated by strips of the frame bearing the inscriptions
Sibylla eritrea and Sibylla cvmana, the Erythraean and
Cumaean Sibyls (Plates 86, 87, 88, 90, 94-95).
Each panel 84¾ inches (215 cm) high, 15 inches (38 cm) wide,
the pictures of the Room being 47¼ inches (120 cm) high and
those of the Sibyls 30¾ inches (78 cm).
On the scroll of the Erythraean Sibyl: Nil mortale sona⟨n⟩s
afflata es numine celso.
On the scroll of the Cumaean Sibyl: Rex adve⟨n⟩iet p⟨er⟩
sec⟨u⟩la futur⟨a⟩ sci⟨licet⟩ i⟨n⟩ carne. On her collar:METAPARO.

THE SIGNATURE (Fig. 87)

On the lower edge of the frame of the pictures in the lower row
on the outside of the altar-piece the signature appears, in four
lines:

> . . . ubertus .eyck maior quo nemo repertus
> incepit pondusq iohannes arte secundus
> . . . . . . iodoci vyd prece fretus
> versu sexta mai vos collocat acta tueri

The last line is a chronogram. The letters here underlined
were painted on the original in red instead of black and, added
together, give the year 1432.
All readings (and suggestions for completing it) of this inscription, which in its essence can only have one meaning, that
Hubert began the work, while Jan completed it at the request

---

[4]Under the strips of the frame separating the Annunciation scene
from the Prophets, the oak-wood without any grounding is visible.

87. *The Signature of the Ghent Altar-Piece*

of Jodocus Vyd, are given in: P. Coremans and A. Janssens de Bisthoven, *Van Eyck, L'Adoration de l'Agneau mystique* (Antwerp 1948). The theory advanced by E. Renders (*Hubert van Eyck, Personnage et légende*, Paris and Brussels 1933, and *Jean van Eyck*, Bruges 1935), that the inscription is a forgery made about 1620 (*cf.* p. 22, note 3) is contradicted by, among other things, the character of the letters.

Cf. P. Faider, *Revue Belge de Philologie et d'Histoire*, 12, 1933, p. 1274; Hulin de Loo, *Revue archéologique*, 1934, p. 62 ff, L. Scheeve, *Hubert und Jan Van Eyck, Ihre literarische Würdigung bis ins 18. Jahrh.*, The Hague 1933, and *Zeitschrift für Kunstgeschichte*, III, 1934, p. 139.

According to A. Hirsch (*Repertorium f. Kunstwissenschaft*, 42, 1920, p. 77) the last line gives Friday 16th May 1432 (not 6th May) as the day on which the work was completed.

History of the Work

According to M. van Vaernewijk (1568), the altar-piece was restored in 1550 by Lancelot Blondeel and Jan van Scorel. The same author mentions a predella completely destroyed by a restorer, representing Hell, painted by Jan van Eyck in watercolours (*cf.* Friedländer XIV).

Until the iconoclastic riot on 19th August 1566, the work was in the chapel of Jodocus Vyd in St. Bavon (formerly dedicated to St. John) at Ghent; it was then removed to the Stadthuis and was brought back to the Cathedral in 1584.

It was restored by Antoine van der Heuvel in 1663.

The Adam and Eve panels were separated from the rest of the altar-piece in 1781.

In 1794 the centre portion (Adoration of the Lamb, God the Father, the Virgin Mary, St. John) was removed by the French and taken to Paris (in the Musée Central in 1799).

In 1816 the centre portion was once more installed in St. Bavon In the same year the wings (without Adam and Eve) were sold to the art-dealer L. C. Nieuwenhuys and by him to the English collector Solly. In 1821 they were bought by the Berlin Museum.

The centre portion in St. Bavon, after a fire in 1822, traces of which are still visible on the Adoration of the Lamb, was restored in 1825, 1829 and 1859.

In 1861 the Adam and Eve panels were purchased by the Belgian Government and assigned to the Musée des Beaux-Arts in Brussels.

The wings in the possession of the Berlin Museum were sawn apart about 1900.

In accordance with the treaty of Versailles (1919) the wings then belonging to the Prussian State were ceded to Belgium. The whole altar-piece was once more installed in the chapel in St. Bavon. Its effect is there seriously impaired by the baroque marble facing, which makes the interior of the chapel too narrow for the work. On 11th April, 1934 the wing-panel of the Just Judges, together with the sawn-off back (St. John the Baptist), was stolen. The thief deposited the back at a public depot, sent in his receipt in order to prove that he was in possession of the front, and demanded a ransom. The back was recovered at the indicated place, but the authorities refused to pay the ransom. The front has never been found, a modern copy being substituted for it in St. Bavon.

In 1936-37 the Adam and Eve panels were cleaned by J. van der Veken. During the 1939-45 war the altar-piece was removed. The Belgian government brought it to France. From there the German authorities took it away in 1942 and sheltered it in 1944 in the Aussee salt mines in Austria.

In 1951 the four centre pictures (Adoration of the Lamb, God the Father, St. Mary, St. John) were freed of yellowed varnish and of some over-paintings; the cleaning and the restoring were done with great skill by M. Albert Philippot.

Earliest Mentions of the Altar-piece

1495—Hieronymus Münzer, *Itinerarium et peregrinatio . . . .* (copy in the Staatsbibliothek at Munich, CLM 631, published by Voll, *Die Werke des Jan van Eyck*, Strassburg 1900).

1517—Antonio de Beatis (*cf.* L. Pastor, *Die Reise des Kardinals Luigi d'Aragona . . .* Freiburg im Breisgau 1905).

1521—Albrecht Dürer, in the diary of his journey to the Netherlands.

1559—Lucas de Heere, *Den hof ende Boemgart der Poesien* Ghent 1565.

1567—Luigi Guicciardini, *Descrizione di tutti i paesi bassi . . . .* Antwerp 1567.

1568—Marcus van Vaernewijk, *Spieghel der Nederlandscher Audtheyt*, Ghent 1568.

1604—Karel van Mander, *Het leven der . . . . Nederlandtsche Schildern*, Haarlem 1604.

Recent Literature

A complete bibliography of the Altar-piece will be found in: P. Coremans and A. Janssens de Bisthoven, *Van Eyck, L'Adoration de l'Agneau mystique*, Antwerp 1948.

1. *Iconography, etc.*

Can. van der Gheyn, *L'Interprétation du Retable de Saint Bavon à Gand* (Brussels 1920).
L. Clysters, *Kunst en Mystiek, de aanbidding van het lam* (Tongerloo 1935).
Hulin de Loo, Le sujet du retable des frères van Eyck à Gand: La glorification du Sauveur (Annuaire des Musées Royaux des Beaux-Arts de Belgique 1940-41).
L. Aerts, *De Aaanbidding van het lam Gods*, Diest 1943.

2. *Design and Execution*

Dvořák (*Jahrbuch d. kunsth. Sammlungen*, XXIV, Vienna 1904) attributes to Hubert van Eyck: God the Father, The Virgin, St. John and, in the Adoration of the Lamb, the foremost plane and the centre of the picture (with the exception of a few angels).
Voll (*Altniederländische Malerei*, 1906) declared himself unable to find anything pointing to the participation of two artists.
Weale (p. 56): 'The only portions of the altar-piece entirely due to John are both sides of the shutters on the face of which Adam and Eve are represented.'
Heidrich (*Altniederländische Malerei*, 1910): Not by Jan: God the Father, the Virgin, St. John, the Adoration of the Lamb. 'Begun by Hubert' and 'completed or worked over by Jan?': the choirs of angels and the Annunciation.
Friedländer (I, p. 85): thinks it nearly impossible to differentiate clearly the hands of the two artists.
Winkler (*Altniederländische Malerei*, 1924): The altar-piece, as we see it today, must be held to be the work of Jan.
Beenken (*Wallraf-Richartz Jahrbuch*, 1933-34). Executed by Hubert: in the Adoration of the Lamb, the upper part with the landscape, the Holy Bishops and Confessors and the Holy Maidens; in the wing-panels, the landscape backgrounds.
Panofsky (*The Art Bulletin*, XVII, 1935) follows Dvořák as regards the parts of the Adoration of the Lamb to be assigned to each of the two masters, and Beenken in his hypothesis that Hubert planned a work consisting of the lower row only. 'Hubert may be responsible for the basic composition of the wings'. Panofsky suggested a separate retable ('almost entirely completed by Hubert'), with God the Father, the Virgin and St. John; supposing that the two panels of angels (which may originally have been wings of an organ) were begun by Hubert and finished by Jan. To Jan Panofsky assigns Adam and Eve and the outside.
Tolnay (p. 22): 'toute la partie centrale, en haut comme en bas . . . . exécutée par Hubert van Eyck'.
Friedländer (XIV, p. 77) would like to consider the hypothesis that the 'elder brother' painted . . . the predella[1] . . . which was painted in water-colours. According to Friedländer, L. de Heere says that Hubert began this work, 'as was his custom'. The author thinks it permissible to interpret this . . . statement[2] as meaning: 'Hubert began the work in the usual, traditional tempera technique'. On the basis of this interpretation one may assume that he was the author of the predella.
Hulin de Loo (*Annuaire des Musées Royaux des Beaux-Arts de Belgique*, 1940-41). Inside: by Hubert, the centre portion of the picture and the design for the angels singing and making music; the whole of the outside, by Jan.
L. van Puyvelde (*L'Agneau Mystique*, 1946): 'Les panneaux des Anges et de l'Annonciation sont traités d'une manière plus rapide et même superficielle en comparaison des autres. Ceci

---

[1] 'Door Joannes van Eyck van waterwerwe gheschildert' (van Vaernewijk, 1568). If the chronicler speaks of water-colours which bad painters spoilt ('uut gevaecht') by washing, it is more likely that he is speaking of the very easily destroyed water-colour technique on linen which was then very much in vogue, and not of the solid tempera technique on oak of Jan van Eyck's predecessors, which he would hardly have known.
[2] Only van Vaernewijk speaks of the predella and its technique. It is not mentioned in L. de Heere's work or anywhere else.

contredit des nombreux érudits, qui attribuent précisément ces panneaux à Jan van Eyck, le réaliste minutieux . . . . En présence de ces dissimilitudes nous restons circonspect et nous n'oserions préciser ce qui fut la part de Jean et ce qui fut celle d'Hubert van Eyck'.
F. J. Mather jnr. (*Gazette des Beaux-Arts*, 1946, I, p. 269 ff.; II, p. 75 ff.): 'In the five panels of the lower order of the open altar-piece . . . nothing that conforms to Jan's style. Adam, the singing Angels, Isabella Borluut by Jan van Eyck; Eve, the playing Angels, Jodocus Vyd attributed to Hubert', etc. etc.
Th. Musper (*Untersuchungen zu Rogier van der Weyden und Jan van Eyck*, n.d.): 'Ein nicht ganz einheitliches Werk Jans'.
E. Schenk (*Zeitschrift für Kunstgeschichte* III, 1949, p. 15 f.): The exterior designed and executed by Jan. As to the interior Jan created the lower wings and completed the Adoration of the Lamb as early as during his Dutch period (*i.e.* before 1425!), whereas in the upper row only Adam and Eve are his work, painted shortly before the installation.
E. Renders (*Jean van Eyck et le polyptyque*, Bruxelles 1950): Jean van Eyck seul a reçu de Jean de Bavière la commande du retable de l'Adoration de l'Agneau . . . Il reçut également des commandes d'autres retables non achevés. Jean offrit à Philippe le retable de l'Adoration de l'Agneau, composé de cinq panneaux, mais celui-ci ne pouvait lui convenir parce que les personnages de marque qui figurent à cheval sur un des panneaux du retable représentent des dignitaires étrangers à sa cour. Plus tard, Jean van Eyck trouve acquéteur du retable de l'Adoration et de sept panneaux disparates. C'était Josse Vydt, qui voulut en faire un ensemble éblouissant. Pour réaliser cette pièce montée, il fallait évidemment des aménagements . . . Tout l'intérieur du polyptyque a été peint en Hollande, avant le départ de Jean pour Bruges en 1425 . . . l'extérieur a été peint à Bruges après 1430 par ordre de Josse Vydt.
L. Baldass (*The Art Quarterly*, Detroit, 1950: The basic theory of Chapter III of this book, *i.e.* the attempt to clarify the shares of the brothers in both design and execution, has there been expounded. Only so far as the execution is concerned, some points had to be revised in Hubert's favour, as I had the opportunity to see all the pictures from near at hand in Brussels in May 1951.

*   *   *

The Share of the Brothers

A. *The Design:*

1. By Hubert:

The Adoration of the Lamb. The composition is perfectly homogeneous. For the sake of a closed arrangement each of the two groups of standing figures in the foreground is placed so near the group of kneeling worshippers in front of it as to produce the optical impression of one block on either side of the well. The density of the blocks gives to the whole picture a static effect.
God the Father, St. Mary and St. John.
The Angels singing and making music (without details).
The Annunciation on the reverse (the figures and the spatial image of the main room).

2. By Jan:

(*a*) Additions to Hubert's design:
The distant landscapes in the background of the Adoration of the Lamb (Plate 17, Fig. 49), the sceptre of God the Father (Plate 69), the music-desk and other details of the Angel's panels (Plates 72—79), the side rooms and the town views in the Annunciation pictures (Plates 92—95).

(*b*) His own designs:
Interior: the Warriors of Christ, the Just Judges, the Holy Hermits, the Holy Pilgrims, Adam, Eve, the Sacrifice of Cain and Abel, Cain slaying Abel.
Exterior: the two St. Johns, the donors, the Prophets, the Sibyls.

B. The Execution:

1. By Hubert:

The Adoration of the Lamb. The work must have been in an advanced state of execution when Jan undertook to complete it. It is obvious that Hubert must have executed the altar of the Lamb, the surrounding angels, the well, the kneeling apostles and prophets (Plates 16, 20, 21, 24, 26, 27). The essential parts of the two groups in the second plane with the Holy Bishops and Confessors (Plates 17, 18) and the Holy Maidens (Plate 22) and parts of the group of the Holy Martyrs on the right-hand side of the foreground (Plate 23) also seem to have been painted by him. Probably his work also are the turf (Plate 36), the clusters of bushes on the left (Plate 17, *cf.* Plate 7), and the town views, especially those on the right near the upper edge (Plates 40, 41).

God the Father, St. Mary and St. John. Besides the overpainted parts, most of the execution must be due to Hubert. The details are obviously more conventional and devoid of Jan's verve.

The singing Angels. The three heads in the second line (Plate 74) are less marked in colour as well as in expression than those in the first line. It seems probable that here Hubert has done more of the execution, or that Jan has made fewer alterations.

2. By Jan:

The Adoration of the Lamb. After Hubert's design, Jan painted large portions of the Holy Patriarchs (Plate 19), several of the heads of the Holy Martyrs and also the foremost of the Holy Maidens (Plate 25). The execution of the flowers above the heads of the Holy Martyrs (Plate 37) and of the landscape on the right near the upper edge (Plate 42) seems to be by his hand.

God the Father, St. Mary and St. John. Here, as in the Adoration of the Lamb, Jan's activity was mostly confined to applying many assimilating glazes, serving to create a homogeneous effect.

The Angels. Most of the execution seems to be by Jan.

The Annunciation. Only Jan's execution can be discerned.

Dated 1432.
Cf. Chapter III, p. 34–49.
Plate 14–103. Figs. 35–49.

II. THE WORKS OF HUBERT VAN EYCK[1]

2

THE THREE MARIES AT THE SEPULCHRE

Left wing of a diptych or central panel of a polyptych (*cf.* p. 24). Vierhouten, D. G. van Beuningen collection.
According to Weale, the picture was formerly in the following collections: Jacob Wynckelman (auctioned at Bruges in 1770) Bauwens (auctioned in 1826); Middleton (auctioned in London in 1872); J. C. Robinson; Sir Francis, Sir Frederick, Sir Herbert Cook (Richmond).
Wood. Height 28¼ inches (71.5 cm), width 35 inches (89 cm). In the right bottom corner, the coat of arms (added later) of Philippe de Comines, surrounded by the chain of the Order of St. Michael, founded in 1469 by Louis XI of France.
Since the last sale, the picture has been freed from overpainting and its authenticity now seems to me to be beyond all doubt.

Weale (p. 201) claims to have been the first to attribute it to Hubert.
Hulin de Loo, in *Catalogue critique* of the 1902 Bruges exhibition: Hubert van Eyck.
Heidrich (*Altniederl. Malerei*, 1910, p. 266): Jan(?) van Eyck.
Weale and Brockwell (*The van Eycks*, 1912): 'by Hubert, but left uncompleted'.
Friedländer (I, p. 77): in the early van Eyck style.
Panofsky (*The Art Bulletin*, 1935): by Hubert van Eyck, or else a replica.
Beenken: By Hubert van Eyck.
Tolnay: 'D'après Hubert van Eyck'.
Baldass (*The Art Quarterly*, 1950): By Hubert van Eyck (with reasons for this attribution).

Painted hardly before 1420, but before the design for the Adoration of the Lamb.
Plate 1 shows the picture before it was cleaned.
Fig. 22, Plates 2–6 show it after cleaning.
Cf. p. 23–24.

3

* THE ANNUNCIATION

New York, Metropolitan Museum of Art.
Formerly in the collections of the Prince de Charleroi, Duke of Bourgogne; Parent, Paris; Countess O'Gorman, Paris;

Philip Lehman, New York; Colonel M. Friedsam, New York.
Wood. Height 30½ inches (77.5 cm), width 25⅝ inches (66.4 cm). Inscription on the steps of the church: REGINA CELI LET⟨ARE⟩.
The composition has probably been cut at the top. A letter from the Metropolitan Museum, signed Margaretta M. Salinger and dated 9th March 1950, says: 'Before it came here, the painting had been mounted on a thin panel, apparently of mahogany, and the back of this extra panel had been cradled. All four edges have been concealed by added strips, made, at the top and bottom, of mahogany, and at the sides, of oak. There is a fairly good indication that the right edge is original, because a ridge of gesso at that side suggests that this edge always ran into a moulding at that point'. According to this, only the right edge is original, but from the composition it can be deduced that any cuts below and on the left can only have been trifling.
Panofsky (*The Art Bulletin*, 1935): Hubert van Eyck (after an exhaustive stylistic comparison with the Three Maries at the Sepulchre (Plate 1) and with the Adoration of the Lamb, and not, as M. J. Friedländer (XIV, p. 77) maintains, 'after considering it from the point of view of Hubert's method of construction', which Panofsky 'could only have deduced from the upper row of the Ghent altar-piece'.
Beenken (*The Art Bulletin*, 1937, p. 222 ff.): Petrus Christus, probably after a design by Hubert van Eyck.
Tolnay considers the authorship doubtful and detects the influence of Robert Campin.
Friedländer (XIV): Petrus Christus. The composition being extremely archaic, Petrus Christus may have copied an original dating from some time before.[2]
Harry B. Wehle and Margaretta Salinger (*A Catalogue of Early Flemish Paintings*, Metropolitan Museum 1947): '... early Jan van Eyck, perhaps in collaboration with helpers'.
Baldass (*The Art Quarterly*, 1950, Note 31): The Composition undoubtedly by Hubert van Eyck.

The picture is stylistically more advanced than No. 2, but of earlier design than the Adoration of the Lamb.
Plates 7, 8.
Cf. p. 24–25.

---

[1] See also No. 60, Durrieu XIII and p. 32, note 1.
[2] No other examples of Petrus Christus making direct copies are known; his Madonna pictures in New York and Berlin are free renderings of compositions by Jan van Eyck, the Madonna by the Fountain and the Madonna with a Carthusian.

III. THE WORKS OF JAN VAN EYCK

A. *RELIGIOUS PICTURES*

4

THE VIRGIN IN THE CHURCH

Berlin, Kaiser Friedrich Museum.
Acquired in 1874, together with the Suermondt Collection (Aachen).
Wood. Semicircular top. Height 12½ inches (32 cm), width 5½ inches (14 cm).
According to Burger (*Gazette des Beaux-Arts*, 1869, II, p. 12) identical with the picture then belonging to the architect Nau at Nantes, described by L. de Laborde (*Les Ducs de Bourgogne*, Paris 1849–51, and *La Renaissance des Arts à la Cour de France*, I, 1855) as being in the possession of F. Cacault. Laborde says that it measured 43 × 25 cm (which, if we assume that the frame was 5.5 cm wide, would correspond to the present measurements).
According to the Berlin Catalogue, the frame bore the inscriptions: MATER HEC EST FILIA PATER HI⟨C⟩ EST NATVS QVIS AVDIVIT TALIA DEVS HOMO NATVS and FLOS FLORIOLORVM APPELLARIS. According to the same Catalogue the frame was lost on the occasion of a theft of the picture.
In the left lateral niche of the rood-screen is an altar with a statuette of the Virgin.
In the left-hand gable of the rood screen is a relief of the Annunciation; in the centre gable, one of the Coronation of the Virgin.
Above the rood-screen is a Crucified Christ with the Virgin and St. John (only small portions of the Apostle are visible). Copies, each as the left half of a diptych (*cf.* p. 26, note 2), in the Antwerp Museum (dated 1499) and—enlarged at the right edge—in the Galleria Doria in Rome (from the beginning of the sixteenth century, ascribed by Friedländer to Jan Gossaert).

Heidrich (*Altniederländische Malerei*, 1910, Fig. 11): By Hubert?
Hulin de Loo (*Heures de Milan*, 1911): By Hubert.
M. J. Friedländer, I: 'In the early van Eyck style'.
Panofsky (*The Art Bulletin*, 1935, p. 408, Note)72: 'About 1430'.
Tolnay: By Jan van Eyck, 'antérieur à ses travaux de Gand'.
Beenken: By Jan van Eyck, about 1420–25.

Painted about 1425.
Plate 10, Fig. 28.
Cf. p. 26–29.

5

** ST. JEROME IN HIS STUDY

Detroit, Institute of Arts.
According to M. J. Friedlaender, formerly in the possession of a noble family in North Germany.
Wood. Height 8 inches (20 cm); width 5 inches (13 cm).
On the wall to the right of the chair, Richardson (*Flemish Paintings of the fifteenth and sixteenth centuries*, The Detroit Institute of Arts, 1936) and Valentiner (*Masterpieces of Art*, New York World's Fair, 1939) deciphered the date 1442 in very small figures (*cf.* p. 98, note 6).
Facius (1456) mentions having seen in the collection of King Alfonso of Naples (*cf.* No. 52) a wing picture of St. Jerome in his study by Jan van Eyck. Vasari mentions a St. Jerome by Jan van Eyck belonging to Lorenzo de' Medici (No. 56). This picture is described in the 1492 inventory as follows: 'Una tavoletta di Fiandra suvi uno San Girolamo a studio chon un armarietto di piu libri propettiva e uno lione a piede, opressa di maestro Giovanni di Brugia, cholorita a olio, in una guaina, f. 30'. According to Guicciardini (1567) Lorenzo's pictures by the master were among those sent by van Eyck to the King of Naples, the Duke of Urbino and other Italian princes.
There is no direct connection between this picture and the painting by Colantonio showing St. Jerome in his study extracting a thorn from the lion's paw (Naples, Museum). Ghirlandaio, as M. J. Friedländer was the first to note, probably borrowed from this composition for his 1480 fresco in the church of the Ognissanti at Florence.
The composition was used in a modified form for a miniature (one of those destroyed by fire) of St. Thomas Aquinas in the 'Heures de Turin' (*cf.* Cat. No. 60, Durrieu XL).

M. J. Friedländer (*Kunstwanderer*, May 1927, p. 297): by Petrus Christus.
W. R. Valentiner (*Bulletin of the Detroit Institute of Art*, March 1925, pp. 58–59)
F. Winkler (*Festschrift für M. J. Friedländer*, 1927, p. 94 ff.): by Petrus Christus after Jan van Eyck, with alterations. He compares it with MS. Fr.166, Paris, B.N. (Fig. 24), without establishing any connection.
Baldass (Belvedere, 1927, p. 82): 'Besides the supposition that Petrus Christus in this case copied a work by Jan van Eyck, and in doing so surpassed by far the execution of all his other works, it seems worth while considering whether this is not an early work by Jan himself, created before he began work on the Ghent altar-piece'.
Tolnay: a copy by Petrus Christus after Jan van Eyck.
Baldass (*The Art Quarterly*, 1950): 'An early composition by Jan van Eyck'.

The design of the picture must date from about 1425.
Plate 9, Fig. 25.
Cf. p. 25–26.

6

* ST. FRANCIS RECEIVING THE STIGMATA

Philadelphia, Pennsylvania Museum of Art, John G. Johnson Collection. Formerly in the collection of Lord Heytesbury (according to Weale, purchased at Lisbon about 1830).
Wood. Height 4⅞ inches (12·5 cm), width 5¾ inches (14·5 cm). Before the restoration by Roger Fry, the picture was larger (6 5/16 × 8¼ inches).
Weale (p. 130) mentions a will made on 10th February 1470 by Anselm Adornes, lord of Corthuy, Ronsele and Ghendbrugge and afterwards burgomaster of Bruges, who was born in Bruges of a family of Genoese origin. In his will he left to each of his two daughters, who had entered two different convents as nuns, a little picture—'Sinte Franssen in portrature van meester Jans handt van Heyck'—stipulating that the portraits of himself and his wife should be carefully painted on the wings. Whether Jan van Eyck painted two pictures of St. Francis—the will does not state whether the compositions were identical—is a question that must remain unanswered. In any case, the larger version in Turin (Fig. 30; height 28 cm, width 33 cm), the authenticity of which has already been doubted by Kämmerer (p. 108) and by Weale, is an old copy (*cf.* p. 29).
Pointing out that both monks are wearing not the original grey habit of the Franciscans, who for this reason were known in the Netherlands as the Grey Friars, but the brown habit of

the reformed Franciscans, whose first convent in the Nether-lands was not founded until the end of the fifteenth century,[1] Weale concluded that the painting must have been executed in Southern Europe. As to the style, it seems quite possible that it may have been executed during Jan's journey to Portugal.

M. J. Friedländer (I): About 1438 ('the steep and harsh lines of the folds are drawn in a way reminiscent of the Rothschild Madonna, especially of the robe of St. Barbara in that picture').
Tolnay: 'Les formes nettes et cristallisées de cette composition révèlent la maîtrise des dernières années' (about 1438–39).
Beenken: 'Jan's earlier period' (before the Ghent altar-piece).
Baldass (*The Art Quarterly*, 1950): 'In the photograph only the singularly graphic, that is to say unpainterlike, treatment of the clouds seems strange'.

Before 1430.
Plate 13.
Cf. p. 29–30.

7

THE MADONNA IN HER CHAMBER

Melbourne (Australia), National Gallery of Victoria.
Formerly in the Weld-Blundell Collection, Ince Hall, where it was seen in 1854 by Waagen and mentioned in 1857 by Crowe and Cavalcaselle. On the back, according to Weale, there is a contemporary note, saying, that the panel was pledged in Italy on the 2nd July, 1619.
Wood. Height 10⅜ inches (26·4 cm); width, 7⅝ inches (19·4 cm).
On the wall at the back, on the left above the signature: COPLETV ANO D MCCCCXXXIIJ P JOHEM DE EYC BRVGIS; on the right, the motto: AΛC IXH XAN.

Tschudi (*Repertorium für Kunstwissenschaft*, XVI, 101) points out that the signature was probably copied from the original frame.
Voll (*Altniederländische Malerei*, 1906): The inscription, crudely inserted in the picture itself, is recognizably not genuine.
Friedländer (*Repertorium für Kunstwissenschaft*, XXIX, p. 574): Inscription copied from the original frame.
Friedländer (I, p. 53 f.) cites a statement by the restorer (G. F. Zink, 1922), according to which the signature proved to be con-temporary with the whole, and refers to a copy, bearing the same inscription in the same position. According to Weale this copy was found in Sicily and transferred to the collection of the heirs of the Duke of Verdura in Rome.
Winkler (*Pantheon*, 1931, p. 258) claims that the amplified copy, with altered details, in the Collegiata at Covarrubbias, near Burgos (published by S. Reinach, *Burlington Magazine*, 43, 1923, p. 15) is derived from a lost second version by Jan van Eyck.

Dated 1433.
Plate 104, Fig. 52.
Cf. p. 51–52.

8

TRIPTYCH

The Virgin and the Child in the Church, with St. Michael, the (secular) donor and St. Catherine.
On the backs of the wings, the Annunciation, in grisaille.
Dresden, Gemälde Galerie (since 1765).
Wood. Height 10½ inches (27.5 cm); width: centre panel 8¾ inches (21.5 cm); wings 3¼ inches (8 cm).
On the scroll of the Child, the inscription: Discite a me qvia mitis sum et hvmilis corde (St. Matthew, xi, 29).
On the throne are two bronze figures, Abraham's Sacrifice and David and Goliath, with a pelican and a phoenix beneath. The meaning of the figures on the capital in the left wing-picture has not yet been discovered.

On the original frame of the centre panel the inscription:
HEC EST SPECIOSOR SOLE + SUP⟨ER⟩ O⟨MN⟩EM STELLARV⟨M⟩ DISPOSICIONE⟨M⟩ LVCI COMPA⟨RA⟩TA I⟨N⟩VE⟨N⟩IT⟨VR⟩ PRIOR: CA⟨N⟩DOR E⟨ST⟩ ENI⟨M⟩ LVC⟨I⟩S ETERNE + SPEC⟨V⟩L⟨V⟩M S⟨INE⟩ MACVLA DEI MAIESTATIS EGO QVASI VITIS FRVCTI-FICAVI SVAVITATE⟨M⟩ ODORIS: E⟨T⟩ FLORES MEI F⟨RV⟩CTVS HONORIS + HONESTATIS EGO M⟨ATE⟩R PVLCHRE DIL⟨E⟩C-⟨TI⟩O⟨N⟩IS + TIMORIS + MAGNITVDINIS + S⟨AN⟩C⟨T⟩E SPEI.
On the original frame of the right wing the inscription:
HIC EST ARCHANGELVS PRINCEPS MILICIE ANGELORVM CVIVS HONOR PRESTAT BENEFICA P⟨O⟩P⟨V⟩LORV⟨M⟩ E⟨T⟩ OR⟨ACI⟩O P⟨ER⟩DVCIT AD REGNA CELORV⟨M⟩ HI⟨C⟩ ARCHANGELVS MICHAEL DEI NVNCI⟨V⟩S DE A⟨N⟩I⟨M⟩AB⟨V⟩S IVSTIS, GRA⟨CIA⟩ DEI ILLE VICTOR IN CELIS RESEDIT A PACIS.
On the original frame of the left wing the inscription:
VIRGO PRVDENS ANELAVIT AD SEDEM SIDEREA⟨M⟩ VBI LOCVM P⟨RE⟩P⟨ARA⟩VIT, LINQVENS ORBIS AREAM GRANVM SIBI RES-ERVAVIT VENTILA⟨N⟩DO PALEA⟨M⟩, DISCIPLINIS EST IMBVTA PVELLA CELESTIB⟨V⟩S NVDA NVDV⟨M⟩ E⟨ST⟩ SECѵTA CERTIS X⟨CHRISTI⟩ PASSIB⟨V⟩S DV⟨M⟩ MV⟨N⟩DA⟨N⟩IS E⟨ST⟩ EXVTA.
Here on the frame at the top on the right is a coat of arms, which Woerman, in the 1908 Dresden Catalogue, and Weale explain as being that of the Genoese family of the Giustiniani.
C. Benoit (*Chronique des Arts*, 1899, p. 152) identifies this little altar-piece as No. 266 of the inventory, dated 17 July 1696, of the Everard Jabach collection in Paris, in which it is attributed to Hubert van Eyck.
Kämmerer (p. 78): Very closely akin to the St. Barbara of 1437.
Friedländer (I, p. 101): Between 1434 and 1436.
Tolnay: About 1433 (shortly before the Melbourne Madonna).
Beenken: About 1427–1430.

Between 1430 and 1434.
Plates 105–107, Figs. 53, 55.
Cf. p. 52–53.

9

* THE ANNUNCIATION

Probably the left wing of an altar-piece.
Washington, National Gallery of Art (Mellon Collection).
From the Hermitage at Leningrad.
Formerly in the collection of King William II of the Nether-lands († 1850); said to have been found in 1819 in a church at Dijon.
Transferred from wood to canvas. Height 36¾ inches (93 cm); width 14½ inches (37 cm).
Inscription close to the Angel's mouth: AVE GR⟨ATI⟩A PLENA; close to the Virgin's mouth (upside-down): ECCE ANCILLA DNI.
On the floor are medallions showing signs of the Zodiac (Gemini, Cancer, Leo, Scorpio, Sagittarius) between com-partments showing Samson slaying the Philistines with the jawbone of an ass, Samson and Delilah: DALIDA VXOR S, Samson pulling down the pillars of the temple of Dagon: SAMSON MVLTAS GENTES I⟨N⟩TERFECIT I⟨N⟩ ⟨CON⟩VIVIO, David slaying Goliath, with Saul and his warriors looking on from the tent: DAVID.
In the spandrels between the pointed arches of the rear wall are medallions showing Isaac and Jacob.
In the glass window, Christ with the sceptre and an open book, standing upon the orb: on the latter, ASIA. Above, two angels.
On either side of the window a mural painting—on the left, the Finding of Moses: PHARAONIS PHILIA F⟨I⟩SCELLA MOYSES; on the right, Moses (MOYSES) receiving the tablets of the Law, on which is inscribed the second commandment: NON ASSVMES NOMEN DOMINI DEI TVI IN VANVM.

Voll (*Altniederländische Malerei*, 1906): about 1426.
Heidrich (*Altniederländische Malerei*, 1910, p. 266): relatively early.
Friedländer (I. p. 104): about 1434.

---

[1] In the Turin picture, St. Francis is wearing a brown and his com-panion a grey habit.

Panofsky (*The Art Bulletin*, 1935, p. 473): A few years before the Ghent Annunciation; (*ibid.*, p. 418, Note 72): Around 1425–6.
Tolnay: About 1433.
Beenken: About 1436–37.

About 1432–35.
Plates 113–115.
Cf. p. 54–55.

IO

THE MADONNA AND CHANCELLOR ROLIN

Paris, Louvre.
(Removed from the Cathedral of Autun in 1800.)
As the picture is mentioned in 1778 as being in the sacristy of Notre-Dame at Autun (*cf.* p. 56, note 2) and as Rolin came from Autun and his son Jean was Bishop of Autun in 1436, the assumption that the picture was donated by the Chancellor or his son to that church cannot be disregarded.[1] The town shown in the picture has been identified, but not convincingly, as Maastricht, Liége, Utrecht, Lyons, Geneva and Autun (on this point, see Trimmer, *Oud Holland*, LXI, 1946, p. 5 ff.).
Wood. Height 26 inches (66 cm); width 24½ inches (62 cm). Thick, brown-coloured varnish.
Inscription on the Virgin's mantle: EXALTATA SVM IN LIBANO.
On the capitals of the pillars on the left: Expulsion of Adam and Eve from Paradise; Sacrifice of Cain and Abel; the Drunkenness of Noah.
Nicolas Rolin, 'venu de petit lieu', born 1376 at Autun, was Chancellor to Duke Philip the Good from 3rd Dec. 1422, died 18th Jan. 1462 at Autun (*cf.* Abord, *Nicolas Rolin, chancelier de Bourgogne au siècle*, Dijon 1898).
Kämmerer (1898, p. 91): About 1437.
Voll (*Altniederländische Malerei*, 1906): About 1425.
Weale (1908, p. 99): Before 1430.
Friedländer (I, p. 96): More likely after than before the Van der Paele Madonna.
Tolnay: Between the Washington Annunciation and the Van der Paele Madonna.
Beenken: About 1435.

About 1434–35.
Plates 116–119; Frontispiece.
Cf. p. 55–57.

II

THE ANNUNCIATION

Lugano-Castagnola (Villa Favorita), Schloss Rohoncz Foundation (Baron Thyssen).
Wood. Each wing 15½ inches (39 cm) high; 9½ inches (24 cm) wide. In grisaille. Very well preserved.
Inscribed on the frame above the angel: AVE GRA⟨TIA⟩PLENA D⟨OMI⟩N⟨V⟩S TECV⟨M⟩ B⟨E⟩N⟨E⟩D⟨I⟩C⟨T⟩A TV I⟨N⟩ MVLIE…,
and above the Virgin: ECCE ANCILLA DOMINI FIAT MIHI S⟨E⟩C⟨VN⟩D⟨V⟩M V⟨ER⟩BV⟨M⟩ TV⟨VM⟩.
Introduced into the literature by M. J. Friedländer (*Burlington Magazine*, LXV, 1934, p. 3) as the outside of a lost triptych dating from the time between the Ghent altar-piece and the Antwerp Madonna. According to the 1949 catalogue of the Schloss Rohoncz collection, the pictures are not the outer wings of an altar-piece, but, as the treatment of the backs (chalk ground with marbling) reveals, a self-contained work, which probably served as 'aufklappbarer Hausaltar' (a folding altar-piece meant for devotion in the home).

[1] It would explain why the influence of this most important among the paintings of the Madonna by Jan van Eyck can be discerned on two occasions only, namely in the adoption of certain landscape motives in the Rothschild Madonna (Cat. No. 18) and of the whole scheme of composition in the Madonna with St. Luke by Rogier van der Weyden, who subsequently painted the Beaune altar-piece for the Chancellor Rolin.

Sulzberger (*Revue Belge d'Archéologie et d'Histoire de l'Art*, XIX, 1950, p. 67)

About 1434–36.
Plate 112.
Cf. p. 59.

12

THE MADONNA IN HER CHAMBER

Frankfurt, Städelsches Kunstinstitut.
Formerly in the collections of the Duke of Lucca, the art-dealer Nieuenhuijs (1841–42) and King William II of the Netherlands (†1850).
Wood. Height 25¼ inches (65·5 cm); width 19½ inches (49.5 cm)
On the throne, the lions of the throne of Solomon.
Weizsäcker (*Catalog der Gemälde des Städelschen Kunstinstituts*, 1900): probably dates from the years 1435–40.
Friedländer (I, p. 97): About 1437.
Tolnay: About 1436–37.
Beenken: About 1438.

About 1435–36.
Plate 126.
Cf. p. 57.

13
THE MADONNA
WITH CANON VAN DER PAELE

Bruges, Musée des Beaux-Arts.
(Formerly in the church of St. Donatian at Bruges.)
Wood. Height 48 inches (122 cm); width 61¾ inches (157 cm).
Restored in 1934 by Joseph van der Veken (*cf.* L. van Puyvelde, *Pantheon*, XIII, 1934, p. 175).
Signed and dated on the lower edge of the original frame: Hoc op⟨us⟩ fecit fieri mag⟨iste⟩r georgi⟨u⟩s de pala hui⟨u⟩s ecclesi⟨a⟩e canoni⟨cu⟩s p⟨er⟩ iohanne⟨m⟩ de eyck pictore⟨m⟩: et fundavit hic duas capell⟨an⟩ias de gremio chori domini m°cccc°rxriiij; c⟨om⟩p⟨le⟩t⟨um⟩ an⟨no⟩ 1436.
In the corners of the frame are the arms of Canon van der Paele and of the Carlijns family (to which, according to Weale, the Canon's mother belonged).
On the top edge of the frame: HEC EST SPECIOSIOR SOLE SVPER OMNEM STELLARVM DISPOSICIONEM LVCI COMPARATA INVENITVR PRIOR CANDOR EST ENIM LVCIS ETERNE + SPE-CVLVM SINE MACVLA DEI MAIESTATIS.
On the left edge of the frame; SOLO P⟨AR⟩TV NON⟨V⟩S FR⟨ATRV⟩M MERS⟨VS⟩ VIV⟨VS⟩ REDDIT⟨VR⟩ ET RENAT⟨VS⟩ ARCHOS P⟨AT⟩R⟨V⟩M REMIS CONSTITVITVR QVI NV⟨N⟩C DEO FRVITVR.
On the right edge of the frame: NATVS CAPADOCIA XPO MILITAVIT MVNDI FVGIE⟨N⟩S OCIA CESVS TRIVMPHAVIT HIC DRACONEM STRAVIT.
On the chamfer of the frame: SCS DONATIANS ARCHIEP⟨ISCO-PV⟩S and SCS GEORGIVS MILES XPI.
On St. George's ruff: ADONAI.
On the Madonna's throne, little figures of Adam and Eve, above, the Murder of Abel and Samson slaying the lion.
Mentioned by Guicciardini (1567) as being in the church of St. Donatian at Bruges.

Completed in 1436.
Plates 120–125, Fig. 57.
Cf. p. 58, 59.

14

ST. BARBARA

Brush drawing on chalk ground, probably as a preparation for a painting. Antwerp, Musée des Beaux-Arts.
In 1769 in the possession of M. Joz. Enschedé, Haarlem, subsequently in the Ploos van Amstel, Oyen and van Ertborn collections (*cf.* S. Sulzberger, *Gazette des Beaux-Arts*, 1948, p. 289).

Wood. Height 12¾ inches (34·2 cm); width 7¼ inches (18·6 cm). The sky partially sketched in colour (at a later date).

Signed and dated on the lower edge of the frame: IOH⟨ANN⟩‑ES DE EYCK ME FECIT·1437.

Hymans (*Le Livre des Peintres de Carel van Mander*, 1884, p. 40) identifies the picture as the small painting, of which Carel van Mander gives a brief description: in the house of Lucas de Heere in Ghent, the portrait ('contrafeytselke') of a woman with a small Landscape ('een Landschapken') behind her, which was only underpainted ('ghedootverwet'), but was yet unusually attractive and smooth. Surprising though it may seem that Carel van Mander should describe the seated figure of St. Barbara as a portrait and make no mention of the tower, nevertheless the emphasis laid on the underpainted state of the picture is striking.

Against this identification: A. Sjöblom (*Die koloristische Entwicklung in der niederländischen Malerei*, Berlin 1928, p. 48). Winkler (*Pantheon*, IV, 1929, p. 493) thinks that there is hardly any justification for considering this work as unfinished. [1]

Dated 1437.
Plate 127, Fig. 59.
Cf. p. 59–61.

15
THE MADONNA BY THE FOUNTAIN

Antwerp, Musée des Beaux-Arts.
In 1830 in the possession of the vicar of Dickelvenne (East Flanders); afterwards in the van Ertborn collection.
Wood. Height 7½ inches (19 cm); width 4¾ inches (12·2 cm). Well preserved, except for slight flaking off of the colour, partly restored. Pronounced craquelé.
Signed and dated on the original frame.
Inscription at the top: A⋀C IXH XAN; below: IOH⟨ANN⟩ES DE EYCK ME FECIT C⟨OM⟩PLEVIT ANO 1439.

Probably identical with a picture mentioned in the 1516 inventory of the collection of the Archduchess Margaret: 'Une petite Notre-Dame faite de bonne main estant en un jardin ou il a une fontaine', and in the 1523 inventory of her collection: 'ung aultre petit tableau de Nostre Dame tenant son enfant lequel tient une petite patenostre de coral en sa main fort, anticque ayant une fontaine empres elle et deux anges tenant ung drapt d'or figure derriere elle'.

O. Kerber's assertion (*Hubert van Eyck*, 1937, p. 317 f.) that the date was originally 1420 and was then falsified into 1439, does not correspond with the facts.

Dated 1439.
Plate 128.
Cf. p. 61.

16
** CHRIST AS KING OF KINGS

(With light coming from the left.)
Executors of the late O. S. Swinburne.
Exhibited in 1923 at the Mauritshuis in The Hague, and in

May–June 1951 at the Hatton Gallery, King's College, Newcastle-upon-Tyne.
Wood. Height 9½ inches (24 cm); width 6¼ inches (16 cm).
On the ground at the top: A ω.
On the back, according to M. J. Friedländer, is a slip of paper (This head was pain. . . by John van Eyc . . 30 January 1440, his name and date of the year was written by himself on the frame which (my father) sawed off. T. T. West [1784]). On an old copy, not contemporary, in the Museum at Bruges (according to Weale the date 1637 on the back was written by the painter or by a previous owner), the lost original frame is copied on the surface of the picture. It bears the following inscriptions:
Below, in the fluting: SPECIOS⟨VS⟩ FORMA P FILIIS HO⟨M⟩I‑⟨NV⟩M.
On the upper plane: ·IHESVS VIA·IHS VERITAS·IHESVS VITA·
On the lower plane: A⋀C IXH XAN Johes de eyck Inventor anno 1440 30 Januarij.
Conway (*Burlington Magazine*, 1921, II, p. 253): By Jan van Eyck.
Friedländer (I, p. 116 f.): Might be an original and in any case represents the type in its purest form.

The original painted in 1440 (*cf.* No. 35).
Plate 131.
Cf. p. 61.

17
** THE MADONNA
WITH NICHOLAS VAN MAELBEKE

Paris, Private Collection.
Except for the Ghent Altar-piece this is the only work by van Eyck of which we have an apparently complete history. Mentioned as a work by Jan van Eyck in the church of St. Martin at Ypres by Lucas de Heere (1559); by Mark van Vaernewijk (1562); by Guicciardini (1567) and by Carel van Mander (1604). Described by Sanderus in 1718 as being in the choir of St. Martin's; removed between 1757 and 1760 (according to Weale) to the Bishop's palace in Ypres. Subsequently in the following Belgian collections: Wallwyn (Ypres); Bogaert-Dumortier (Bruges); v.d.Schrieck (Louvain); Schollaert; Helleputte (Kessel-Loo).
Wood. Height 67¾ inches (172 cm); width 39 inches (99 cm). semicircular top.
Underwent several restorations, especially in the sixteenth and nineteenth centuries; the latest, shortly before 1929 (*cf.* No. 14, Note 1).
On the lower hem of the mantle Weale (p. 95) read the following inscription: ANTE SECVLA CREATA SVM ET VSQVE AD FVTVRVM SECVLVM NON DESINAM ET IN HABITATIONE SANCTA CORAM IPSO MINISTRAVI ET SIC IN SION FIRMATA SVM.
On the child's scroll: Discite a me qvia mitis sum et humilis corde iugum enim meum suave est et onus meum leve.

On the frame the inscription: SANCTA MARIA SVCCVRRE MISERIS IVVA PVSILLANIMES: REFOVE FLEBILES ORA PRO POPVLO: INTERVENI PRO CLERO: INTERCEDE PRO DEVOTO FEMINEO SEXV: SENTIANT OMNES TVVM IVVAMEN QVI‑CVMQVE CELEBRANT TVAM COMMEMORATIONEM HEC VIRGO MARIA EX SEMINE ABRAHE ORTA: EX TRIBV IVDA: VIRGA DE RADICE IESSE: EX STIRPE DAVID: FILIA IHERVSALEM: STELLA MARIS: ANCILLA DOMINI: REGINA GENTIVM: SPONSA DEI: MATER CHRISTI: CONDITORIS TEMPLVM. SANCTI SPIRITVS SACRARIVM.

The wings, which are not in the van Eyck style, were not painted before 1460 and were left unfinished: Above in the spandrels, the expulsion of Adam and Eve from Paradise and the Annunciation. On the left, above: the Burning Bush rvbvs

---

[1] Winkler deduces this from the different manner of execution of the Maelbeke Madonna (No. 17), which in the course of centuries has undergone many restorations. As regards this, it should be noted that it would be necessary to see this Madonna after cleaning in order to be able to give a definite opinion as to the authenticity of the execution and the eventual participation of pupils (cf. Friedländer, *Cicerone*, 1929, p. 432 ff.). Moreover, the unfinished wings of the Maelbeke painting have nothing to do with Jan's art, but were created later. Well-preserved works by Jan, such as the Wings of the Adoration of the Lamb, the Dresden triptych and the Madonnas with Chancellor Rolin and Canon van der Paele, prove that Jan must always have prepared his pictures with similar meticulousness. As we possess no work by Jan van Eyck or any other Netherlandish painter left unfinished at the same stage of preparation as the St. Barbara, it is impossible to say why the colouring of the picture was not even begun. From the glued-on frame with the signature we may only conclude that the artist had the painted frame bearing his signature glued on to the prepared panel before he began work on the execution.

arⱱens et non combⱱrens; below: Gideon with the Angel and the Fleece ⱱcllⱱs gcⱱconis; on the right, above: Aaron before the altar with the budding rod ⱱirga aaron florens; below, The Closed Gate of the Temple porta cзccbiclis. claⱱsa. On the outsides, in grisaille: Augustus and the Tiburtian Sibyl.
Nicholas van Maelbeke was abbot of the abbey of St. Martin from 1429 to 1445.

Weale (p. 100 ff.) draws attention to the silverpoint drawing, of very high quality, in the Albertina (dating from the middle of the fifteenth century), and to another in Nuremberg, which are derived from this picture (the drawing in both cases being only partially elaborated), and points out the differences.
Friedländer (I, p. 107): The drawings give valuable hints as to the original state of the painting.
Benesch (*Albertina Catalogue*, II, 1928, No. 13): van Eyck left the picture unfinished.
Winkler (*Pantheon*, 1929, p. 490 ff.): At the time of Jan's death, the completion of the middle picture had made good progress, the wings were quite unfinished. The outsides of the wings executed about 1500.
Friedländer (*Cicerone*, 1929, p. 432 ff.): Unfinished, participation of pupils.
Steinbart (*Oud Holland*, 1929, p. 257 ff.): The whole altarpiece by Jan van Eyck.
Van Puyvelde (*Burlington Magazine*, 1930, I, p. 3): Jan van Eyck.
Wescher (*Pantheon*, XVII, 1936).
Baldass (*Die graphischen Künste*, new series, II, 1937, p. 18): An excellent, unfinished copy, executed not before the last decade of the fifteenth century, of a lost work by Jan.
Tolnay: 'Dans l'état ou se trouve le tableau, nous ne pouvons reconnaître la main de Jean van Eyck. Toute la surface visible est dans le style du milieu du XVIe siècle'.

The original about 1440.
Plate 129.
Cf. p. 61.

18

** THE MADONNA WITH SAINTS BARBARA AND ELIZABETH OF HUNGARY AND A CARTHUSIAN AS DONOR

Heirs of Baron Robert de Rothschild.
(Mentioned as being in the Rothschild Collection at Paris in 1857, by Mündler [according to Weale] and in 1872 by Crowe and Cavalcaselle.) Transferred from wood to canvas. Height 18½ inches (47 cm); width 24 inches (61 cm); widened on either side by about five-eigths of an inch (1·5 cm).
The fundamental lines of the landscape on the right (river-bank etc.) are derived from the Rolin Madonna (Plate 116). According to documents published by H. J. J. Scholtens (*Oud Holland*, 1938, p. 49 ff.), the donor is Dom. Jan Vos, from 1441 to 1450 Prior of the Carthusian monastery of Genadedael near Bruges. According to Scholtens, Vos, when he went to the Carthusian monastery at Utrecht in 1450, took the picture with him and installed it on the altar of St. Barbara in the Carthusian church at Utrecht. Scholtens also believes that the Madonna with a Carthusian by Petrus Christus (Berlin)—the picture only repeats the Madonna and the left half of the painting and shows the same Carthusian at a maturer age—must have been painted for the Carthusian monastery near Bruges to replace the picture that had been taken away. The tiny proportions of Petrus Christus' picture (7½ inches high, 5½ inches wide; 19 × 14 cm) and the altered form of the picture detract from the probability of this hypothesis.
The picture has been hypothetically identified by Weale (p. 113) with a painting of the Madonna with St. Bernard and an Angel mentioned as being by 'Rupert' van Eyck in the 1595 inventory

of the art treasures belonging to Archduke Ernest, Stadt-holder of the Netherlands. The Berlin catalogue of 1931, however, relates this notice to the above-mentioned Madonna with a Carthusian by Petrus Christus.
Kämmerer (p. 93 ff.): By Petrus Christus.
M. J. Friedländer (I, p. 99): Decline of formative power; about 1440.
Exhibition: 'De van Eyck à Bruegel', Paris 1935, No. 39.
Wescher (*Pantheon*, XVII, 1936, p. 34): Report on the condition of the picture.
Tolnay: 'Jean van Eyck aurait-il laissé ce tableau inachevé et un élève, Petrus Christus par exemple, l'aurait terminé?'
Beenken: Probably not completed until after the death of the master.

About 1440.
Plate 132.
Cf. p. 61.

B. *PAINTED PORTRAITS*

19

CARDINAL ALBERGATI

Vienna, Picture Gallery of the Kunsthistorisches Museum.
From the collection of Archduke Leopold Wilhelm, 1659.
Wood. Height 13½ inches (34.1 cm); width 10¾ inches (27.3 cm). The four corners were sawn off about 1720 and restored again before 1783. The background has been over-painted near the edges.
As the portrait is mentioned in the Archduke Leopold's inventory as: 'Ein Contrafait van Oehlfarb auf Holcz des Cardinals von Sancta Cruce, von Johann van Eyckh' (a portrait in oil colour on wood of the Cardinal of Santa Croce, by Jan van Eyck) and as a Cardinal bearing this title was Legate to the Burgundian court at the end of 1431, the identification is clear.

Niccolò Albergati was born in 1375 at Bologna; in 1426 Pope Martin V appointed him Cardinal of the titular church of the Holy Cross in Jerusalem and in 1431 he was sent as legate of the Holy See to the Kings of England and France and the Duke of Burgundy, in order to negotiate a peace between their countries. The identification was made by Weale (*Burlington Magazine*, V, 1904, pp. 190–198).
Cf. the preliminary drawing in Dresden, No. 28 (Plate 133).

Painted in 1431–32.
Plate 134, Fig. 69.
Cf. p. 69–71.

20

PORTRAIT OF 'TYMOTHEOS'

London, National Gallery (purchased in 1857 from the land-scape painter Carl Ross, Munich).
Wood. Height 13½ inches (34.3 cm); width 7½ inches (19 cm). Very yellow varnish; well preserved.
On the stone sill at the foot the dedication: LEAL SOVVENIR ('loyal souvenir'); above it the name: TYM-ⱳⱭEOC; beneath this, the signature: Actu ano ⱱni 1432, 10 ⱱic octobris a job ⱱc cⱱck.
On the back is a sign, probally the mark of a former owner.
Weale (1908, p. 63 f.).
A. Burroughs (*Art Criticism from a Laboratory*, 1938, p. 178 f.): Note on the technique by means of X-ray.
Martin Davies (*National Gallery Catalogues, Early Netherlandish School*, London 1945, p. 35): 'The sitter would not seem to be Flemish'.
G. Münzel (*Zeitschrift für Kunstgeschichte*, X, 1941–42, p. 188): interprets the inscription as a motto TYMⱳ ΘEON (I fear God).
Panofsky (*Journal of the Warburg and Courtauld Institute*, 12,

30
JOHN IV, DUKE OF BRABANT
Vierhouten, D. G. van Beuningen Collection.
Silverpoint. Height 8 inches (20·4 cm); width 5 inches
(12·8 cm).
Inscribed: Le Duc Jehan brabant.
Cf. No. 29.
Plate 148.

31
* PHILIP, DUKE OF BRABANT
Formerly in the Mannheimer Collection; destroyed by fire.
Silverpoint. Height 8 inches (20·4 cm); width 5 inches
(12·8 cm).

Inscribed: Le duc philippe de brabant.
Cf. No. 29.
Plate 149.

32
* PHILIP, COUNT OF NEVERS
Formerly in the Mannheimer Collection; destroyed by fire.
Silverpoint. Height 8 inches (20·4 cm); width 5 inches
(12·8 cm).
Inscribed: philips cont nevers.
Cf. No. 29.
Plate 150.

IV. COPIES AFTER LOST WORKS BY JAN VAN EYCK

A. *MINIATURES* [1]

33
THE AGONY IN THE GARDEN
Turin, Museo Civico.
Cf. No. 60; Hulin XXIII.

Georges H(ulin) de Loo (*Les Heures de Milan*, 1911): An early
work by Jan van Eyck.
Winkler (*Altniederländische Malerei*, 1924): Jan van Eyck.
Friedländer, I: Doubts the dating before 1416 and the artistic
value.
Tolnay: 'Style d'Hubert . . . exécuté par un élève'.
Beenken: Jan van Eyck.

Copy after a lost picture by Jan van Eyck, painted about 1430.
Plate 12, Fig. 33.
Cf. p. 30–32.

34
THE CRUCIFIXION
Turin, Museo Civico.
Cf. No. 60; Hulin XXIV (and also Durrieu XX).

Derived from the same lost original (obviously a panel-painting)
as a fifteenth-century Netherlandish copy, with slight variations, painted on wood; height 17¾ inches (45 cm), width 11¾
inches (30 cm), in the Franchetti collection (formerly in a
private collection at Padua), now at the Cà d'Oro, Venice
(Plate 11); *cf.* P. Wescher, *Pantheon*, XVII, 1936, p. 34: 'by an
artist close to Jan van Eyck'), and an unfinished copy from the
end of the fifteenth century in the Museo Civico at Padua
published by F. Schottmüller (*Jahrbuch d. preuss.Kunstsamm-
lungen*, XXIII, 1902, p. 33 ff.) and not convincingly described
as Italian; 'Niccolo di Giolfino ?' (*cf.* Bodenhausen, *Jahrbuch d.
preuss. Kunstsammlungen*, XXVI, 1905, p. 111 ff. and Weale
Brockwell, p. 187).

Literature as for No. 33 except Tolnay: 'parmi les miniatures . . .
la seule qui puisse être de Jean van Eyck'.

The lost original was painted by Jan van Eyck about 1430.
Fig. 31.
Cf. p. 30–32.

---

[1]See also Cat. No. 60, Durrieu XXV, XXIX, XLI, XXVIII.
**

B. *PAINTINGS*

35
CHRIST AS KING OF KINGS
(With light falling from the right.)
Berlin, Kaiser Friedrich Museum.
Acquired in 1821 from the Solly Collection (according to
Weale, originally came from a monastery in Burgos, later in
Segovia).
Wood. Height 17¼ inches (44 cm); width 12½ inches (32 cm).
Inscription on the hem of the mantle: REX REGUM
Above, on the ground A ω.
Below: I F (Initium, Finis).
On the old frame painted to resemble stone, above, VIA
VERITAS VITA.
Below: PRIMVS ET NOVISSIM⟨VS⟩.
Signed and dated on the chamfer of the frame: Johes de eyck
me fecit et aplevit anno 1438 31 Januarij and AME IXH XAN.
The second and third letters of the motto seem to indicate
that the copyist did not understand it and therefore substituted Latin letters of similar form for the Greek characters
of the original. The peculiar fact that the signature as well
has been copied, recurs again in the Bruges copy (*cf.* No. 16),
though in its case with the addition of the word 'inventor'.
As to style, the old copy in the Pinakothek in Munich certainly
originating from the fifteenth century (the original frame being
lost) is closer akin to Jan's art (*cf.* No. 16) than is the artistically
superior copy in Berlin.

Voll (*Altniederländische Malerei*, 1906, p. 44): Another copy in
the Pinakothek at Munich gives the most faithful reproduction
of the lost original.
Weale (1908, p. 166): 'The Munich version is the earliest and
the best copy of the lost original'.
Friedländer (I, p. 116 f.): As regards the Berlin picture, it has
been objected not without reason that van Eyck wrote the word
'als' in Greek characters.
Durrieu (*Gazette des Beaux-Arts*, 1920, p. 70): The method of
painting is all the more difficult to judge because the head is
sprinkled with retouchings.
Tolnay: After Jan van Eyck: the version in Berlin being the
best.

The lost original was painted in 1438.
Plate 130.
Cf. p. 61.

36

LADY AT HER TOILET

One of the paintings depicted by Willem van Haecht in the 'gallery picture' of the Antwerp collector Cornelis van der Geest, now in New York, van Berg Collection, formerly in the collection of Lord Huntingfield (Heveningham).
The 'gallery picture' is signed and dated 1628 (39 × 53 inches).
Reproduced in: *The Arundel Society*, No. 20, and also in *The van Berg Collection of Paintings*, New York 1947.

Weale p. 175.
M. Davies (*National Gallery Catalogues, Early Netherlandish School*, London 1945, p. 34).

The lost original was painted about 1435.
Figs. 79, 80.
Cf. p. 84–86.

C. *DRAWINGS*

37-48

THE TWELVE APOSTLES

Vienna, Albertina.
Formerly in the 'Praun Kabinet', Nuremberg; engraved in 1779 by Prestel.
Pen-drawings.
Height 8–8⅛ inches (20·3–20·6 cm); width 5⅜–5½ inches (13·6–13·9 cm).
Six of the Apostles (Peter, Paul, Andrew, James the Great, John, Thomas) are standing and six (James the Less, Philip, Bartholomew, Matthew, Simon, Judas Thaddaeus) seated.
Made after lost drawings by van Eyck, which were probably preliminary sketches for small sculptures (*e.g.*, for a shrine).
All the twelve drawings reproduced by O. Benesch, Albertina Catalogue, II, 1928, Nos. 1–12.
F. Winkler (*Jahrbuch d. preuss. Kunstsammlungen*, 37, p. 297 ff.) introduced these drawings into the van Eyck literature.
Friedländer (I, p. 126): The originals made shortly before 1430.
Winkler (*Pantheon*, 1931, p. 258) draws attention to a second, incomplete series of Apostles (Louvre and Musée Bonnat, Bayonne), which he thinks to be likewise derived from originals by Jan van Eyck.

The lost originals were probably made between 1430 and 1434.
Plates 108–111.
Cf. p. 53, 54.

49

JAEL AND SISERA

Brunswick, Herzog Anton Ulrich Museum.
Pen and brush.
Height 5¾ inches (13·6 cm); width 4 inches (10 cm).

Winkler (*Der Meister von Flemalle und Rogier van der Weyden*, Strassburg 1922, p. 3 f.): 1400–25, or not much later, copy after the Master of Flémalle.
Flechsig (*Zeichnungen alter Meister im Landesmuseum zu Braunschweig*, Prestel VII, Frankfurt am Main 1923, No. 46).
Friedländer (I, p. 127): About 1425, draughtsman very close to Jan van Eyck and Petrus Christus.
Tolnay: 'Copie d'après une composition de Robert Campin'.

Only the principal group is in the style of Jan van Eyck.
The lost original drawing may be supposed to date from about 1430–35.
Fig. 50.
Cf. p. 50, note 1.

50

MAN WITH CHAPERON

Paris, Louvre (No. 20653). Stolen in 1929.
Silverpoint.
Height 4¾ inches (12 cm); width 3¾ inches (9·5 cm).

Weale (p. 210): 'Possibly a copy of a work by Jan van Eyck'.
Friedländer (I): Can be considered an original work of Jan van Eyck.
Tolnay: 'Dessin apocryphe'.
Popham (*Drawings of the Early Flemish school*, London, 1926, No. 7): Jan van Eyck(?) perhaps the portrait of Barthélemy Alatruye (*cf.* the portrait No. 531 in Brussels, an old copy after R. Campin).

The original was made about 1432.
Plate 152.
Cf. p. 78.

51

THE FALCONER

Frankfurt am Main, Städelsches Kunstinstitut.
Silverpoint.
Height 7⅜ inches (18·8 cm); width 5⅝ inches (14·3 cm).
Attempts to identify the person represented as Henry van Eyck or William VI, Count of Holland, have no valid foundation.

Weale (p. 24): 'Henry van Eyck' "jaghermeester" at the Hague in 1425, in the service of Philip of Burgundy in 1426 and mentioned in 1433 and 1436 as "L'espriveur" and "espriveteur," died 11 November 1466'.
Weale-Brockwell (1912, p. 122): 'Drawing bearing directly on an Eyckian painting'.
Friedländer (I, p. 124): Outstanding original by Jan van Eyck about 1425.
Popham (*Drawings of the Early Flemish School*, 1926, Plate 5): By Jan van Eyck ? ('in Jan's circle not convincing').
Tolnay: 'Dessin apocryphe'.
Beenken: After van Eyck's lifetime, as it corresponds in its spatial conception to the portraits of Petrus Christus (*cf.* the portrait of Edward Grymeston).
Degenhart (*Europäische Handzeichnungen*, 1943): By a follower of Jan van Eyck.
E. Schenk (*Zeitschrift für Kunst*, 1949): Hubert van Eyck.
Winkler (*The Art Quartlery*, 1950, p. 216): 'Copy from a painting, a lost work by Rogier van der Weyden'.
O. Kurz (*Burlington Magazine*, July, 1951, p. 238): 'There seems to be no cogent reason why this splendid drawing should be a copy—"the suspicious strip at the lower edge" is the parapet frequent on Quattrocento portraits—and it is difficult to discover any relation to Rogier's style'.

Drawn by an excellent artist after a lost picture. Only the head is in Jan van Eyck's style of about 1435.
Plate 151.
Cf. p. 78, note 5.

V. LOST WORKS BY JAN VAN EYCK KNOWN ONLY FROM LITERARY REFERENCES[1]

52
ALTAR-PIECE

Centre panel: *The Annunciation*; on the wings: *St. John the Baptist; St. Jerome in his Study* (*cf.* No. 5). On the outside: The Donors: Battista Lomellino and his wife. Mentioned by Facius in 1456 as being in the possession of King Alfonso V of Naples.

Facius' text is reprinted in Crowe and Cavalcaselle, *History of Old Netherlandish Painting*, German edition by A. Springer, Leipzig 1875, p. 412 f.

Cf. p. 68 note 1, 79 note 1.

53
MAPPA MUNDI

Painted, according to Facius, for Duke Philip of Burgundy.

Cf. p. 86.

54
WOMEN BATHING

Mentioned by Facius as being in the possession of Cardinal Ottaviano in 1456.

Cf. p. 83, 84.

55
ST. GEORGE SLAYING THE DRAGON

Purchased by King Alfonso V of Naples in 1445 (according to Cassella's '*La Novela den Sampere*', IX, in '*Veu de Catalunya*', Barcelona 1906).

Cf. p. 50.

[1] *Cf.* L. Scheeve, *Hubert and Jan van Eyck*, The Hague 1933. For other lost pictures, see Weale-Brockwell (1912, p. 195 f.). *Ibid.*, in Appendix B a list of pictures sold by auction since 1661 under the name 'van Eyck'. See also Denucé, *Kunstausfuhr Antwerpens im 17. Jahrhundert, Die Familie Forchoudt* (*Quellen zur Geschichte der flämischen Kunst*, I, Antwerp 1931).

56
ST. JEROME IN HIS STUDY

(Identical with one of the wings of No. 52?)
In the possession of Lorenzo il Magnifico de' Medici in Florence (according to the 1492 inventory of Lorenzo's collection) (*cf.* No. 5).

Cf. p. 104 and Cat. No. 5.

57
THE BEAUTIFUL PORTUGUESE LADY[2]

(Identical with the portrait of the Princess Isabella, painted in 1429?[2]).
Tempera on canvas.
In the possession of Don Diego de Guevara and the Archduchess Margaret (according to the inventories of the latter's collection).

Cf. p. 78, note 2.

58
LANDSCAPE WITH OTTER-HUNT

Padua, in the house of the philosopher Leonico Tomeo (according to Marcantonio Michiel).

Cf. p. 86.

59
LANDOWNER SETTLING ACCOUNTS WITH HIS MANAGER

Half-figures, dated 1440. Milan, in the house of Niccolo Lampognano (according to Marcantonio Michiel).

Cf. p. 87.

[2] The drawing of the princess Isabella, third wife of Duke Philip the Good in the Royal Library in Brussels (Weale-Brockwell), Plate XXXIV) does not agree with the descriptions in the inventories of the Archduchess (*cf.* p. 68, note 3).

VI. WORKS ATTRIBUTED BY SCHOLARS TO HUBERT OR JAN VAN EYCK AS ORIGINALS OR COPIES, BUT NOT GENERALLY ACCEPTED

A. *MINIATURES*
60
THE 'HEURES DE TURIN'

Book of hours made for Jean Duke of Berry, begun about or shortly after 1400, completed long after his death (in the second half of the fifteenth century); subsequently taken to pieces. Each page: 11 inches (28 cm) high; 7½ inches (19 cm) wide.

1. *The Portion destroyed by fire*

Destroyed in 1904 on the occasion of the fire at the Biblioteca Nazionale, Turin. *Cf.* Durrieu, *Les Heures de Turin*, Paris 1902.

Durrieu XIII: *God the Father in the canopy of Heaven, surrounded by Angels*. In the marginal miniature: *Angels making music*.

Hulin de Loo: By Jan van Eyck.

Tolnay: 'Style d'Hubert van Eyck, exécuté par un élève'.

After a model connected with Hubert's art and created about 1420–30 (*cf.* p. 32, note 1).

Durrieu XV: *The Betrayal of Christ*.

In the initial beneath: *The Agony in the Garden*.

In the lower margin: *The Denial of St. Peter and the Mocking of Christ* (Fig. 85).

By the Chief Master. *Cf.* p. 94.

The two chief motives of the figural composition (Judas kissing Christ and St. Peter attacking Malchus) may point back to a lost model, which was also used in a rather crude miniature of a Bible (Brussels, Bibliothèque Royale Ms.9020–30; publ. by de Wit, *Jahrbuch der preussischenKunstsammlungen* 1937, p. 123) dated 1431. The whole composition, the setting included, is used in a Dutch manuscript at Liége (*cf.* Winkler, *Jahrbuch der Kunsthist. Sammlungen*, Vienna, 1915, p. 324 ff.).

Durrieu XVIII: *Christ bearing the Cross.*

Probably earlier version of the lost original of the copy in Budapest (No. 63, Plate 166). Pictures with other variants, also in vertical format, in Aachen, Suermondt Museum (published by Kern, *cf.* p. 96 note 2) and in the Metropolitan Museum in New York (*cf. ibidem*) published by F. Winkler (*Jahrbuch der preussischen Kunstsammlungen* 37), see also Zimmermann (*Amtliche Berichte*, Berlin 1917) *cf.* p. 96 note 2).

Durrieu XX: *The Crucifixion.*

The figure of Christ and the city of Jerusalem are copied from a miniature in the preserved portion (Cat. No. 34, Fig. 31, Hulin XXIV).

Durrieu XXV: *Christ as Redeemer.* (*Salvator Mundi*) standing. The figure is in the style of Jan van Eyck (*cf.* p. 90).

Durrieu XXIX: *The Lamentation.*

Hulin de Loo: By Jan van Eyck.

Tolnay: 'Style d'Hubert van Eyck, executée par un élève'.

Probably altered copy of a lost picture by Jan, painted about 1430 (*cf.* p. 33).

Cf. p. 33, note.

Durrieu XXX: *The Voyage of St. Julian.*

By the Chief Master (Fig. 83, *cf.* p. 93 f.).

Durrieu XXXVI: *The Virgin and Child surrounded by Maidens.* The initial is probably by another hand. In the lower margin: The Maidens approaching the Lamb.

The marginal miniature (Fig. 83) was also by the Chief Master and derived iconographically from the centre panel of the Ghent altar-piece. In the main picture Dvořák detects deviations from the style of the Chief Master.

This is the only page in the 'van Eyck style' with contemporary (instead of older) framework.

By the Chief Master. *Cf.* p. 92, note 4.

Durrieu XXXVII: *God the Father appearing to Horsemen on the Seashore.*

In the initial: Christ blessing, with the Dove.

In the lower margin: Horsemen in a flat landscape (Fig. 82).

By the Chief Master. *Cf.* p. 91–92.

Durrieu XXXVIII: *Christ teaching the twelve Apostles the Lord's Prayer.*

Influenced by Jan van Eyck.

Durrieu XL: *St. Thomas Aquinas.*

Free borrowing from Jan van Eyck's St. Jerome (Cat. No. 5, Plate 9).

Durrieu XLI: *Christ Enthroned as King of Kings.*

In the style of Jan van Eyck (*cf.* p. 90).

Durrieu XLIII: *French King praying before a battle.*

Perhaps by the same artist who painted Hulin XXIII, XXV, XVIII (*cf.* p. 91 note 2).

2. The Preserved Portion.

a. Paris, Louvre.

Durrieu XXVIII: *God the Father between Christ as the Man of Sorrow and the Virgin Mary.*

Winkler (*Jahrbuch d. preuss. Kunstsammlungen*, 1916, p. 195): Copy of a picture by Jan van Eyck.

Tolnay: 'Copie d'après Jean van Eyck'.

After a model executed about 1420–30 (*cf.* p. 33).

b. Turin, Museo Civico

(Formerly in the collection of Prince Trivulzio, Milan. *Cf.* Georges (Hulin) de Loo, *Les Heures de Milan*, Brussels 1911.)

Hulin XVIII: Margin: *Jonah and the Whale.*

Independent work by the same artist who painted Hulin XXIII and XXIV. Fig. 32.

Hulin XX: *Nativity of St. John the Baptist.*

In the Initial: God the Father.

In the margin: The Baptism of Christ.

Plates 157, 159.

By the Chief Master. *Cf.* p. 92–94.

Hulin XXI: *Requiem.*

In the initial: The Last Judgement.

In the lower margin: Benediction of the Churchyard.

Plates 158, 160.

By the Chief Master. *Cf.* p. 93–94.

Hulin XXII: *The Finding of the Holy Cross.*

In the initial: Christ on the Cross.

In the margin: Resurrection of the Dead.

Hulin : La lettre et le bas de page ne sont probablement pour l'exécution ou l'achèvement que des oeuvres d'élève . . . mais semblent au moins été peints sur de croquis de Hubrecht.

Dvořák points out stylistic differences in the main picture. See also Pigler in *Phoebus*, III, 1950, No. 1.

By the Chief Master.

Plate 161. *Cf.* p. 94.

Hulin XXIII: *The Agony in the Garden* (Cat. No. 33).

Attributed by Hulin de Loo to Jan van Eyck himself, but is nevertheless by a miniaturist contemporary with the Chief Master and copied from a lost picture by Jan van Eyck (dating from about 1430, *cf.* p. 30–32).

In the initial: The Flagellation.

In the margin: The Miraculous Draught of Fishes; both by the same hand, but not after Jan van Eyck.

Plate 12, Fig. 31.

Hulin XXIV: *The Crucifixion* (Cat. No. 34).

Attributed by Hulin de Loo to Jan van Eyck himself, but is nevertheless by a miniaturist contemporary with the Chief Master and copied from a lost painting by Jan van Eyck (*cf.* p. 30–32).

In the margin: The Sacrifice of Isaac (by the same hand, but not after Jan van Eyck).

Fig. 31.

Cf. p. 30.

*   *   *

The Chief Master

Hulin de Loo attributed seven miniatures (*i.e.* seven main pictures, five initials and six marginals) to one master and relying on the evidence of the coats-of-arms, which he assumed to point to their having been executed on behalf of William IV, Count of Holland (†31.5.1417), identified him as Hubert van Eyck.

Dvořák (*Kunstgeschichtliche Anzeigen*, 1910, p. 102: 'There is not the shadow of a proof that the brothers van Eyck should themselves have participated in the illumination of the manuscript.

Dvořák (*Jahrbuch d. preuss. Kunstsammlungen*, XXXIX, 1918): Executed two decades later, probably in Holland, may be early works by Ouwater.

Zimmermann (*Amtl. Berichte v. d. preuss. Kunstsammlungen* 1917): By Albert Ouwater.

Baldass (*Jahrbuch d. kunsth. Sammlungen in Wien*, XXXV, 1919): By Ouwater.

Winkler (*Altniederlandische Malerei*, 1924): By Hubert van Eyck.

Friedländer (I, p. 68 ff.): By Jan van Eyck.

Tolnay: Attributed to Ouwater.

Beenken: By Hubert van Eyck.

For the date of the miniatures *cf.* Hulin (l.c.), Dvořák (l.c.) Duverger (*Oud Holland* 1933, p. 64), Tolnay (note 83), K. de Wit (*Jahrbuch der preussischen Kunstsammlungen*, 1937, p. 115), and Th. Musper, who dates them 1420–25 (*Untersuchungen zu Roger van der Weyden und Jan van Eyck*, n.d.).

Plates 157–161, Figs. 82–85.
Cf. p. 90–97.

B. *PAINTINGS*

1. RELIGIOUS SUBJECTS

6I

CHRIST ON THE CROSS BETWEEN THE VIRGIN AND ST. JOHN

Berlin, Kaiser Friedrich Museum.

Acquired in 1897 from an English art-dealer (Mr. Buttery).

Canvas, transferred from wood.

Height 17 inches (43 cm): width 10¼ inches (26 cm).

Tschudi (*Jahrbuch d. preuss. Kunstsammlungen*, XIX, 1898, p. 202 f.): By Jan van Eyck.

Weale-Brockwell (1912, p. 157): 'Painting of doubtful authentictiy'.

Friedländer (I, p. 78): Panel-painting in the early van Eyck style.

Tolnay: 'Attribuée à Ouwater'.

Beenken: By Hubert van Eyck.

By the Chief Master of the 'Heures de Turin'.

Plate 162.
Cf. p. 95.

62

* THE CRUCIFIXION; THE LAST JUDGEMENT

Two wings of an altar-piece.

New York, Metropolitan Museum.

Formerly in the Hermitage, Leningrad.

Acquired by the Ambassador Tatistcheff in Spain and bequeathed to the Hermitage in 1845. The centre panel, showing an Adoration of the Magi, is said to have been stolen.

Transferred from wood to canvas. Each panel 22¼ inches (56·5 cm) high; 7¾ inches (19·7 cm) wide. Passavant (Kunstblatt 1841) notes on the backs of the wings traces of paintings in grisaille, showing two figures standing on pedestals.

Inscriptions on the Last Judgement: On either side of the lower part of Christ's body: venite benedicti p⟨at⟩ris mei

On St. Michael's shield: ΑΔѠΝΑΙ ΤΕΤΓΡΑ ΜΑΘѠΝ ΑΓΛΑ +Α

On the wings of Death: CHAOS MAGNV⟨M⟩ and VMBRA MORTIS.

On either side of St. Michael: ite vos maledicti in ignem eternvm.

In Hell: ME OBLIVI!

The original frames of the two wings bore inscriptions: *i.e.* On the frame of the Crucifixion:

DOMINVS POSVIT I⟨N⟩ EO INIQVITATE⟨M⟩ OMNIVM N⟨OS-T⟩RVM : OBLATVS E⟨ST⟩ QVIA IPSE VOLVIT + NON APERVIT

OS SVV⟨M⟩: SICVT OVIS AD OCCISIONE⟨M⟩ DVCET⟨VR⟩: + Q⟨VA⟩SI AGNVS CORAM TONDENTE SE OBMVTESCET: P⟨ROP⟩T⟨ER⟩ SCEL⟨VS⟩ P⟨O⟩P⟨V⟩LI MEI PERCVSSI EV⟨M⟩: ET DABIT IMPIOS PRO SEPVLTVRA ET DIVITES PRO MORTE SVAVSAE: ⟨T⟩R⟨ADI⟩D⟨I⟩T I⟨N⟩ MORTE⟨M⟩ A⟨N⟩I⟨M⟩AM SVA⟨M⟩: + CV⟨M⟩ SCELERATIS REPV⟨T⟩ATVS E⟨ST⟩: ET IP⟨S⟩E P⟨E⟩CC⟨ATA⟩ MVLTORVM TVLIT: + PRO TRANS-GRESSORIBVS ORAVIT (Isaiah LIII. 6-12).

On the frame of the Last Judgement: DED⟨IT⟩ MORS MORTVOS ECCE TABERNACVL⟨V⟩M DEI CV⟨M⟩ HO⟨MIN⟩IBVS + H⟨AB⟩I-TAB⟨IT⟩ CV⟨M⟩ EIS IP⟨SE⟩ P⟨O⟩P⟨VLVS⟩ EI⟨VS⟩ ERVNT + IP⟨SE⟩ D⟨EV⟩S CV⟨M⟩ EIS E⟨R⟩IT EOR⟨VM⟩ D⟨EV⟩S: ET ABST⟨ER⟩G⟨ET⟩ ⟨DEVS⟩ O⟨MN⟩EM LAC⟨RIM⟩A⟨M⟩ AB OC⟨V⟩LIS EOR⟨VM⟩: MORS VLT⟨RA⟩ NON E⟨R⟩IT: N⟨EQVE⟩ LVC⟨TVS⟩ N⟨IE⟩Q⟨VE⟩ DOLOR E⟨RI⟩T VLTRA. DEDIT MARE MORTVOS SVO⟨S⟩. CONGREGABO S⟨VPE⟩R EOS MALA. SAGITTAS MEA⟨S⟩ ⟨C⟩O⟨M⟩PLEBO I⟨N⟩ EIS: ⟨C⟩O⟨N⟩SV⟨M⟩E⟨N⟩T⟨VR⟩ FAME + DEVORAB⟨VN⟩T EO⟨S⟩ . . . . DENTES BESTIAR⟨VM⟩ ⟨IM⟩ MITTA⟨M⟩ IN EOS CV⟨M⟩ F⟨VR⟩ORE T⟨RA⟩H⟨EN⟩TIV⟨M⟩ S⟨VPE⟩R T⟨ERRAM⟩ A⟨T⟩Q⟨VE⟩ S⟨ER⟩PE⟨N⟩-TIV⟨M⟩. (Rev. xx, 13; xxi, 3-4; Deut. xxxii, 23-24).

Passavant (*Kunstblatt* No. 3, 1841): By Hubert and Jan van Eyck.

Waagen (*Gemäldesammlung in der Eremitage*, 1864, p. 16): By Petrus Christus.

Crowe and Cavalcaselle (*Early Flemish Painters*, 1872): By Petrus Christus.

C. Justi (*Zeitschrift f. bild. Kunst*, 1887): By Jan van Eyck.

Kämmerer (p. 52 ff.): A miniaturist of lively spirit and temperament; an unsolved riddle.

Dvořák (*Jahrbuch d. preuss. Kunstsammlungen*, 1918, p. 66 ff.): 'A work of the Chief Master of the Turin Book of Hours'.

Weale: In the writer's opinion the work of a contemporary . . . probably a North Netherlander.

Weale-Brockwell (1912, p. 13): 'Painting of doubtful authenticity'.

Friedländer (I, p. 76 f.): Panel-painting in the early van Eyck style.

Tolnay: 'Attribuée à Ouwater'.

Beenken: By Hubert van Eyck.

Harry B. Wehle and M. Salinger (*A Catalogue of Early Flemish Paintings*, Metropolitan Museum 1947): By Hubert van Eyck.

By the Chief Master of the 'Heures de Turin'.

Plates 163–165.
Cf. p. 95–96.

63

CHRIST BEARING THE CROSS

Budapest, Museum of Arts.

Acquired in 1904 from the Péteri (Ignatz Pfeffer) Collection, Budapest.

Wood. Height 38½ inches (98 cm); width 51 inches (130 cm).

Copy dating from the second quarter of the sixteenth century; *cf.* No. 60. Durrieu XVIII, Nos. 78 and 79.

Winkler (*Jahrbuch d. preuss. Kunstsammlungen*, 37, 1916, p. 288 ff.): Copy after van Eyck.

E. H. Zimmermann (*Amtliche Berichte d. Berliner Museen*, 39, p. 15 ff.): The execution in the manner of the 'Brunswick monogrammist'.

M. Dvořák (*Jahrbuch d. preuss. Kunstsammlungen*, 39, 1918, p. 66 ff.): The lost original was a work of the Chief Master of the 'Heures de Turin'.

P. Post (*Repertorium f. Kunstwissenschaft*, XLIV, 1924, p. 16 ff.).

Friedländer (I, p. 121): 'Eyckisch'; designed about 1420.

Saxl (*Belvedere* IX, X, 1926 p. 142): The painter must have known an Italian composition similar to that of Andrea da Firenze's fresco in the Spanish Chapel at Florence.

Winkler (*Festschrift für M. J. Friedländer*, 1921): The Bearing of the Cross in Budapest, respectively the Eyckian model, reappears in the Horarium of Catherine of Cleve (Prince d'Arenberg collection).

de Wit (*Jahrbuch d. preuss. Kunstsammlungen*, 1937): The Utrecht miniaturist of the Horarium of Catherine of Cleve (Prince

d'Arenberg collection) takes two figures of the composition, considerably altering the figure of Christ.
Tolnay: 'Copie d'après Ouwater'!
Pigler (*Phoebus*. III, 1950–51): Copy after a panel-painting by Jan van Eyck: about 1420.[1]).

After a lost panel-painting by the Chief Master of the 'Heures de Turin'.
Plate 166.
Cf. p. 96.

64

ST. CATHERINE BENEATH A BALDACHIN

Full-length; probably the right wing-panel of an altar-piece.
In a private collection in Belgium (formerly in the Maurice d'Alta collection, Brussels).
Wood. Height 23¼ inches (59 cm); width 11¾ inches (30 cm).
Published as by Jan van Eyck by A. Dezarrois (*La Revue de l'Art*, LXII, No. 340, Dec. 1932, pp. 170–176), who quotes a certificate by Hulin de Loo ('Petrus Christus comme créateur possible') and a letter from M. J. Friedländer ('Plutôt . . . . Petrus Christus que . . . Jean van Eyck'). According to the owner, and to *Pantheon*, XI, 1933, p. 37, Hulin subsequently excluded it from the work of Petrus Christus, attributing it to Jan van Eyck, and F. Winkler also declared for Jan van Eyck. Owing to the present condition of the picture it is impossible to give a definite opinion. The figure of the Saint shows stylistic relationship to Hubert's Three Maries at the Sepulchre (Plates 1, 2), and to the Holy Maidens in the Adoration of the Lamb (Plate 22). Similar spatial images are not known before Jan van Eyck. Unusual is the view of a garden, through the right-hand window-opening only, whereas there is a closed glass window on the left. The treatment of the folds and the high horizon are not in the style of Petrus Christus.

65

THE WELL OF LIFE

Madrid, Prado.
Acquired in 1838 from the Hieronymite convent near Segovia.
Wood. Height 71¼ inches (181 cm); width 45¾ inches (116 cm).
One of the Angels is holding a scroll inscribed: can 4 ffons ortorum puteus aquarum vivencium.
The figures of God the Father and the Virgin Mary reveal the influence of the Ghent altar-piece.

---

[1]Pigler claims to recognize portraits among the horsemen. Induced by the cut of the beard and despite the evidence of a different type of nose, he identifies the leader of the cavalcade, mounted on a white horse, as the Emperor Sigismund, and the beardless rider seen in profile in the second row as Duke John of Bavaria, Count of Holland, basing this assertion on a page of the 'Recueil d'Arras', which, however, would appear to be derived from a genealogical representation rather than from a portrait. A meeting between the Emperor and the Duke at Liége in 1416 would be, according to Pigler, the starting point. 'What could be more natural than that Duke John, after taking possession of the provinces, should have had the Bearing of the Cross painted, including portraits of his mighty liege-lord and himself'. (Thus, according to Pigler, the Duke would have undertaken to honour the secular head of Christendom by having him depicted as the leader of the band of Christ's executioners. Saxl already assumed that the painter wanted to give the figure of the leader an appearance of wicked character.) In the view of Jerusalem with the church of the Holy Sepulchre, Pigler sees a representation of the city of Liége, assuming that the painter cut off the view at the very point where the Meuse flowing through the town would have become visible. The chief arguments in support of the identification are a fork in the road on the hill behind the town which is found in this picture and in an etching of Liége dating from 1616, and a double wall enclosing the road leading to the gate. The ornamental letters on the harness of the horse of the rider wearing a turban Pigler reads as ONAZARA on the top line and as MIN. HEER VAN below, from which he deduces that this full-bearded Oriental must be Philip of Ozara (Filippo Scolari), Sigismund's army-commander.

Generally held to be an old copy of a lost original. The original is believed to have been the picture seen by Ponz in 1783 in the cathedral of Palencia.

Weale (1908, p. 162 ff., p. 202): 'Very difficult to say if it is a copy after a lost original by Hubert van Eyck or an early work by a contemporary Netherlander painted in imitation of the Ghent polyptych'.
Friedländer (I, p. 117 ff.) dates the original about 1430.
Post (*Jahrbuch d. preuss. Kunstsammlungen*, 33, 1922, p. 120 ff.): About 1420.
Winkler (*Pantheon*, 1931, p. 188 ff. and 255 ff.): Copy after Jan van Eyck.
Tolnay: 'Œuvre contestée'.
Musper (*Untersuchungen zu Rogier v. d. Weyden und J. v. Eyck*. Stuttgart, p. 97).

The original was painted by a follower of Jan van Eyck (*cf*. Cat. No. 74).

2. PROFANE REPRESENTATIONS

66

THE FOOL

Vienna, Picture Gallery of the Kunsthistorisches Museum.
From the collection of Archduke Leopold Wilhelm in 1659.
Wood. Height 14¼ inches (36 cm); width 9½ inches (24 cm).
Brockwell (*The Connoisseur*, December 1949, p. 78): By Jan van Eyck.

No other work by the painter of this picture, executed about 1440–50, has hitherto come to light.
Cf. p. 72 note 4.

67

HUNTING FESTIVAL OF DUKE PHILIP THE GOOD

Versailles, Musée.
Acquired in 1898.
Sixteenth-century copy.
Wood. Height 63⅜ inches (161 cm); width 46 inches (117 cm.)
Another copy on canvas, measuring 86¼ inches (219 cm) by 46½ inches (118 cm), belonging to the same museum is now in the château of Azay-le-Rideau.
According to Roblot-Delondre (*Revue Archéologique*, 1910, p. 52 f.), the original was seen and described in 1582 by Argote de Molina, in the palace of the Pardo near Madrid (destroyed by fire in 1608). That Philip the Good is here represented is rendered probable by the fact that in the 'Recueil d'Arras' the figure of this Duke's fool is copied from the fool in the right foreground of this picture.

According to Post (*Jahrbuch der preussischen Kunstsammlungen*, 1931, p. 120 ff.), derived from a lost picture by Jan van Eyck. On the date which Post assigns to the original, see p. 82, note 2.
Tolnay: 'D'après Jean van Eyck'.

The original was painted by a Franco-Flemish artist, about 1425.
Fig. 77.
Cf. p. 82.

3. PORTRAITS

68

JEAN SANS PEUR, DUKE OF BURGUNDY

Antwerp, Museum, van Ertborn bequest.
Wood. Height 8¼ inches (21 cm); width 5½ inches (14 cm).
Additions on right and left.
John of Burgundy, born 1371, became Duke in 1404, murdered in 1419. Father of Duke Philip the Good.

Beenken (*Pantheon*, 1937, p. 116): By Hubert van Eyck.

Excellent enlarged copy, executed about 1440 by a pupil of Rogier van der Weyden, of a lost bust portrait without hands (of which there is a copy in original size in the Limpurg-Stirum collection, published by Post in *Jahrbuch d. preuss. Kunstsammlungen* 1921, p. 73) in the style of 1415.

Fig. 62.

Cf. p. 67.

69
THE MAN WITH THE PINKS

On his breast the sitter is wearing the cross of the Brotherhood of St. Anthony, founded in 1382 by Albert of Bavaria, Count of Hainault.

Berlin, Kaiser Friedrich Museum.

Acquired in 1874 from the Suermondt Collection; Engels auction-sale, Cologne, 1867.

Wood. Height $15\frac{3}{4}$ inches (40 cm); width $12\frac{1}{4}$ inches (31 cm).

Voll (*Altniederländische Malerei*): A work of the end of the fifteenth or the beginning of the sixteenth century.
Weale-Brockwell (1912, p. 80): 'By Hubert or John'.
Friedländer (I, p. 93 f.): 'By Jan van Eyck, between 1422 and 1425'.
Tolnay: 'Œuvre contestée'.
Beenken: By a follower of Jan van Eyck, about 1435–45.
Cornette (*De Portretter von Jan van Eyck*, Antwerp, 1947): 'A youthful work of Jan?'
Schenk (*Zeitschrift für Kunst*, III, 1949): Hubert van Eyck's self-portrait(!).

By a follower of Jan van Eyck.
Plate 156.
Cf. p. 78 note 3.

70
PORTRAIT OF A DONOR

Leipzig, Museum der bildenden Künste; bequest of Frau Amalia von Ritzenburg, 1878.

Wood. Height $10\frac{3}{8}$ inches (26·4 cm); width $7\frac{5}{8}$ inches (19·5 cm). Fragment (?).

The fact that the sitter is turned towards the right makes it permissible to suppose that a female counterpart was lost.

Weale-Brockwell (1912, p. 183): Under 'Copies, Variants, Derivatives and Imitations'.
Friedländer (I, p. 95): Even as a fragment, not perfectly preserved, showing all the qualities of the mature van Eyck style.
Tolnay: 'Œuvre contestée'.
Beenken: By Jan van Eyck, about 1422–28.

By a follower of Jan van Eyck.
Plate 155.
Cf. p. 79.

71
* PORTRAIT OF A CLERIC

Montauban, Musée Ingres (attributed to Ouwater).

Wood. Height $10\frac{1}{4}$ inches (26 cm); width $7\frac{1}{2}$ inches (19 cm).

Bredius (*Oud Holland*, 12, 1904, p. 90): By Hans Memling.
Durant-Gréville (*Hubert et Jean van Eyck*, 1910, p. 95): By Hubert.
Weale-Brockwell (1912, p. 187): Under 'Copies, Variants, Derivatives and Imitations'.
Friedländer (I, p. 108).
P. Wescher (*Pantheon*, 20, 1937, p. 352): Close to van Eyck.
Tolnay: 'D'après Jean van Eyck'.
Beenken: 'Doubtful'.

By a follower of Jan van Eyck.
Plate 153.
Cf. p. 78 note 3.

72
* PORTRAIT OF A MAN

Philadelphia, Pennsylvania Museum of Art (John G. Johnson Collection).

Wood. $7\frac{1}{4} \times 5\frac{5}{8}$ inches (18.4 × 14.3 cm); dimensions of the picture $5 \times 4\frac{1}{2}$ inches (12.7 × 11.4 cm).

Weale (p. 208).
Valentiner (*The Johnson Collection*, II, p. 315).
M. Conway (*The van Eycks and their Followers*, 1921, p. 67): By Jan van Eyck.
Tolnay: 'D'après Jean van Eyck'.

Netherlandish school, about 1430–40.
Plate 154.
Cf. p. 76, note 4.

73
PORTRAIT OF A YOUNG MAN
WITH A RED ROSE

Berlin, Kaiser Friedrich Museum.
Presented in 1900 by Alfred Beit, London.
Wood. Height $7\frac{1}{8}$ inches (18 cm); width $4\frac{3}{4}$ inches (12 cm).

Friedländer (I, p. 165): 'Dates from Jan van Eyck's period. The vacuity of the form makes it impossible to attribute the painting to him'.
Beenken: (*Pantheon*, 1937, p. 116): By Hubert van Eyck.

Netherlandish school, about 1430–40.

74
PORTRAIT OF A MAN

Berlin, Kaiser Friedrich Museum.
Acquired in 1895 from an Italian art-dealer.
Wood. Height $4\frac{1}{2}$ inches (11·5 cm); width $3\frac{1}{2}$ inches (8·8 cm). Apparently a fragment.
The person represented is to be found again on the 'Well of Life' in Madrid (No. 65).

Weale-Brockwell (1912, p. 162): 'Painting of doubtful authenticity'.
Friedländer (I, p. 95): Unsigned panel-painting in the mature van Eyck style.
Tolnay: 'Oeuvre contestée'.

Netherlandish school, 1430–40.

75
* PORTRAIT STUDY OF AN ELDERLY MAN

Copenhagen, Statens Museum for Kunst (known to have been there since 1690).
Tempera on parchment. Height $5\frac{1}{8}$ inches (13 cm); width $4\frac{3}{4}$ inches (12 cm).

K. Madson (1922 Catalogue, No. 68): By a follower of Jan van Eyck.
F. Winkler (*Pantheon*, 1931, p. 258): Has a claim to be considered as having been executed by Jan van Eyck himself.
J. Dupont (*Revue de l'Art*, 69, 1936, I, p. 261): By the Master of the Aix Annunciation.
Ring (No. 96): 'Closer to the style of Jan van Eyck than to anything French or even Franco-Flemish.'

The only point which can be definitely established is the close relationship to the realistic Flemish style prevalent about 1430–40.

C. DRAWINGS

1. RELIGIOUS SUBJECTS

76

THE BETRAYAL OF CHRIST

London, British Museum.
Silverpoint on light grey ground.
Height 4⅝ inches (11·7 cm); width 5⅛ inches (13 cm).
Popham (*Drawings of the Early Flemish School*, London 1926, No. 2): 'Franco-Flemish, about 1410'.
Winkler (*Thieme-Becher Lexikon*, XIII): By Paul de Limbourg.
Popham (*Old Master Drawings*, 1932, p. 59): 'Near to Paul de Limbourg'.
Beenken (*Old Master Drawings*, 1932, p. 18).
Tolnay: 'Attribuée à Ouwater'.
Beenken: By Hubert van Eyck.
Ring (No. 35): 'Attributed to Paul de Limbourg'.

Presumably a work by the first teacher of the Chief Master of the 'Heures de Turin' or an early work of his own invention, created before 1420, still under the strong influence of Paul de Limbourg.
Plate 169.
Cf. p. 94–95.

77

THE ADORATION OF THE MAGI

Berlin, Print Room.
Pen-drawing. Height 5⅞ inches (15 cm); width 4⅞ inches (12·4 cm).
Modified copies in a Prayer-Book (Museum Meerman-Westrheenen den Haag) and in a Dutch Bible at Vienna (cod. 2772, published by F. Winkler, Vienna, *Jahrbuch* 1915, Pl. XXI).

Friedländer (I, p. 125): 'Stylistically coincides with the miniatures in Turin and Milan . . . which I have endeavoured to explain as early creations of Jan van Eyck's.'
Winkler (*Festschrift für M. J. Friedländer*, p. 98): After Hubert van Eyck.
B. Martens (*Meister Francke*, Hamburg, 1929): Netherlandish, about 1416–18.
Tolnay: 'Attribuée à Ouwater'.
O. Kerber (*Hubert van Eyck*, 1937): By Hubert van Eyck.
Beenken: At the most a free copy of a composition by Hubert. The rocky ground has nothing of van Eyck.

After a lost picture by the Chief Master of the 'Heures de Turin'.
Plate 168.
Cf. p. 95.

78

THE ADORATION OF THE MAGI

Amsterdam, Rijksmuseum.
Silverpoint on green ground. Height 5 inches (12·6 cm); width 4⅞ inches (12·5 cm).
Fürbringer (*Die künstlerischen Voraussetzungen des Genter Altares*, Weida 1904, p. 99 ff.): Pencil note on the cartoon: Jan van Eyck. Hypothetically accepted as an early work of Jan's.
Schmidt-Degener (*Burlington Magazine*, XIX, 1910, p. 255): 'Copy after a lost work by Hubert van Eyck'.
Friedländer (I, p. 125): Deserves consideration as an original by the hand of the miniaturist Jan van Eyck.
Popham (*Drawings of the Early Flemish School*, London 1926, Plate 3): Hubert van Eyck(?).

After a lost picture by the Chief Master of the 'Heures de Turin', but hardly after the lost centre-piece of No. 62.
Plate 167.
Cf. p. 95.

79

CAVALCADE FROM THE 'BEARING OF THE CROSS'

Brunswick, Museum.
Silverpoint. Height 5¼ inches (13·2 cm); width 4½ inches (11·5 cm).
Winkler (*Jahrbuch d. preuss. Kunstsammlungen*, 37, 1916, p. 290): Copy after Jan van Eyck.
Friedländer (I, p. 121): A drawing probably made after the original, but in any case not after the Budapest copy.
Ebbinge-Wubben (*Catalogus der Tentoonstelling : Tekeningen van Jan van Eyck tot Rubens*, Rotterdam, Boymans Museum, 1948–49): After Jan van Eyck.
After the Chief Master of the 'Heures de Turin'. *Cf.* No. 63.
Plate 170.
Cf. p. 96.

80

GROUP FROM THE 'BEARING OF THE CROSS'

Vienna, Albertina.
Pen-drawing. Height 8 inches (20·4 cm); width 10⅞ inches (27·6 cm).
Winkler (*Jahrbuch d. preuss. Kunstsammlungen*, 37, p. 292): Under the influence of the original of the Budapest 'Bearing of the Cross' (No. 62).
Benesch (*Jahrbuch d. preuss. Kunstsammlungen*, 46, p. 181): May be by the same hand as a drawing in the Louvre representing Hell.
Benesch (*Albertina Catalogue*, II, p. 22): By a Dutch Master, 1450–1460.
O. Kerber (*Hubert v. Eyck*, Frankfurt, 1937, p. 208): 'Die Konzeption Jan zuzuschreiben.'

Skilfully executed drawing from the beginning of the second half of the fifteenth century after the main groups of a variant of the lost original of No. 63, with still more figures and in the counter-sense. The advanced realism and pronounced plasticity of the individual figures contradict the assumption that this variant was also painted by the Chief Master of the 'Heures de Turin'.
Cf. p. 96, note 2.

81

* CHRIST ON THE CROSS BETWEEN THE VIRGIN AND ST. JOHN

Copenhagen, collection of Graf Moltke.
Barely 2¾ inches (7 cm) high, gummed on to a sheet of parchment of a late sixteenth-century miniaturist (according to Winkler, George Hoefnagel).
On the parchment the inscription: BELGARV SPEDOR JOANNES DE EYCK AO 1430.
Winkler (*Festschrift für M. J. Friedländer*, 1927, p. 91 ff.): By Jan van Eyck.
Tolnay: 'd'après Jean van Eyck'.

Has merely a stylistic relationship to the art of Jan van Eyck.
Cf. p. 95, note 2.

82

** CROWNED HORSEMEN (CAVALCADE OF THE MAGI)

Weimar, Goethehaus.
Pen and wash, dated 1521.
Schöne (*Jahrbuch d. preuss. Kunstsammlungen*, 58, 1937, p. 157): Has a stylistic relationship to the 'Bearing of the Cross' in Budapest.

Is only remotely akin to the art of Jan van Eyck.
Cf. p. 92, note 2.

83

* THE ANNUNCIATION

Wolfenbüttel, Library.
Silverpoint. Height $7\frac{7}{8}$ inches (20 cm); width $5\frac{5}{8}$ inches (14·2 cm).

H. Zimmermann (*Jahrbuch d. preuss. Kunstsammlungen*, 36, 1915, p. 215): By Jan van Eyck, shortly after 1426.
Friedländer (I, p. 126 f.): Original by Jan van Eyck about 1428, at the same time as the original of the Well of Life in Madrid (No. 64).
Tolnay: 'Dessin apocryphe'.

By a follower of Jan van Eyck, the interior influenced by No. 4.
Cf. p. 90, note 3.

84

ST. CHRISTOPHER

Paris, Louvre.
Pen-drawing. Height $7\frac{1}{2}$ inches (19 cm); width $5\frac{1}{2}$ inches (14 cm).

Brising (*Quinten Metsys*, Upsala 1909, p. 150): By Quinten Metsys.
Winkler (*Jahrbuch d. preuss. Kunstsammlungen*, 37, 1916, pp. 296-7): Derived from a work by Jan.
Friedländer (I, p. 125 f.): 'Original by a great master about 1420. I believe that Eyck was the creator of it.
Baldass (*Jahrbuch d. kunsthistorischen Sammlungen*, VII, 1933, p. 154): More likely to be a drawing made by an artist after a painting than a preliminary drawing for a painting or a self-contained work. The style of the landscape is only slightly prior to 1500 and the figures must have been modelled on originals dating from the time of the foundation of Old Netherlandish painting.
Beenken (*Old Master Drawings*, 1932): Copy or original by Jan van Eyck.
Tolnay: 'Copie de 1500, d'après Jean van Eyck'.
Ebbinge-Wubben (*De Tentoonstelling : Tekeningen van Jan van Eyck tot Rubens*, p. 14 f.).

About 1500. Only the figures are derived from a model by Jan van Eyck, or, more probably, by one of his followers. The lansdcape reveals the influence of the art of Gerard David.

2. PORTRAITS

85

PORTRAIT OF A WOMAN

Rotterdam, Boymans Museum (known to have been there since 1852).
Silverpoint. Height $5\frac{1}{4}$ inches (13·2 cm); width $3\frac{1}{2}$ inches (8·9 cm).
P. Haverkorn van Rijsewijk (*Jaarsverslag Museum Boymans* 1903): By Rogier van der Weyden.
Schmidt-Degener (*Burlington Magazine*, XIX, 1911, p. 256): By Jan van Eyck.
Friedländer (I, p. 127): Certainly an original.
Popham (*Drawing of the Early Flemish School*, 1926, No. 6): Jan van Eyck.
Tolnay: 'Dessin apocryphe'.
Ebbinge-Wubben (*Catalogus der Tentoonstelling : Tekeningen van Jan van Eyck tot Rubens*, Rotterdam 1948-49).

Netherlandish school, about 1440.
Cf. p. 78, note 1.

86

JACQUELINE OF BAVARIA

Frankfurt am Main, Städelsches Kunstinstitut.
Silverpoint. Height $6\frac{3}{8}$ inches (16,3 cm); width $5\frac{1}{4}$ inches 13,4 cm).

Jacqueline of Bavaria, daughter of Philip IV of Bavaria, Count of Hainault and Holland, born 1401, died 1436. The Rogieresque motive of the hands is even more evident in the drawing made from this in the 'Recueil d'Arras'.
G. Glück (*Mitteilungen d. Gesellschaft für vervielfältigende Kunst*, 1905, p. 1): In the Städel Institute attributed to Rogier van der Weyden. By an unknown contemporary artist, who has more in common with the art of Jan van Eyck about 1432.
Weale (1908, p. 182): 'A copy'.
Friedländer (I, p. 124): Deserves consideration as an original drawing by Jan van Eyck.
Tolnay: 'Dessin apocryphe'.

Drawing made after a Netherlandish picture of about 1430, of which painted copies (Vienna, Kunsthistorisches Museum) are also extant.
Cf. p. 78 note 1, 79.

87

* TWO FEMALE HEADS

Turin, formerly in the Palazzo Reale.
Winkler (*Der Meister von Flémalle und Rogier van der Weyden*, 1913, p. 54): By an artist very near to Rogier.
Friedländer (I, p. 128): Rightly photographed (Anderson 9803) as 'study by Jan van Eyck'.
Tolnay: 'Dessin apocryphe'.

Netherlandish school, about 1440.
Cf. p. 78 note 1.

88

PORTRAIT OF A MAN WITH A CHAPERON

London, British Museum (Malcolm Collection).
Acquired from the Galichon Collection.
Silverpoint. Height $8\frac{1}{2}$ inches (21·5 cm); width $5\frac{5}{8}$ inches (14·4 cm).

Friedländer (I, p. 125): May be included in the œuvre of van Eyck as a work of the early period.
Popham (*Drawings of the Early Flemish School*, London 1926, Plate 9): School of Jan van Eyck.
Popham (*Catalogue of the Early Flemish School*, 1932, p. 17): 'Original work of a somewhat primitive artist (more primitive than Jan van Eyck)'.
Tolnay: 'Sans aucun rapport direct avec le style de Jean van Eyck'.

By an independent South Netherlandish or Northern French master, about 1430.
Cf. p. 78 note 1.

D. Engraving

89

'THE LARGE GARDEN OF LOVE'

Engraving. By the 'Meister der Liebesgärten.' L. 27.
Height $8\frac{5}{8}$ inches (21·8 cm); width 11 inches (28·1 cm).
The so-called 'Master of the Gardens of Love', an engraver, probably worked in the Netherlands towards the end of the first half of the fifteenth century. The only existing print of 'the Large Garden of Love' is in the Cabinet of Engravings in Berlin.

Lehrs (*Geschichte und kritischer Katalog des Kupferstichs im XV. Jahrhundert*, I, p. 324, No. 21).
J. Schüler (*Der Meister des Liebesgartens*, Amsterdam 1934, p. 3 f.).
Schöne (*Jahrbuch d. preuss. Kunstsammlungen*, 58, 1937, p. 357 ff.).
Tolnay: 'D'après Jean van Eyck'.

The hypothesis that the work is derived from mural paintings by Jan van Eyck in the palace of the Count of Holland at The Hague (1422-24) cannot be proved.
Fig. 78.
Cf. p. 82, 87.

INDEX OF PLACES

In order to facilitate the use of this Index, references to the works of the brothers Van Eyck are given only for pages on which a painting or drawing is discussed in some detail. Pages on which a work is mentioned in passing only are not quoted. Under the heading of each collection, the works of the brothers Van Eyck are listed first, followed by works of other Masters in historical order.